LIZ LOCHHEAD

Liz Lochhead was born in Lanarkshire in 1947 and educated at Glasgow School of Art. Her collections of poetry include *Dreaming Frankenstein*, *The Colour of Black & White* and *True Confessions*, a collection of monologues and theatre lyrics.

Her original stage plays include *Blood and Ice*, *Mary Queen of Scots Got Her Head Chopped Off*, *Perfect Days* and *Good Things*. Her many stage adaptations include *Dracula*, Molière's *Tartuffe*, *Miseryguts* (based on *Le Misanthrope*) and *Educating Agnes* (based on *L'École des Femmes*); as well as versions of *Medea* by Euripides (for which she won the Scottish Book of the Year Award in 2001), and *Thebans* (adapted mainly from Sophocles' *Oedipus* and *Antigone*). All of these plays are published by Nick Hern Books.

Other Titles in this Series

Howard Brenton
ANNE BOLEYN
BERLIN BERTIE
FAUST – PARTS ONE & TWO
after Goethe
IN EXTREMIS
NEVER SO GOOD
PAUL
THE RAGGED TROUSERED
PHILANTHROPISTS *after* Tressell

Caryl Churchill
BLUE HEART
CHURCHILL PLAYS: THREE
CHURCHILL PLAYS: FOUR
CHURCHILL: SHORTS
CLOUD NINE
A DREAM PLAY *after* Strindberg
DRUNK ENOUGH TO SAY
I LOVE YOU?
FAR AWAY
HOTEL
ICECREAM
LIGHT SHINING IN
BUCKINGHAMSHIRE
LOVE AND INFORMATION
MAD FOREST
A NUMBER
SEVEN JEWISH CHILDREN
THE SKRIKER
THIS IS A CHAIR
THYESTES *after* Seneca
TRAPS

Ariel Dorfman
DEATH AND THE MAIDEN
PURGATORIO
READER
THE RESISTANCE TRILOGY
WIDOWS

Helen Edmundson
ANNA KARENINA *after* Tolstoy
THE CLEARING
CORAM BOY *after* Gavin
GONE TO EARTH *after* Webb
THE HERESY OF LOVE
LIFE IS A DREAM *after* Calderón
MARY SHELLEY
THE MILL ON THE FLOSS *after* Eliot
MOTHER TERESA IS DEAD
ORESTES *after* Euripides
SWALLOWS AND AMAZONS
after Ransome
WAR AND PEACE *after* Tolstoy

Debbie Tucker Green
BORN BAD
DIRTY BUTTERFLY
RANDOM
STONING MARY
TRADE & GENERATIONS
TRUTH AND RECONCILIATION

Liz Lochhead
BLOOD AND ICE
DRACULA *after* Stoker
EDUCATING AGNES ('The School
for Wives') *after* Molière
GOOD THINGS
MARY QUEEN OF SCOTS GOT
HER HEAD CHOPPED OFF
MEDEA
after Euripides
MISERYGUTS ('The Miser')
& TARTUFFE *after* Molière
PERFECT DAYS
THEBANS *after* Euripides & Sophocles

Linda McLean
ANY GIVEN DAY
ONE GOOD BEATING
RIDDANCE
SHIMMER
STRANGERS, BABIES

Joanna Murray-Smith
BOMBSHELLS
THE FEMALE OF THE SPECIES
HONOUR

Rona Munro
THE HOUSE OF BERNARDA ALBA
after Lorca
THE INDIAN BOY
IRON
THE LAST WITCH
LITTLE EAGLES
LONG TIME DEAD
THE MAIDEN STONE
MARY BARTON *after* Gaskell
PANDAS
STRAWBERRIES IN JANUARY
from de la Chenelière
YOUR TURN TO CLEAN THE STAIR
& FUGUE

Amanda Whittington
BE MY BABY
LADIES' DAY
LADIES DOWN UNDER
SATIN 'N' STEEL

LIZ LOCHHEAD

Five Plays

Blood and Ice
Mary Queen of Scots Got Her Head Chopped Off
Quelques Fleurs
Good Things
Perfect Days

NICK HERN BOOKS
London
www.nickhernbooks.co.uk

A Nick Hern Book

Liz Lochhead: Five Plays first published in Great Britain as a paperback original in 2012 by Nick Hern Books Limited, The Glasshouse, 49a Goldhawk Road, London W12 8QP

Blood and Ice first published in an earlier version in 1985 in *Plays by Women: Vol. 4* by Methuen Drama and in this version in 2009 by Nick Hern Books; *Mary Queen of Scots Got Her Head Chopped Off* first published in an earlier version in 1989 by Penguin Books, and in this version in 2009 by Nick Hern Books; *Quelques Fleurs* first published as part of *Scotland Plays* in 1998 by Nick Hern Books and slightly revised for this edition; *Perfect Days* first published in 1998 by Nick Hern Books and in this version in 1999; *Good Things* first published in 2006 by Nick Hern Books, and slightly revised for this edition.

Cover design: Ned Hoste, 2H

Typeset by Nick Hern Books, London
Printed and bound in Great Britain by Mimeo Ltd, Huntingdon, Cambridgeshire PE29 6XX

ISBN 978 1 84842 294 0

Contents

Foreword

The five plays in this book – when cast well and directed by directors whose main, and proper, impulse is to tell the story – seem to work very well with audiences. There is, it seems, life in them. Despite their flaws, they have been, to varying extents, and in, to me, often surprising ways, *popular*. Oh, not universally of course, but what is?

Because it is (truism coming) from the audience that one learns everything about one's plays, I now know a lot more about their flaws than I did, as I am lucky enough to be able to say that all five in print here together in this volume have had several diverse outings – professional, student and amateur – over the thirty years since *Blood and Ice*, the earliest in this volume, was first produced.

I have always tried, once I thought I understood them, to remedy these flaws, rewriting obsessively, often late into the night and generally not even with the excuse of a new production in sight – madness – sometimes finding a solution, but sometimes having later to admit I've succeeded only in stamping out some of the raw, imperfect life in the original.

Nevertheless, I am finally willing to stand by *these* versions of these five plays. All 'original' plays of mine.

Only five? Well, this does not seem to be a great cache after exactly thirty years (I was a late starter) in the Scottish theatre. I am, clearly, not very prolific. I'm trying, though, to console myself right now by reminding myself that over the years I have done quite a few more of my own, original plays – honest! – than these five you have here in your hand.

Including, just last year, one I liked a lot! (Perhaps because it's the most recent?) It is about the very long and very private life of the Scottish poet Edwin Morgan, who died almost two years ago at the age of ninety. The protagonist of the play is his biographer and friend, and it is about this good man's struggle with the question of what he is entitled to make of the life of another, and about his struggle to keep Morgan alive and creative right up to the very end. The audiences found it very moving – well, it *is* a great story, a wee play about very big and universal things, and we certainly hope to revive it. There were originally only five performances for a festival called Glasgay here in Glasgow last November.

Though, can I really with any justice call it original or my own? The three absolutely fantastic actors – it's simply not recastable, this play – were even more involved in the construction of the piece than is usual for me. Oh, the play was all my idea, but so much of the material came straight out of James McGonigal's Morgan biography, *Beyond the Last Dragon*, with its author's permission and generous help. Maybe it was another one of those pieces of my work that should properly come under the banner of adaptation?

For since the mid-eighties, I've spent much of my time – most of my time? – in the theatre working on translations and adaptations and, especially, versions of great classic plays for particular, mainly Scottish companies of actors – and, yes, I have very, very much enjoyed this, found my delight and amazement just grow and grow as I worked on the genius of Molière or Chekhov or Euripides. I have always tried hard, of course, to get right inside the original, felt a great responsibility to the play and its nature, but been relieved that these great plays were classics which have had, and would continue to have, many other versions. I always felt, doing this work, perfectly creatively fulfilled.

But I must admit there is nothing to beat the enjoyment, or the scary lonely excitement and the passion – and the mess – of working on your own on a new play of your own.

Writing *Blood and Ice*, my first play, and the first in this volume, was exactly like that. More of this story later, in my intro to that play.

The next, *Mary Queen of Scots Got Her Head Chopped Off* was written for a company, and even a cast, already extant. A company whose style I knew and loved, and with a lot of input from both Gerry Mulgrew, the genius of Communicado, and from that cast, but it was written by me. There was a lot of improvisation went into the staging, but not into the writing. More of *that* story too later in this volume.

I then worked for a couple of years for a couple of other theatres on a couple of other projects before rejoining Communicado on what was, for me at the time, a mistake. But one that led to me knowing more about what I believed in, how I needed to work.

Jock Tamson's Bairns, Communicado and Gerry Mulgrew's 1990 Glasgow City of Culture cast-of-thousands site-specific theatre piece for the vast Tramway, is something remembered by many people as immensely powerful – I've even heard 'the best thing I've ever seen'. The music, from the newly created, eclectic Cauld Blast Orchestra, was truly wonderful. Certainly it was visually stunning. Before its time in its poetic, non-narrative structure. A poetry that came out of the rhythm of performance itself.

And I think, had I not been involved, I would have found it mighty impressive as an event. But as I was 'the writer' on the project, never had a clue what I was supposed to be doing, was just aware that I wasn't giving Gerry anything he needed or wanted (not that he could ever explain to me what that might be) – well, all I knew was I was utterly and totally letting him, and myself, down. And after *Mary* being such a success for all of us too…

This time, I was supposed to write *from* things that emerged from improvisation during the long, long rehearsal period, but what I remember is being just alternately miserable and totally terrified as the opening night approached, and so I'd stay up all night and write speeches, scenes, scraps, take them in, they'd be read through once by the company and discarded. There's an old cabin trunk somewhere literally stuffed full of *Jock Tamson's Bairns* drafts and scribbles, and I have no more desire to open it – even now – than to open Pandora's box.

I definitely thought at the time: if that's writing in the theatre, it's just not for me. Never again. Which led, a year later, as my courage and appetite recovered, to *Quelques Fleurs,* the third play printed here.

It was written at all, came out like this, a tight two-hander, a reaction, unashamedly static and all words, all story, all about these specific characters, precisely *because* of *Jock Tamson's Bairns*.

I even put up the money myself and performed as Verena at the Edinburgh Festival Fringe alongside my friend Stuart Hepburn who had been Bothwell in *Mary Queen of Scots Got Her Head Chopped Off* and in *Jock Tamson's Bairns* too. A 'profit-share', and – this is unheard of! – we actually made a (very small) profit, then were invited by Philip Howard to put it on for a run at the Traverse that Christmas as a very anti-festive show for adult pantomime refuseniks. The just-out-of-drama-school David McVicar (will I have to call him Sir David now?) loved it and picked it up as an easy touring show for his short-lived small-scale Glasgow-based theatre company. Lewis Howden, a then new-to-me actor I've worked with frequently since, took over as Derek, insisting that I had been missing an obvious trick with the drama, a plot point I'd been, quite mistakenly in his voluble opinion, avoiding.

When he got his rewrite, two days before we opened, he, temporarily, had his regrets, but I've never had any. Big improvement, Lewis, I was the first to admit it.

This is a play about two people, one of whom talks and talks (all year!) to *not* say what matters to her, until, after all that repressing, out it comes; and one who, in a single day at the end of that year, is taken backwards in time from being incoherently drunk and almost home to what we know will be hell, back to being sober and telling us the whole truth at the beginning of his journey. At the end of the play.

Sound confusing? The interlaced structure, with its two different time frames, one for each character, is, I admit, hard to bring off. A flaw I see no solution for. The audience do seem to catch on fine, though.

The first three plays in this volume are, I think, very different from each other indeed. But the last two, *Perfect Days* and *Good Things*, ought to have something in common, as they were conceived as part one and part two of a loose trilogy of popular comedies, romantic comedies, about the lives of modern women as they approached what the women's mags would have us regard as big milestones – fear of forty, *Perfect Days*, and fear of fifty, *Good Things*.

Perfect Days I wrote for the Traverse Theatre and my friend Siobhan Redmond. She was just brilliant in it, although anybody less like Barbs Marshall in real life would be hard to find. Maybe that's why she enjoyed playing her so much? It toured and even went to the West End for a short run, which was a big thrill. It was translated into many different languages, had several foreign productions – Japan, Finland! – and was on in Poland till last year. There have been quite a few other really terrific professional productions in different parts of Britain over the years. It was a great rep play. Wish I could write another one of these.

Good Things is gentler, more bittersweet and poignant perhaps, and Susan Love isn't either as abrasive, or as quirky, as Barbs in *Perfect Days* but is, in her own way, just as proactive and energetic an everywoman protagonist. One who sets out, in new ways totally accepted and commonplace these days, to get what she wants. And finds, like Barbs, that life is what happens while you're making other plans.

Good Things was written for, and developed by, a terrific popular touring theatre company called Borderline. Not at all well-off even then, it has now been effectively shut down by the funders. The extensive doubling, originally for reasons of economy, done by two of the actors, which means that they are literally never off the stage except for the most bravura of quick changes, well, this doubling was for me the point of it, the structural fun in the writing of it. And I expected this to be much of the fun for the audience, too. But so good was Molly Innes at going from Doris to

Marjorie to Policewoman, etc., that it was actually the curtain before quite a lot of the audience realised they had seen only four actors, two of them, between them, playing thirteen parts! The audience, quite properly, were only interested in the story.

Pitlochry Festival Theatre revived this play in their 2009 summer season with great popular success. I do think there is more life in it, and am slightly puzzled – what with its bonny only-four-actors economy – why it hasn't, so far, had the country-wide repertory-theatre success *Perfect Days* enjoyed in its first flush.

But because there are actually fifteen parts, some of them tiny, this play has already proved popular with amateur dramatics societies all over the country. I've seen some really excellent ones that absolutely caught the tone.

What about the third in the trilogy? Fear of sixty?

Vow: either – by my own sixty-fifth birthday in six months' time – I get a draft of this as-yet-unborn play with the title I love but am not telling and the characters I know inside out and the setting that actually does deeply interest me, or I dump, for once and all, into the bin, the unconnected contradictory scenes, the inconsistent tone, all I've so far managed to get down, all these characters, the unexplored narrative possibilities and the whole idea.

Writing plays, in whatever 'artistic climate', does not get any easier with age or experience.

Why would it?

I'm hopeful though.

Liz Lochhead
June 2012

BLOOD AND ICE

Introduction

Blood and Ice, my first play, was performed in its first full incarnation at the Edinburgh Festival Fringe in August 1982 at the Traverse Theatre in Edinburgh with Gerda Stevenson perfectly cast as Mary. She was lovely. Young, heartbreakingly young was how she played it, in love with a poet and with a poetic ideal, earnest, passionately enquiring, passionately committed to living a life that secretly terrified her.

Nevertheless, the play, even by its kindest critics – and, yes, there were some of those – could not possibly be called an unqualified success. It was far too long for one thing, and was, literally, all over the place. I, for one, must admit that I can't, now, make head or tail of the original script, although within its excesses I can see it also contains what proved to be the still-beating heart of the whole creature, which is an exploration of the sources, and the consequences for its creator, of an enduring and immortal myth.

Mary Godwin Shelley lived at the cusp of reason and romanticism. She was the daughter of two great Age of Reason radical philosophers of freedom: William Godwin, author of *Political Justice*, and Mary Wollstonecraft, author of *A Vindication of the Rights of Woman,* a founding feminist who died of puerperal fever just one week after giving birth to Mary. This legacy weighed heavily upon the child. As did, later, her own female biological destiny.

So much for free love. From the age of sixteen, when she ran away with him, married already as he was, until the death of Shelley eight years later when she was only twenty-four, she herself was almost constantly either pregnant, recovering from miscarriage or mourning the death of a child. (Only one, the delicate Percy Florence, was to survive into adulthood.) So many deaths. The suicides of her own Shelley-obsessed sister and Shelley's deserted wife were sore enough but, far worse, the deaths of so many little innocents – their own, and the child of her stepsister and Byron too, all dragged around Europe in that ultimate romantic pursuit of their progenitors. No surprise perhaps that, prescient as she must have been – many, though not all, of these griefs lay ahead of her – this particular seventeen-year-old girl should have come up with a deep-felt fantasy of *a new way of creating life*. She was already, I'm sure, subconsciously aware of pushing herself beyond her own natural boundaries. Therefore the myth emerged as far from Utopian, but one of horror and terror of Science, a myth that remains potent for our nuclear age, our age of astonishment and unease at the fruits of perhaps-beyond-the-boundaries genetic experimentation.

That garbled first script of mine nevertheless contains, more or less verbatim, many of the scenes which are still extant in this version, the umpteenth and, I have promised myself, final version, which was completed for a 2003 production in the Royal Lyceum Theatre in Edinburgh instigated by, and directed by, Graham McLaren, with whom in the last decade I have collaborated on several versions of classic plays for Theatre Babel.

Many young directors, many young actors, university students and struggling new fringe companies have, since 1982, taken on the challenge of this play. I have met quite a few since who were keen to tell me: 'This was the first play I found for myself and just knew I had to direct it'; or 'I played Byron'; or 'I was Shelley'; or 'I loved playing Mary.' Many of these productions, the ones I saw at any rate, had wonderful *moments*. They'd fire me up and get it going again for me. I got on with trying to write other plays, but, all through the 1980s, like a dog returning to its own vomit, I'd go back to it, trying, abortively, to solve the problem of the structure, find what would finally seem the satisfactory form, keeping up the pursuit myself – for its own sake, whether there was an upcoming production or not – happily scribbling away through long lonely nights, just as obsessively, I had to own, as half-mad Frankenstein himself labouring with his unlovely creation, looking for the spark of life.

That spark came towards the end of the decade when, in 1988, David McVicar, now world-famous as a director of opera, but then a second-year student at Glasgow's Royal Scottish Academy of Music and Drama, phoned me up and said he wanted to direct the play and had a cast together for a production at the Edinburgh Festival Fringe.

I remember saying, 'Don't do it. Yes, it has great ideas in it, and a couple of great scenes, but it doesn't actually *work*.'

David said, 'I know, but I think I can see what's wrong with it. Can we have a coffee and talk?'

I met David. Then went to a rehearsal and fell in love with the cast. It had to be a real ensemble piece and they were a real ensemble. So young, so talented and full of fire. I felt: hey, this lot might actually be about to crack it...

They got me doing, for nothing of course, but happily, obsessively again, loads and loads of work, more midnight oil, on a new script, one very, very like this one published here.

David McVicar's production in its Edinburgh Fringe Scout Hall venue was thrilling. It was alive! Candlelit, and in 1960's cheesecloth shirts and loon pants and simple long hippy-chick dresses for the girls, it had an amazing *coup de théâtre* when, from under the alpine peaks of an unmoving heap of muslin, the Creature, at the end of the first act, naked and beautiful as a baby, suddenly stood up and made the audience gasp – and terrified Mary into sitting down to write.

The cast were fantastic. Wendy Seager's Mary, Daniela Nardini's Claire (for the first time not *merely* an annoying idiot of a millstone for Mary but also passionate, and pitiable, a convincingly whole, if not well-rounded, person asserting, painfully, her own right to love), John Kazek's brooding Byron and John Straiton's incandescent Shelley were all so young and so beautiful they had charm enough to make us actually care about this set of self-indulgent, if brilliant, adventurers.

They were invited to perform their production at the Traverse that autumn, and RSAMD gave them leave of absence from the final year of their course to do so. It was sold out and there were queues for returns. When they had graduated, *Blood and Ice* was the first production of David McVicar's far too short-lived touring company Pen Name.

A ghost, for me, was laid to rest.

When, half a dozen years ago, Graham McLaren came to me wanting to do *Blood and Ice* on the big stage of Edinburgh's Royal Lyceum, I said, '… yes – but, oh, it's practically impossible to bring off, the actors must be really, really young, and also credibly these brilliant poets, and be gorgeous, and charming, especially Shelley, whom I haven't ever managed to make so enough in the script, and they must all be human and vulnerable, even Byron – and you'll have to make sure they find a lot of laughter and lightness in the opening scene, and some playful, joyful and easy sensuality too, because there is so little of that shown as the play begins at the point the cracks are appearing, and because there is so much darkness ahead in the journey. And, Graham, for the big stage, I'll really have to have a wee go at the *structure…*'

Graham's production, with another lovely young cast, was very beautiful, very spooky, very romantic and made me very happy.

It's exactly thirty years since I first took down from a library shelf Muriel Spark's *Child of Light*, her wonderful biography of

Mary Shelley, and, shortly after, began my own pursuit. Could I make a play…? Naively, I was, at the time, quite blithely unaware that I wasn't the first, and certainly wouldn't be the last, to be fired by the dramatic possibilities of this moment in history, that iconic stormy summer of 1816 by the shores of the lake and beneath the high Alps. There is, apparently, a 1969 novel called *A Single Summer with L.B.* by Derek Marlowe, which since someone told me about it twenty-odd years ago, I've always meant to read. And now that I really am finally through with these characters for myself, I will. There was a fairly terrible Ken Russell film called *Gothic* in 1986; and also Howard Brenton's 1989 stage play *Bloody Poetry,* which focused on Shelley's radical romantic politics – and Byron. But, as for *Blood and Ice,* this published version is the very last word from me on these characters, this particular dilemma.

Unless, David McV, you know someone you can persuade this old play of mine could be a brilliant, blazing brand-new opera…?

Liz Lochhead
July 2009

This version of *Blood and Ice* was first performed at the Royal Lyceum Theatre, Edinburgh, on 24 October 2003, with the following cast:

MARY SHELLEY	Lucianne McEvoy
SHELLEY	Phil Matthews
BYRON	Alex Hassel
CLAIRE CLAIRMONT	Susan Coyle
ELISE	Michele Rodley
Director	Graham McLaren

Characters

MARY SHELLEY
PERCY BYSSHE SHELLEY
CLAIRE CLAIRMONT
LORD BYRON
ELISE, *a maid*
THE CREATURE
NURSE

ACT ONE

In an England of darkness and loneliness, MARY SHELLEY*, a young widow in her late twenties, is stretched out asleep.*

The 'nightmare is upon her', the image is that of the famous Fuseli painting and there is perhaps an actual and physical manifestation of the smothering homunculous on her chest that appears momentarily in a flash of lightning and disappears again in the beat of darkness that follows it. Certainly, shadows move. A dream whisper breaks her sleep.

CREATURE'S VOICE. Why did you make me?… Frankenstein?

MARY *wakes with a gasp of fear. Dead silence. She breathes, listening. Wind blows the window open, it bangs once, twice, three times. She gets up and, barefoot, pads across the floorboards to fasten it, her relief palpable.*

Ideal or important pieces of set and furniture are a double-sided oval mirror on a stand (a cheval glass) and a nightmarish perhaps oversized rocking horse. It rocks now of its own will, but when MARY *turns around, it stops.*

MARY (*sighing relief*). Nothing.

CREATURE'S VOICE (*a whisper*). Frankenstein?

MARY. Such dreams.

Night after night, such bad dreams.

I go to my new book, for I will write it, I must!

And dreams of that old one, the one that's done and dusted, in print and out there in the world, making whatever stumbling way it can, for better or worse – dreams of my infamous creation come back to haunt me.

Come back to haunt me and I cannot shake it off.

I have the strongest presentiment something terrible is about to happen.

Last night I dreamed, I dreamed I was seventeen, we were back in Poland Street, I found my little baby, my firstborn, it was not dead but… cold merely. Shelley and I rubbed it before the fire and it lived! Awoke and found no baby.

No Shelley.

CREATURE'S VOICE. Why?

MARY. Don't think of him.

When they found him washed up, his eyes, his face, all parts of him… not protected by his clothes were eaten away, they only knew him by – in his pocket they found… that volume of Keats he carried with him always.

Sometimes I wake up. Cold. Bathed in a moon sweat. And I rub myself slowly to life again.

The dead of night.

Don't think of him.

More movement, shadows, and suddenly:

SHELLEY'S VOICE. Oh, Mary! You don't seem to care how much it grieves me that you won't sail with me…

Come and see her.

New arrived from Genoa, *The Ariel*, the bonniest boat that ever sailed the seas!

MARY. Don't think of him.

She goes to her writing desk with great effort of will.

Loud cries of 'Mama, Mama, Mama' and suddenly a very flesh and blood bonny wee six-year-old CHILD *with girlish soft long fair hair, runs in, capering with a toy windmill or a ball, some toy in motion.* MARY, *laughing, runs and catches him up and tickles him. He giggles and squirms.*

Oh, Perciflo, you rascal! Your mama's best boy, her only! What am I to do with you! Your mama is busy, she must write her new storybook and earn lots of pennies for her big bonny best boy!

Nurse! Nurse! Come and fetch him, please!

NURSE *appears, a quick in-and-out shadow of a girl who takes the* CHILD, *kicking, under her arms, and exits with him.* MARY *calls offstage after them.*

See Percy Florence gets to bed again and has himself a proper night's sleep – and no argument about it, my naughty little, my nice little, my naughty little man!

Alone again, she sits at her work.

My sweet, sweet boy, my only consolation…

Oh, how am I to take care of you, all by myself?

This new book of mine will save us both. Must! *The Last Man…* such a good fantastical idea for a philosophical and terrifying novel. If I work constantly on this one and manage a mere thousand words a day, then in only a hundred days… allow two more months for copying and revisions and… surely on the strength alone of the stir that surrounded my last publication –

CREATURE'S VOICE. Frankenstein, why did you make me?

MARY. Well, it wasn't for the money anyway. Nor for the wager, or the challenge of the competition –

Shadows move.

BYRON'S VOICE. I'll set us a little contest. Why should we content ourselves with translated, traditional horrors, all bookish and stilted. Home-grown ones are the best. Who can make the most stirring unnatural tale?

MARY. There were three of us.

SHELLEY'S VOICE. Mary!

BYRON'S VOICE. Mary!

CLAIRE'S VOICE (*a giggle*). Mary!

MARY (*as if silencing her*). There were *three* of us!

Shadows move.

ELISES'S VOICE. Mrs Shelley, madame! Milord Byron's man says he is here to fetch both the ladies –

MARY *firmly suppresses these voices from the past.*

MARY. There was Shelley… and Byron… and me.

CREATURE'S VOICE *overlaps and echoes.*

CREATURE'S VOICE. Me… Me… Me!… Tell me about the night you made me, Frankenstein.

MARY *blows out the candle, casts off her heavy, dark dressing gown and is a laughing eighteen-year-old in white muslin back in Switzerland, 1816 – summer, daytime, in a totally bright and different light. The lake and Mont Blanc above it.*

Wet and naked, capering, SHELLEY, *a boy of twenty-two, wrapped only in a lace tablecloth, spins her round and kisses her.*

SHELLEY. Mary Godwin, you are such a prude! Such blushes! Come here until I kiss them better.

MARY. Shelley, how could you? Honestly… put some clothes on.

SHELLEY. Swimming, Mary. I want to learn to swim.

MARY. Walking naked across the terrace, all tangled up with weeds and –

SHELLEY. I forgot. I forgot they were coming.

MARY. You did not! You only wanted to be outrageous –

SHELLEY. Oh, what does it matter, Mary!

MARY. It matters to me! She was a great friend of my mother's.

SHELLEY. Old humbugs, pretending to be shocked!

MARY (*fighting laughter*). I thought La Gisborne would have an apoplexy!

SHELLEY. And the other old goose! Lord, I thought she was going to burst her goitre.

MARY (*laughing*). Thank goodness they've gone! They didn't stay a minute after your grand apparition, though! It was make excuses and off before they'd drained their first teacup. Oh, Shelley, how could you have! Naked!

SHELLEY. I covered myself! Just as soon as I saw you had company to tea. I had two choices. I could brazen it out, or hide myself behind the maidservant. So I –

MARY. What Elise must have thought I cannot imagine!

SHELLEY. Oh, so not content with fretting over the old dowagers, now we are to agonise over the imagined offence to the servant girl! Well, at least we don't have to worry about what the neighbours will say.

MARY. It's his influence makes you so careless of the regard of others!

SHELLEY. No, Mary, you know I never cared for the world's approval. Not in such… silly and private matters. And neither did you! The Mary I met…

MARY. Did not go deliberately out of her way to offend elderly ladies in such… silly and trivial ways!

SHELLEY. I covered myself. Dodging behind the maidservant, swaddling myself in her apron strings. I twirled around and, sleight of hand, snatched out the topmost tablecloth like a conjurer ere she put down the tea things and sat myself down, decently draped in dimity and lace, to adequate small talk amid the tinkling cups. I do not see how you can begin to complain of me!

MARY. I was surprised enough when they called in the first place. You know how our position makes us vulnerable to… of course, Maria Gisborne was a follower of Mama's, certainly she is of more liberal opinions than most middle-aged matrons, but it was kind of her to call.

SHELLEY. Kind! Now don't you think Mrs Gisborne might just have been moved by curiosity, not to speak of the passing expectation of perhaps a glimpse of our illustrious… no, our infamous neighbour?

MARY. Shelley, it was very kind – !

SHELLEY. So, they can certainly tell all the English Community that no, they never saw so much as an eyelash of Lord Byron…

He runs to the terrace door and throws off the tablecloth.

…but they saw every inch of Percy Shelley, the whole natural man!

MARY. Shelley!

SHELLEY (*laughing*). Mrs Gisborne! Come back! Maria! Look at me, am I not a pretty sight? Look what the sea threw up! What? You've never seen a naked man in all your sixty summers. She's fainted, smelling salts? Come here, I'll give you a sniff of the sea.

ELISE, *the maid, enters from the terrace, exactly from where she'll have had a good view of the naked* SHELLEY. *He is laughing and unabashed, she professionally deadpan.* MARY *is not amused.*

ELISE. Madame? Shall I clear the tea things?

MARY. Yes, yes, you may, Elise, of course.

SHELLEY *is still trailing the tablecloth.*

SHELLEY. Yes, and bring in the brandy, Elise.

MARY. Oh no, dearest!

ELISE. Yes, sir.

She takes the tea tray and exits again to where she's come from.

MARY. We do not take alcohol, you say yourself – !

SHELLEY. No, we have no need of intoxicants. A failure of the imagination I call it, but when we have guests –

MARY. No, Shelley, no brandy, not tonight, I don't want him to come!

SHELLEY *grabs her, spins round and hugs her in a mad dance, wrapping her up in the tablecloth too.*

SHELLEY. Do we care anything for prudish old hypocrites?

MARY. No!

SHELLEY. Prime ministers and poltickers?

MARY. No!

SHELLEY. Papas who go back on every principle they have ever published and are suddenly scandalised by love freed from the shackles of marriage? What do we care for them?

MARY. Nothing!

SHELLEY. Less than nothing. Let love know no limits!

They twirl and kiss, euphoric.

MARY. Now, go and change!

SHELLEY. Come with me, Mary.

MARY. Change!

SHELLEY. C'mon, Mary…

MARY. I have to feed William!

SHELLEY. Kiss me.

They kiss.

MARY. Your lips are cold! Oh, Shelley, you made me shiver.

They kiss again, longer. An intrusion of movement in the shadows.

Who's there?

Stillness. Silence.

SHELLEY. Nobody. It's nothing. What's the matter? Kiss me.

He kisses her again. She responds passionately. ELISE *enters with brandy on a tray, and coughs.*

ELISE. Madame…

MARY (*embarrassed*). Yes, Elise?

ELISE. Milord Byron's man, madame, he says he has come to fetch you both.

MARY (*to* SHELLEY). You go!

SHELLEY. Mary! He'll be offended…

MARY. You go with him.

SHELLEY. Mary –

MARY. I have to feed Willmouse.

SHELLEY. I'll stay with you.

MARY. Go and sail with Byron on the lake. You know you want to.

SHELLEY. Tonight I promise you I'll make you shiver, Mary.

Exit SHELLEY. *From far away, calling:*

CLAIRE. Elise! Elise!

ELISE *begins to go.* MARY *stops her.*

MARY. Oh, Elise!

ELISE. Yes, madame.

MARY. You must have thought Mr Shelley's behaviour somewhat strange?

ELISE. No, madame.

MARY. Tell me, are you at home here, Elise?

ELISE *shrugs.*

ELISE. S'pose so, madame. I am at home. I was born here in Switzerland.

MARY. No, Elise, I meant… (*In a blurt.*) you must not be surprised at anything Mr Shelley does, he is… I think you know we are not, he is not bound by normal conventions, he cares nothing for them, neither of us do! But he is a good, good man, he is against all viciousness and cruelty and tyranny and ownership. What is nakedness compared to…

ELISE *withholds her reassurance. Eventually:*

ELISE (*shrugging*). It's only nature, madame.

MARY. Thank you, Elise.

ELISE. May I go, ma'am?

ELISE *begins to go again.*

MARY. Oh, Elise! Elise, in the packing today, that arrived from England, there is such a pretty shawl… and a bonnet that – yes, I'm sure – would look very fetching on you!

ELISE. Thank you, madame.

CLAIRE (*a voice still far away*). Elise! Elise, where are you, you tiresome creature? Come and help me make myself pretty!

ELISE. Can I go, madame? Mam'zelle Claire, she –

MARY. Of course you may. And do take away the brandy, please, we'll have no need of it this evening.

ELISE. Yes, ma'am.

MARY *goes to the terrace and out.* ELISE *takes up the tray with the decanter again, murmurs under her breath, but quite audibly:*

Yes, madame, no, madame, take it, leave it. A bonnet! A bonnet! Very fetching, I'm sure…

Exit ELISE.

Transition: lights change back to that opening scene, present time, again. Widow MARY*, shawled, dressing-gowned, at her desk. There's movement in the shadows again.*

MARY. We were so happy then, always, Shelley and I, even with Claire, our ever-constant companion.

CREATURE'S VOICE. You should love this. The creator should not shun his creature.

MARY. Oh, Claire Clairmont, you were always so jealous of me. Everything I had, you had to have it too. Everything…

CREATURE'S VOICE. Why? Why?

MARY. Perhaps I am unjust to her? My millstone and my sister. Since I was three years old. My papa married her mama.

'You are to be sisters now. Share your doll.' It's my doll. It's my book. I'm clever!

'You may be cleverer but I'm prettier, my mama says so. *Your* mama is dead.'

Mama. My dead mama. All the time of my growing up the legend of my dead mama. And she died giving birth to me.

Rivers of blood. I heard the cook tell the parlourmaid when she thought I wasn't listening. Puppies at her breasts so they'd suck until the afterbirth came away. No use. She died.

CREATURE'S VOICE. Who made me? Who made This…? Frankenstein.

MARY. Oh, but Claire or no Claire, we were so happy then, always, that summer, Shelley and I, before *he* came!

She actually means BYRON*, but then –*

CREATURE'S VOICE. Frankenstein, why did you make me, why did you make me not beautiful?

Echo and fade. Lights change.

Back in sunlit Switzerland. CLAIRE*, in petticoats, is having her lacing done up by* ELISE*, in obedient ladies-maid mode.* ELISE *has brought* CLAIRE*'s dress.*

CLAIRE *is young, radiant, overexcited.*

CLAIRE. Tight! Tighter! Lace me nice and small, Elise! Make me beautiful.

MARY *comes in from the terrace in her white muslin frock, eating an apple.*

MARY. – And breathless!

CLAIRE. Not me! Now my hair. One hundred strokes so it'll shine! Ow! Elise, you're tugging. Give it to me. Clumsy! Mary, do you not think we are somewhat alike? *Oui?* Yes, we do resemble each other after all.

MARY. How could we, we are not sisters.

CLAIRE. Not in blood, no. But we are closer perhaps than sisters, *oui*? Haven't we always shared everything?

MARY (*murmurs*). Since we were three years old…

CLAIRE. You love to write! And I love to write! You found a passionate poet to be your lover. And I –

MARY. Came with us!

CLAIRE. Mary! *Tu n'est pas gentile!* What else could I do? (*Pause.*) You are such a scarlet lady, Mary. And now I am scarlet too! We are two very scarlet ladies. Tongs, Elise!

MARY. I'm not!

ELISE. Madame. (*Passes the tongs.*)

CLAIRE. Oh yes, you are! In the world's eyes. Not hot enough, silly girl, here! (*Pause.*) Mary found herself a young and beautiful and a passionate poet to be her heart's companion. And Claire found herself a… not *quite* so young but quite as beautiful and quite as passionate a poet to be hers!

MARY. Oh, Claire, be careful!

Elise, do go fetch me that ribbon from next door, please.

ELISE *goes, then – at* CLAIRE, *urgently:*

Why, this morning at dawn I saw you running through the gap in the hedges back through the garden to the kitchen quarters, all disordered with your hair loose, losing your shoe like Cinderella –

Re-enter ELISE *unseen by* MARY. *Stands. Listens.*

And that maid presented it back to you with such an ironical little bob of a curtsey and the most insolent smirk on her face.

CLAIRE. So the servants see we too have a little blood in our veins…

ELISE. Ribbon, madame!

CLAIRE. Probably jealous, aren't you, Elise! All England would be jealous of me if they knew. All the ladies in England, at least!

MARY. Jealous! To see you make a fool of yourself, throwing yourself at a man just because he's a scandal – oh, and a famous poet!

CLAIRE. I love him. And I know he loves me. Such a scandal, though! Imagine! Peacocks, packing cases all over the quayside, monkeys escaping from their cages, a piano dangling in mid-air. And the ladies! All the ladies weeping oceans into their cambric handkerchiefs, pressing billets-doux on him, sending little black pageboys to shower him with locks of their hair. Do you know, Mary, some ladies even cut off –

MARY. There can be only one outcome of all this, Claire! He is married already!

CLAIRE (*laughing*). And you are an '*ippocreet*!

ELISE. Careful, Madame Claire, these tongs are very hot!

CLAIRE. Byron loathes and detests Annabel with all his heart. Byron has far less truck with Annabel after only a month or two's parting than Shelley has with his Harriet after nearly three years!

MARY. Harriet is the mother of his children. He cannot leave her destitute, his children bereft – I would not for a moment wish him to. Harriet is…

CLAIRE. His wife, *n'est ce pas*?

MARY (*gentler*). Claire, don't let's quarrel. I… I cannot bear it when we do.

CLAIRE. No. Don't let's quarrel, Mary. You are so good, of course you are not jealous. I was silly! Of course Shelley must care for

Harriet. Oh, Mary! (*Kisses her.*) I want to love *you*, and Shelley and little William, and... oh, Mary, I feel as though my heart could burst. The moment I met my Albé, that very first instant –

MARY (*bursts*). Would you mother a fatherless child?

CLAIRE *wavers, won't answer for a beat, then:*

CLAIRE. Mary, you do not know how cruel my life was, *vraiment*! You had Shelley to be your protector, I had no one... I told Byron, I wrote to him... once or twice, and told him what his poetry meant to me, how reading it had transformed my whole drab existence and that made him responsible for me – for the Creator should not shun his creature – and I... (*Brazenly.*) I – yes I did! – I arranged that we would go away together and be free and unknown and we could return the following morning!

Well, did not your mama defy convention so?

I am sure she thought it shameful that women must simper and sit in the chimney corner and make mimsy mouths and wait for men to decide to kiss them. I am sure she looked forward to a time when woman as well as man may freely state her desire.

MARY. Of course! But –

CLAIRE. But what? Everything your mother ever thought, everything she wrote – Your mama wanted that women should be free.

MARY. Do you want to be a mother? Because –

CLAIRE. There is no stronger bond between a man and a woman than the making of a child. It is only nature, Mary. (*Pause.*) I think... perhaps... it may have happened already. Oh – I'm sure *not* – don't let's quarrel! You said so yourself. We mustn't quarrel. We must be happy here – the lake, the high Alps – we are a million miles away from tight little *Angleterre*! Hasn't all our luggage been unpacked yet? Elise, hasn't –

ELISE. Madame?

CLAIRE. Our *baggages*! Lord, I'm sure it seems such ages ago we packed it, and I was in such a lather of excitement – I cannot think what we'll find when we open it! Isn't it exciting?

MARY. You know I do not interest myself much in frippery!

CLAIRE. Did you pack the blue, *ma favourite*?

MARY. I can't remember…

CLAIRE. I was always jealous of that dress. Quite green over the blue! A happy dress – you wore it always that summer when we were sixteen and I was the little bird that carried messages between you and Shelley and you walked together in the graveyard.

SHELLEY *enters, for first beat of his presence a strange and frightening shape, then graceful light-footed* SHELLEY, *finger to his lips, holding a blindfold.*

CLAIRE *sees him, smiles, distracts* MARY *by tying, choker-fashion, a thin red-velvet ribbon round her throat.*

Look at me, Mary. Look! Do you not think this is fetching? It is my latest fashion… oh, rather an antique one to be sure, but then something genuinely flattering is surely à la mode for all time… The brave beldams of the French revolution affected it. The thinnest simple crimson-velvet ribbon at the throat… *'À la victime'!* (*Laughs.*) – Don't you love that?

So witty! Such a piquant bit of stylishness. Oh, only a fashion, Mary, but I'm sure the gentlemen will love it!

SHELLEY, *giggling his high-pitched laugh, grabs* MARY *and ties the blindfold over her eyes. She gets a fright but* SHELLEY *and* CLAIRE *begin an at first sweet, childish and innocent 'Blind Man's Buff', calling* MARY *in different voices and dodging under her arms and giggling.* MARY *tries to join in as if it's fun. But soon she's spinning round, grasping, stumbles towards, stops at* ELISE, *who has been standing silent at the edge of the game, an onlooker.*

MARY *feels all down* ELISE*'s face and shoulders and breasts.*

MARY. Claire?

CLAIRE. Not I!

Then she feels who it is and screams slightly.

CLAIRE *and* SHELLEY *are laughing aloud.*

(*From elsewhere.*) You're getting colder!

MARY (*spinning around*). Shelley!

CLAIRE. Getting cold-er! That was only the maid, Mary, and she's not in our game!

MARY (*grasping, desperate*). Shelley!

Giggling, SHELLEY *and* CLAIRE *dodge her, pull* ELISE *out from her grasp too.*

BYRON *limps in silently.* MARY *bumps into him, touching, and then she grasps him, hugging. Holds on.*

Shelley! Oh, darling, free me –

BYRON *kisses her lightly on the cheek and unties her blindfold.*

BYRON. Easily… but it's only me, Mary.

MARY *looks confused, turns away.*

ELISE *helps a suddenly imperious* CLAIRE *into her dress.*

CLAIRE. Byron! Where have you been? I was waiting! When my Albé says he will come over with the poem he wishes me to transpose then I do expect him to come.

BYRON. But I didn't.

Ah! Such a fine sail we had, eh, Shelley? We'll get you your sea legs yet, Shiloh! I was as good as born with them. (*Limps arrogantly across the room.*) It's dry land I find difficult, except when I have strong drink taken and am half-seas-over. Well, ladies, how have you been wiling away the idle hours? Apart from rouging, titivating and bathing in asses' milk and waiting for your sailor boys to return?

CLAIRE *twirls around before him.*

CLAIRE. And don't we look pretty? Albé, don't you admire my necklace?

BYRON. Very diverting, yes. Not so bonny as that gewgaw you wear at your throat, though, Mary. And who is that?

CLAIRE. That's Mary's famous mama!

BYRON *looks at it, holding* MARY *by it close to him.*

BYRON. The writer, eh? She was bonny, but not so bonny as you.

MARY. I do not resemble her.

BYRON. No, she was all russet – fire and earth. You're more… water and air.

MARY *pulls away.*

MARY. And where's Polidori? He doesn't join us this evening?

SHELLEY. Pollydolly says he won't come. I think he's jealous.

BYRON (*laughing at the idea of it*). He says he's busy writing…

MARY. He has never refused to join us before…

SHELLEY. The wild eye, the pale brow, the fevered scratchings and scribblings! (*Laughs.*) A harsh mistress he's taken up with, the Muse, she'll lead him a merry dance, if she don't desert him like she has me these days and nights…

CLAIRE. Shall I go, Albé? I'll charm him into joining us. I'll tell him it won't be the same without him.

BYRON. Without his French volume of ghost stories more likely! Lord, but there are some stirring tales in that book of his – oh, after what you read aloud to us last night, Mary Godwin, all the long night through I slept scarce a wink. Yes, after our… little *soirée*, our cosy little *conversazione* of the supernatural…

SHELLEY (*playful, in a mock-sepulchral voice*). Once upon a time, there was Byron and Mary, and Claire and Shelley. It was a dark and a moonless night –

BYRON. – and all night long I was quite unmanned and unnerved by thoughts of a light pale little girl with silken hair and the strangest stories to tell. All I could see was Mary, Mary…

SHELLEY *is laughing*.

MARY *is held in thrall, but horrified*.

CLAIRE *is jealous, but when, pouting, she goes to try and hang around* BYRON*'s neck, she is shrugged off*.

BYRON *never flinches from his blatant attention to* MARY.

SHELLEY. See, Mary, you are a witch, cast quite a spell on poor old Byron here!

BYRON. Ask poor Pollydolly! I had to summon him in the middle of the night and he had to administer me the strongest draught to make me… lie down and get me to sleep.

Well, dear friends, and shall we eat dinner soon, I'm ravenous. Where's the maid? She's always forgetting to bring the bloody decanter! Elise! Elise! Lord, I am so hungry I could eat a Scotch reviewer. Roasted. Couldn't you? Oh, I forgot, the Shelleys are Utopian vegetarians who won't gorge themselves on anything bloodier than an orange, eh?

ELISE *enters.*

Bring us brandy, my dear, did not you know I was arrived?

ELISE. Yes, sir.

BYRON. Well, surely by now you know how to fulfil my every desire and pleasure?

ELISE. Yes, sir. (*Confused.*) No, sir…

BYRON. Well, just bring the bloody brandy on the double. 'Twould be a start…

ELISE. Yes, sir…

ELISE *exits.*

MARY. Lord Byron! Please don't –

SHELLEY *sees that* MARY*'s really angry, is outraged at* BYRON*'s proprietorial attitude to her servant, and he interrupts, tries to change the subject.*

SHELLEY. Ah, Mary, I wish you had come with us… Today we were right inside that storm, I was part of it.

MARY. I am afraid to sail.

SHELLEY. Nonsense, Mary, you *want* to. I know you do! Remember back there in St Pancras Graveyard we used to blow bubbles and sail paper boats, and plan how we would sail away for ever.

BYRON. Graveyard? That does not sound the most romantic sport for courtship, still –

CLAIRE. That was Mary's secret place. Her mother's grave. She would tell me how her mother would come and haunt me. I never went there.

MARY (*heartfelt*). There, I could be perfectly alone.

CLAIRE. Alone until you began to encourage Shelley to accompany you!

SHELLEY. And I needed little encouragement! (*Kisses* MARY.) You know, Byron, I was half in love with Mary before I even met her. I'd go to Godwin's house. And how I worshipped that man –

CLAIRE. You used to bring Harriet!

SHELLEY. Sometimes.

CLAIRE *turns to* MARY.

CLAIRE. You were away in Scotland then. My mama found you unmanageable!

MARY. I was just fifteen! She sent me away!

SHELLEY. I could not wait to see the daughter of this excellent man I wished was my father!

CLAIRE. That would have made Mary your sister!

SHELLEY. My soul's sister. She is. Has been always!

CLAIRE. If she was your real sister you could not –

BYRON (*laughing*). Not without being the storm in every teacup in Albion – and you may take that from the horse's mouth! Godwin, eh? *Political Justice*!

SHELLEY. The best and bravest and most important book ever written in the English language.

BYRON. High praise!

SHELLEY. Not exaggerated!

BYRON. Poor Mary-Mary! Wearing her mother round her neck and her father on her sleeve.

SHELLEY. Albé, I defy anyone to read that book and not be filled with the certainty that, as sound politics diffuse through society – as they inevitably will – freedom and justice for both men and women then must be universal.

BYRON *laughs*.

BYRON. And do you think I have not read Godwin's great work? Well, I have, when it was fashionable – long before you, Mary, were out of schoolroom pinafores, I had seen that silly book for the euphoric bombast it was.

ELISE *enters with the decanter.*

Ah, Elise, come here. Elise, come help us, we need you to demonstrate.

ELISE *curtseys.*

ELISE. Lord Byron.

BYRON. What do you do, Elise?

ELISE. Sir?

BYRON. For a livelihood, Elise. Who are you?

ELISE. Mrs Shelley's maid, sir.

BYRON. A maid?

ELISE. Yes, sir.

BYRON (*indicating* MARY). Well, Mademoiselle Maid, and who is this?

ELISE. Mrs Shelley, sir.

BYRON. No, indeed, it is not! This is – a Great Man. A... philosopher, let's say.

ELISE. Sir?

BYRON. No one reads him, of course. Can you read?

ELISE. Yes, sir.

BYRON (*amazed*). You can?

ELISE. I'm learning, sir. A little each day. Mrs Shelley, she helps me when William is asleep, and Mr Shelley, sir.

BYRON. He does?

ELISE. In the afternoons, sir. Sometimes.

BYRON. A maid who can read!

ELISE. And write, sir. Mrs Shelley helps me to form my letters...

BYRON. Perhaps we shall have dogs on two legs next, entering the House of Lords, and pissing on its portals.

SHELLEY. Better than the wolves and vipers and crocodiles that we have to contend with currently!

BYRON. Indeed! But we digress! Elise, who is this?

ELISE. A… philosopher, sir.

BYRON. And who are you?

ELISE. A maid.

BYRON. His maid.

ELISE (*very uncomfortably*). Yes, sir.

BYRON. And now I have to decide which one of you to save.

MARY. Byron, this is an abuse – Elise, don't be alarmed, this is but a game of our neighbour's, he –

BYRON. Wishes to demonstrate a philosophical argument of the illustrious Godwin's. And do you know who Godwin is, Elise?

ELISE. He is… Mrs Shelley's father, sir?

BYRON. Indeed. Mary Godwin's famous father. And now we shall examine his concept of justice, ladies and gentlemen! You are both in a burning building and I have to decide which of you to save. Can't you feel the flames catch at your petticoats, lick at your ankles?

ELISE *looks down. She is angry, silent, impotent.*

Can't you feel the thick smoke choke you? Elise, can't you? Answer me, girl!

ELISE. Yes, sir.

BYRON. Now, I am concerned with justice. Godwin's justice.

There is an old maxim, everyone's heard of it, although only you, Claire Clairmont, seem inclined to put it into practice around here: that we should love our neighbour as ourselves.

CLAIRE (*going to his side*). Albé!

BYRON. Keep seated! I'm on the track of justice. You, philosopher, and you, chambermaid, are presumed of equal worth. You are both human beings, are you not?

And entitled to equal attention… in the natural world at any rate. As a general principle? Yes? No? And yet Godwin says I must save –

MARY. Well, I understand why my father advocated the saving of me.

BYRON. The philosopher!

MARY. Yes. There is the consideration that the common good of all mankind for all time will benefit from my work. So save me.

SHELLEY. Bravo, Mary!

BYRON. Ah, but suppose this mere maid were my wife? Or my mother? Yes, or my sister? Certainly I should want to save my beloved sister before some old philosopher.

MARY. My wife, my sister, my mother! What is so magical about the pronoun 'my'? My sister may be a fool… or a harlot… If she be, then what worth is she lent by the fact she is my sister?

BYRON. Where is your heart, Mary? Hear that, Elise? Are you listening, Claire? She'd consign her own sister to the flames. But I don't know I believe her. I think it's Godwin's daughter wishing to convince us – and her papa – that she has her head in the right place!

MARY. Suppose I were myself the philosopher's maid, I should choose to die rather than him.

BYRON. Ah, so you won't grant life to the maid. Elise, tell me who are you going to save? Yourself, or Mister Philosopher?

ELISE. I… I shouldn't like to say, sir.

BYRON. Come, Elise, you are among friends, you can tell us what you think.

ELISE. What would you like me to say, sir?

BYRON. Tell us the truth. Who would you save?

ELISE. I should save myself, sir.

BYRON *bursts out laughing.*

BYRON. Thank you, Elise, that is what I wished to hear.

ELISE. May I go, madame?

MARY. Yes, Elise.

ELISE. Madame, I did not mean… I hope I did not say the wrong thing, madame?

MARY. You are a good girl, Elise.

ELISE. Thank you, madame.

ELISE *exits.*

MARY. It was wicked of us to use her so.

BYRON. Why? She is but a maid.

MARY. But I have not bought the right to abuse her. I ought to act towards all creatures with benevolence.

BYRON. Benevolence by all means, Mrs Shelley. Nicety costs nothing. But recognise that where you are paymaster, benevolence is yours to bestow… or to take away.

SHELLEY. Peddling in human flesh… a vile and a universal thing. To be born poor may be translated: to be born a slave. The lot of the working people! In the new hells of our cities, the mechanic himself becomes a sort of machine. His limbs and articulations are converted into wood and wires.

Surely they must rise up, they shall rise up.

MARY. But Elise is not my puppet. It is my duty to educate her, enlighten her.

BYRON. So she can see the justice of her giving up her own life for you! No, she is not your puppet, Mary. Thank God we may own the body but, although we stuff the head with Latin, algebra and Platonics, we cannot own the heart. (*Pause.*) Nevertheless, if I am honest, and I think I am, I must admit that possession of the odd body does all but suffice. For me. But then I'm no Godwinite. I won't tyrannise the world by force-feeding it freedom.

CLAIRE. I don't like these games, I wish Pollydolly was here.

BYRON. Well, he's not. So we have to otherwise divert ourselves. Pollydolly! Pollydolly, indeed. Honestly, Shelley, I pick me as travelling companion a physician – hoping he can at once apply the pharmaceutical leeches *and* keep the human ones at bay – and what does he do but decide he should forsake his doctoring and take up competing with *me* – and you – at the scribbling. Ah, the Literary Life! And truly, Claire, I think, he *is* a little jealous! Since I found myself such… congenial neighbours and stimulating companions I have little time for Pollydolly. (*Kisses*

CLAIRE *lightly, sarcastically.*) I fear we have begun to tire of one another. Oh, is it not the way of all human intimacy?

Even the best of marriages, you know yourself, Shelley, grows tedious to the combatants.

And even the firmest friendships come unstuck…

CLAIRE. 'True love *differs* from gold and clay. To divide is not to take away.' Shelley's poem, Albé! Remember?

BYRON. Pretty lines!

MARY. It's true! Because… because Shelley loves me, it does not mean he must stop loving Harriet; I should be wrong to wish him to.

SHELLEY. I think if she would only consent to meet Mary she would become her friend.

BYRON. Honestly, Shelley, you do take the Bath bun and the biscuit too! (*Laughs.*) I'm afraid you're not for this world. Shiloh! Love is all on account, debits, debits, precious few credits, and always less in the coffers than one thinks there is – a sudden running-out and not a ha'p'worth left is the common way to the inevitable bankruptcy.

The worst of Annabel's lies and slanders is I'll see her in hell. If only she'd keep a virtuous silence she'd gain the other place, and eternity were not too long a time I'd never see her again…

SHELLEY. There could not have been devised anything – anything! – more hostile to human happiness than marriage.

CLAIRE. Amen!

BYRON. I'll drink to that!

BYRON *polishes off the last drop in his glass.*

SHELLEY. Abolish marriage and all connections between women and men will be natural. And right – because choice and change will be possible – will even be desired by both!

The two women cheer and applaud SHELLEY. MARY *goes to him.*

BYRON. Lord, Shiloh, I'm not much of a one for such airy Platonics. I am a simple man. Ladies, I am as ditchwater dull and tethered to the earth as clodhopper Caliban… I am happy as a pig in… the proverbial acorn wood. I'll gobble up the lot. Shelley here, though, he's a different kettle of nightingales. Oh, we only have to look at him and we dissolve. He's all Light and Grace, is Shiloh! He's Ariel, a pure spirit moving through the changing air, fashioning liquid verse into new forms for freedom. How he will flame and amaze! And how about you, Miranda-Mary?

Friends, how shall we amuse ourselves?

Oh, to hell with Dr Polidori and his German volume of *Fantasmagoriana*! Listen, I'll set us a little contest. Why should we content ourselves with translated, traditional horrors, all bookish and stilted. Home-grown ones are the best. We shall all write a ghost story!

CLAIRE. A story!

She laughs uproariously, clapping her hands, dancing around in circles.

A story, a story! Who can write the most horrid tale! Oh yes, we shall all be terrorists – Claire will, and Mary will, and Shelley will, and Byron, and Claire and Shelley and Byron and Mary…

And fade out as lights change.

Back to widow MARY, *who is back at her writing desk, suffering as she remembers.*

MARY. I did not want to write –

CREATURE'S VOICE. Did I request thee, Maker, from my clay to mould me?

MARY. I did not want to write. I did not want to write. Daughter of *Political Justice*, daughter of *A Vindication of the Rights of Woman*. And I wrote you. If I had known the misery, the terror, the grief I foretold for myself? I did not want to write you anyway. Nothing came to me, no ideas, I was empty. Everybody was engaged on his creation, except me.

Back to Switzerland, 1816 again, a few days later, and much later at night, with the wind outside, summer storms. BYRON *and* SHELLEY *with opium pipes.*

The trio of BYRON, SHELLEY *and* CLAIRE *are all writing.*

SHELLEY (*deep in thought*)…. A beautiful creature, half-man, half-woman. Perfect, therefore terrifying!… (*Writes.*)

BYRON. There's Mad Shelley, and Bad Byron, and Sad Polidori next door, scribbling away like a dervish, muttering 'Vampyre, vampyre.' Why, even *Glad*-eyed Claire is lusting somewhat after cuttlefish ink and quill pens, eh, Claire?

CLAIRE. I tell you, I have begun one.

BYRON. Of course you have. (*Mutters.*) It'd be too much to hope, would it, that girls of eighteen had nought but fertile imaginations…

MARY *comes in to join them.*

And how about you, Mary, have you begun yours?

SHELLEY. Is he asleep at last?

MARY. He's sleeping.

CLAIRE. You should let the maid! Don't they say 'tis a pity to spoil the creatures?

MARY. When you are a mother, Claire, perhaps I'll listen to your advice.

BYRON. Ah! (*Mutters.*) And this may be sooner than you think, apparently…

Never mind. Writing time! The Contest! Creation! I asked you, Mary, how goes your story?

SHELLEY (*bursting out enthusiastically*). Well, all I'll say of mine – it's scarce begun, to tell the truth – but I will say it's something about a dream.

BYRON. A dream, eh? Marvellous! How about you, Mary?

SHELLEY. A dream of a beautiful creature – half-man, half-woman – who lives high, high, on the topmost pinnacle above that awful ravine, where naked power, dressed as a river, pours out of the rock, and down… Remember, Albé, when we finally reached the source of the Arve?

BYRON. Up mountain and glacier! No wonder we're chilled and stiff and ache so that Polidori had to lard us with liniment. Ladies, I'm sure we reek like racehorses…

SHELLEY. It wasn't a river. It was pure, naked, absolute Power. That element. Oh, in the disguise of a river! This time.

The surfaces of things hide from us what they truly are.

MARY *is thrilled by this,* BYRON *laughing at it.*

MARY. Oh yes! The surfaces... of things... hide from us what they really are!

SHELLEY. The same secret strength of things flows through us all, making us work. Just because it's invisible doesn't mean it isn't real...

Think of us! We four.

Oh, there are wires and bonds between us that are as finespun as filigree and as intricately structured as a spider's web and stronger than blood – or Manchester iron.

As imperative as the delicate smells that drag the insect to the nectar.

BYRON. Gossamer, blood, pig-iron and stink! Four very different things in my book.

MARY. Then what's in your book, Albé, is only the tip of the iceberg.

BYRON. Ah, Mary! Brave new world that has such poets in it.

BYRON *drinks to her, toasting her.*

SHELLEY *begins to write again, almost in a trance, staring. A moment or two's silence but for the scratching of the pen nibs.*

I'm asking you, Mary Godwin –

MARY. What?

BYRON. Have you started your story?

MARY. I don't think we would play with such dangerous things.

BYRON. Won't dabble in the dark?

MARY. There is no darkness! There are no forces of evil outside of ourselves. Once we let the clear light of reason sear through... Besides, how can I write when William screams all day?

BYRON. As Claire said, let the nursemaid see to him.

SHELLEY. Naked!

MARY. He needs me, every child needs his mother.

BYRON *notices* SHELLEY, *who's really spooking himself, writing and muttering.*

SHELLEY. Naked! Naked! God! And eyes…

BYRON. *Fan… tas… magor… iana…*! What was that story, Mary? You read it last night. 'And when the moon…' What? 'And by that…' What, Mary?

MARY. Blue and baleful light.

BYRON. 'Blue and baleful light!'

Shelley! Shelley! Does she not make your flesh to creep and your gorge to rise? Oh, I know she does mine! 'He saw that in his arms…' yes?

MARY *is almost in a trance now,* BYRON*'s power has her half-hypnotised – she can't not answer.*

MARY. 'He saw that in his arms he clasped the pale, pale ghost of her he had deserted.'

SHELLEY. No! Who in hell are you? Mary! Not-Mary! Your breasts… you have eyes, eyes in your breasts… don't stare at me! Keep… her away from me!

MARY. Shelley –

But he screams, runs from her. Chaos. BYRON *tries to hold* SHELLEY *in the room,* CLAIRE *begins fighting with* BYRON *to let* SHELLEY *escape.*

CLAIRE. Let him go! Leave him! Mary! Albé! Help him!

SHELLEY *breaks loose and runs screaming from the room.*

MARY *stands, upset, unable to move.*

Shelley? Hush, Shelley, it's me, your Claire, calm, I'm coming!

CLAIRE *runs out after him.* BYRON *stands stock-still looking at* MARY*, she at him.* BYRON *shrugs.*

BYRON. He reads too much.

MARY *belatedly makes to follow* SHELLEY.

MARY. Shelley…!

BYRON *stops her by grabbing her wrist.*

BYRON. No, Mary, let Claire. You are not the right person. You are the subject of his… Waking Nightmare.

MARY. I must go to him. We always have avoided stimulants. Even alcohol, especially alcohol, as well you know! Too much opium…

BYRON. Too much imagination. Let Claire see to him. Claire will calm him.

BYRON *lets* MARY*'s arm go. She stays.*

MARY. I must go to my husband.

BYRON. Ah? Strange, but I thought poor Shiloh had a wife already! Mary, Mary, don't scuttle off like a manhandled maidservant! Don't spurn my company. Lord knows, I've had enough of ostracism in England.

Well, well, I should have honestly thought it impossible to scandalise Shelley, the Anti-Christ's Lady! The Queen of the *Ménage à Trois*!

MARY. What do you mean?

BYRON. Was not… What's-his-name, your dear friend, Mary?

MARY (*involuntarily*)….Hogg?

BYRON. Yes, Hogg. Thomas Jefferson Hogg. Percy Bysshe Shelley's bosom companion. And his rival in love for the affections of their 'participated pleasure' – Mary Wollstonecraft Godwin!

MARY. Hogg was a brother to me…

BYRON. Ah! Fraternal love! I've heard of such things.

MARY. Surely Shelley did not trust you with such a secret?

BYRON. Hush-hush, of course not. Claire did, didn't she – now, it was not unkindly meant, oh, don't break my confidence to you and chide her. It was in an unguarded, not to say unclothed moment…

MARY. You cannot know how cruel you are! He was Shelley's friend. Shelley and I don't believe in… I wanted to show Shelley I felt the same as he did about freedom.

BYRON. Goodness, Mary, what's to get in such a tush about? If you loved Hogg, what's to shock? Surely it was nothing more than the revolutionaries declaring independence from the laws the rest of us humble mortals have to live by – or some of us frolic to flout! Surely it was merely the embracing of your own published principles, Mary Godwin?

MARY. How could a libertine like you understand? It was a noble experiment!

BYRON. The dissection of the affections! The analytical, anatomical dismantling of the human heart!

MARY. We wanted a new way to live. Can't you understand that?

BYRON. Oh yes… Intellectually I can conceive of it, Mrs Shelley. But there is something hideously unnatural in such a cold-blooded, put-together passion, is there not? I cannot believe it can have been a very pretty thing in practice. And I'm all for practice… making perfect.

Mary! Mary, I am a simple soul at heart! None of your rational splits between the heart and the head for me. None of your cold-blooded laboratories of sexual relations, just the head, the heart, the body and soul!

MARY. You have no soul!

BYRON. – The healthy mind in the healthy body! But I do have a soul, Mary. A blackened, burnt-out cinder of a soul perhaps, may it rot in hell. And it has done, it has done.

Don't say you've swallowed Shelley's fallacy of freethinking? So, you're free to agree with your Atheist, allowed to assent to uniting yourself with your Dissenting Angel…

But I, Mary, am like all blasphemers, a true believer! A libertine who breaks the code, but is good and glad it exists to rupture. The Lord knows, were it not for legitimate married love, there would not be a convention worth outraging!

MARY. You are a heartless seducer!

BYRON. Not heartless, just… faint-hearted sometimes. Where it could really… make a difference. Oh, I do tumble the occasional dollymop, that I do freely admit, do the odd bit of hobnobbing below stairs, and below the greasy petticoats of scrubbing scullery wenches – I'm not snobbish!

But it's all just to kill time, Mary.

MARY. Are you trying to make me pity you? For –

BYRON. Not at all! No, Mary, it is not that I am half-hearted in my love affairs. Just that recently… Well, you know all about that, all England knows all about that… recently I have been rather half-witted about who I chose – but do we ever really *choose* who we truly love?

MARY. Your sister!

BYRON. *Half*-sister, Mrs Shelley. But yes, I love my sister Augusta. Too much to subject that love to the warpings of Platonics. Frustrated love perverts, produces monsters! But as for you, Mary, and Shelley, and Hogg, and Claire, with your frigged-up intellectual *notions* of passion!

Oh, it is not love which is dead in my heart, Mary, but hope merely.

Like all highly coloured comedians, I do take a dim view of the world.

MARY. And that is your real sin, Lord Byron. You do… give up too easily!

BYRON. Do I? You mean if I but bide my time, bonny Mary…?

MARY. I mean you give way to pessimism! It is unforgivable! How can you, in a century which has given us Arkwright… and Owen… and Watt…

MARY *and* BYRON. The French Revolution?

BYRON. And the Terror, the heads bounding into baskets, the Jacobins, the Girondins, the Sans-Culottes, the Ruin, the Rot, the Reaction! Did not Sweet Shelley's second honeymoon straddle the charred and blackened corpse of La Belle France? Or didn't he notice? Or didn't you notice, Mary-Mary?

MARY. Our eyes were wide open! My Shelley's no sleepwalking dreamer. He was the first, the only one of his generation quickly to see through Napoleon!

BYRON. Bravo!

MARY. My mother, did you know she travelled to France during the Revolution, she lived in Paris all during…

BYRON. That bloodbath?

MARY. Yes! And she did not give up hope.

BYRON. Mary Wollstonecraft's Cookbook: 'You cannot make an omelette without cracking a few skulls.' Percy Bysshe Shelley's Dreambook: 'It's getting a little better all the time!'

MARY. And should a true poet like Shelley not indulge in dreams and aspirations?

BYRON. Humbug and bubbles, Mrs Shelley! Mary, you are getting good and sick, I know it, of Ariel's head-in-the-clouds hopefulness. Come on, come down to earth where you belong! Come on, come and curl up with old club-footed Caliban!

Hold for a long moment. Till it almost looks as if she will. She steps a step closer to him. He flicks at her mother's pendant on her throat.

Come, write that story, and let me tell you, it won't be made of nebulous ideas, pretty philosophies and pointless, pointless politics!

Everything I write is a Creature who can only live by what he sees, hears, smells, tastes, touches, and grabs, Mrs Shelley. And rather than have him starved and skinny, living on air, I'd have him rich and fat with facts, facts, facts. And any plain fact looked at without flinching is funny. At any rate, one has to laugh. Or doesn't this one? Don't you, Mary? I look at you, Mary, and I see someone who is holding it all within. A lovely lady who yet suppresses every gust, every gale, every giggle. Don't sit on your wit, just to please Shelley.

MARY. 'Like a sword without a scabbard, it wounds the wearer!' What good does wit do a woman? Wit in a woman is always sour.

BYRON. So is my sour wit womanish?

I think *not*, Mary. (*Whispers.*) I'll prove it to you…

CLAIRE *enters. He hears her and turns.*

We'll have Claire here sign an affidavit! Claire, come here! Kiss me.

She does. BYRON *kisses her fully and lewdly on the lips.*

Lord, Lord, I think I have found me Polidori's Vampyre!

You know, Claire, Mary's virtue is much affronted that there is so much… to-ing and fro-ing between your villa and mine. She does not like to be too near the foul sty or the hot breath of the two-backed beast!

He kisses her again, grabbing her breasts and buttocks and pulling up her skirt.

CLAIRE. Albé! Stop! Stop it! Mary's here.

BYRON. Not alone, are we not, Mam'zelle Clairmont, and me so mad with lust for you?

CLAIRE. Albé, I mean it, I'm getting vexed! (*To* MARY.) Polidori came and gave him a sleeping draught. He says we're wicked, winding each other up so tightly, exciting ourselves so. We'll forget all this happened. Come away, Albé! It'll all be better in the morning. Come –

BYRON. Goodnight, Mrs Shelley.

BYRON *chases* CLAIRE *across the stage, catching her, kissing her, laughing, making her shriek. They exit.*

Lights change.

Back to widow MARY *at her desk, remembering.*

MARY. Cold. Cold and lonely. I thought: 'Go to him, go to Shelley… no! He should come to me!' I was as far away from him that night… and him only asleep next door, wound round in laudanum dreams and brandy fumes, and poppy scents of incense. But I was as far away from him as I am now. And him drowned and dead for ever.

I lay down. Not to sleep, I did not sleep, nor could I have been said to dream. Not dreaming… I saw him!

The CREATURE*'s music begins, a slow throb. She senses him behind her, but does not turn round.*

The form he takes – if he is indeed made visible – is shadowy and barely lit.

She goes slowly to and lies down flat on the chaise longue, lies on it as if she is the created one, limp and lifeless. Her eyes are shut. Only her lips move, slowly.

I see him! A pale student of unhallowed arts, kneeling beside the thing he has put together.

Flash of lightning. MARY *sits up as if electrified, speaks out:*

It lives! The artist is terrified, and would rush away from his handiwork, horror-stricken. Begins to hope that, left to itself, the spark of life will fade.

Sleeps a deep and dreamless sleep. Awakens.

Behold, standing right by my bedside, looking down at me with yellow, watery, but hungry eyes…

CREATURE'S VOICE. Cry hallelujah, Frankenstein! Sing out. For you have found this, this has found you. It is easy, describe what haunts you. Frankenstein, you have thought of a story. Mary Shelley, you have seized the spark of life. Now write this.

MARY *goes to the desk begins to write.* MARY *writing, the* CREATURE*'S* VOICE *and* MARY*'s voice together –*

CREATURE'S VOICE *and* MARY. It was on a dreary night in November, that I beheld the accomplishment of my toils.

End of Act One.

ACT TWO

Widow MARY *with candle, quill, at her writing desk again. She has some letters, opens one, reads. Paces, frets.*

MARY. Oh, Percy Florence Shelley, my sweet son, how am I to keep you?

When your grandpapa Godwin, far from supporting us financially, asks us for money just as constantly as he did when Shelley was alive?

And when your grandpapa Shelley threatens he will cut us off without a penny if we bring out your father's poetic productions posthumous before the world and add, in his eyes, yet more infamy to the family name?

But he should know it. I will collect and edit and bring out in a single volume the works of Percy Bysshe Shelley if it is the last thing I do.

Must write!

When creation goes dead and dull, that's the time the author has to force himself to put the long hours in and have the faith that sometime soon the spark surely will return.

The Last Man, oh, Mrs Shelley – if you can but keep your courage – *this* is the book that will make your name, your fame and your fortune.

'The year is 2073, a slowly spreading plague threatens the very existence of human life on earth. Vernay, the hero of our tale –

The Last Man.'

I'll live here lonelier than the last woman alive on earth and I'll write it.

It is so much better an idea than any I ever have had before in all my life.

As for my last monstrosity, my grotesque invention, my scandal, to my surprise my enduring and popular success, no, I didn't invent you, I didn't write you, you came unbidden and I wrote you down.

Movement in the shadows.

CREATURE'S VOICE. Wrap yourself in furs, Frankenstein, for soon such ice and cold. No escape, except by the death of you or this.

MARY. I could never think how to kill you. Night after night, I had done with you, only for you to rise again.

I buried you in an avalanche, I had you leap into the smoking crater of a volcano, I burned you to death in a church.

I did not think of drowning you in the ocean…

I mangled you in the workings of a gigantic mill…

I froze you to death in an Arctic storm. But you would not die.

CREATURE'S VOICE. Come, pursue This, chase This, till This shall catch you…

MARY *picks up the volume,* Frankenstein*, opens it at random and reads with a shudder.*

MARY. 'How can I describe my emotions at this catastrophe, or how delineate the wretch which, with such infinite care I had endeavoured to form? His lips were in proportion, and I had selected his features as beautiful. Beautiful! Great God! His yellow skin scarcely covered the work of muscles and arteries beneath; his hair was lustrous and flowing, his teeth of a pearly whiteness – these luxuriances merely a more horrid contrast with the watery eyes, that seemed almost the same colour as the dun-white sockets in which they were set… his shrivelled complexion and straight black lips… I could not endure the aspect of the being I had created.'

CREATURE'S VOICE. Frankenstein's Frankenstein? Why did you make me? This must know.

MARY. Frankenstein's Frankenstein? Am I? I am! My God! Oh, had I known…

I am responsible.

'It was on a dreary night in November.'

I wrote that, on a stormy night in June. I was happy then, we were all of us happy then. My most congenial companions and I…

They *were* my most beloved congenial companions. Most of the time. And if they were not always… then that is my fault, surely?

'It was on a dreary night in November.'

The book I started on the shores of Lake Geneva that stormy night in June stole me away from the others. Six months later, I was still writing it.

Oh, let the baby cry!

We were back in England then, Shelley and I – with Claire.

It was on a dreary night in December…

Lights change. The desk at which MARY *writes is now in England, December 1816.*

(*The transitions into past time in Act Two happen in an even more fluid fashion.*)

Now CLAIRE *comes; very, very heavily pregnant and bored.*

CLAIRE. Oh, Mary, there you are, still scribbling? Shelley might be back from London soon. Come and I'll crimp your hair for you. Come and I'll make you beautiful for your lover coming home.

MARY. Is that what you've been doing?

CLAIRE. Making myself beautiful for my lover?

MARY. Crimping your hair!

CLAIRE. There's no point in me trying to look pretty in this condition. This kicks! Little monster! Honestly, wouldn't you think there'd be some other way, some better way? No wonder men recoil in horror when they see what they've done! So ugly!

MARY. You're not ugly. How can something so natural be ugly?

CLAIRE. It's ugly!

MARY. Shelley doesn't think it's ugly. Before William was born, when I was first pregnant, with my little girl that died… he used to hold the great globe of my belly as if it were the whole world, and press his face against it.

CLAIRE. Shelley, though, is a man in a million.

Imagine loving a big fat swollen woman!

MARY *is trying to go on writing*. CLAIRE *is lumbering about, bored and clumsy, looking out of the window.*

It has rained and rained for three days and nights without stopping. Not a glimmer in the grey sky. And all the flat sodden grey fields just soak it all up! I hate England. I hate the winter. Why did we come back here?

MARY. Because.

CLAIRE. Yes, I know, but why did the summer have to end?

Silence. MARY *gets another sentence, half-sentence done, crosses it out, scratching her pen*.

I can't even go out! All the villagers whispering about me behind my back, going in and locking their doors. Anyone would think they'd never seen a pregnant woman before.

MARY. They talk about me too! And Shelley. They don't understand, so they gossip.

CLAIRE. You don't care! All you've wanted to do ever since we came home is bury yourself in your damned book! Everything's flat around here. Except my belly.

What are you writing anyway?

Mmm?

CLAIRE *snatches a page*. MARY *tries to grab it*. CLAIRE *avoids her, reading from the manuscript:*

'His yellow skin… the work of muscles and arteries beneath; his hair was lust… his teeth of a pearly whiteness… more horrid contrast with watery eyes… shrivelled complexion and straight black lips.'

God, Mary, what a truly hideous imagination you have. Where do you get it?

MARY. Give it back!

CLAIRE *dodges* MARY, *reads lucidly another passage:*

CLAIRE. 'Here then, I retreated and lay down, happy to have found a shelter, however miserable, from the inclemency of the season and still more from the barbarity of man.' Quite!

MARY. Claire…

CLAIRE. Why didn't I stay there?

MARY. Where?

CLAIRE. In Europe. And follow him? Once his son is born, and I could say: 'Look, here is what we made together… that night we made love in the storm.'

MARY. How do you know it'll be a son?

CLAIRE. Oh, I know. Just as clearly as, that night… I know he loved me!

MARY. Oh, Claire…

CLAIRE. Boring, flat old England. Why did we come back?

MARY. Money.

CLAIRE. Yes, but why did Shelley go to London and leave us here?

MARY. Money.

Silence. MARY *writes, having pointedly taken the sheet of filched paper back from* CLAIRE. *The baby begins to cry.*

CLAIRE. Baby's crying. Ma-ma, Ba-ba wants you! I'll get him, you're too busy.

CLAIRE *comes back with the crying baby, rocking him in her arms.*

There, Willmouse pet. Ssh, where's a lamb? There's your mummy. Mama doesn't love him, does she? Not properly. Mama loves her dream child better, hmm?

Who wants Auntie Claire to give him a little brother to play with?

MARY. Cousin.

CLAIRE. Cousin, brother, what's the difference round here? Oh… Mary… sometimes I'm so frightened.

MARY. What's the use of being frightened?

CLAIRE. Is it terribly, terribly sore?

MARY. It's a pain that one forgets.

SHELLEY, *crying, bursts into the room. He is dishevelled, sobbing.* MARY *leaps to her feet.*

Dear God, Shelley, look what you made me do!

Spilt ink!

She holds up a page stained with red ink like blood.

SHELLEY *is sobbing his distress, and holds out a copy of* The Times, *December 1816.*

CLAIRE. What is it? What is in the newspaper?

MARY. Give it to me!

SHELLEY. No!

CLAIRE *grabs it, reads.*

CLAIRE. 'Tuesday December 10th... Mrs Harriet Shelley, a respectable female far advanced in pregnancy, was taken from the Serpentine River and brought home to her residence in Queen Street, Brompton, having been missed for nearly six weeks... She had a valuable ring on her finger, a want of honour in her own conduct is supposed have led to this fatal catastrophe...'

MARY *is trying to reach out for* SHELLEY.

SHELLEY. Leave me alone!

MARY *recoils, freezes.* SHELLEY *exits.* CLAIRE *looks at* MARY, *appalled, and goes after him.*

Lights change. Back to widow MARY *again.*

CREATURE'S VOICE. Who made This? Who did This?

MARY. God help me, I am the author of her death!

Oh yes, this scandal never left us. Even when we were married and respectable. Respectable! With Harriet dead? The world blamed Shelley. Blamed us both.

Nothing for it, we were hounded back to Italy.

Pursued, we moved on. Shelley, me, our little William, our new little baby Clara, Claire and her little Allegra, with dark curls like her daddy's. One year, two years. My book was finished and forgotten, published in England. We moved on. Lucca, Livorno, marble piazzas, broken columns, sunshine, sewers… and no place we could call our home.

It was not my idea to send Claire's little Allegra to her father. Claire wanted to! She knew it was for the best, the best thing for the child…

Lights change. Back to somewhere in Italy, another new villa, around 1819.

Initial focus is on SHELLEY *with* CLAIRE*, whispering together.* MARY *elsewhere (near the desk), unpacking a box or crate, but she's hearing – and ignoring – them.*

SHELLEY. I will tell her. I'll tell her today. Hush!

CLAIRE. You promised!

She exits.

SHELLEY *goes to* MARY*. She looks up then continues her task.*

SHELLEY. Don't sulk, it isn't like you.

MARY. I'm not sulking, I'm unpacking. For about the twentieth time in five years.

SHELLEY. Not like my best, Mary…

MARY. You encourage her!

SHELLEY. Mary…

MARY. You do! It's pitiful. You heard her: 'Surely Byron will love me again' – it's degrading! After all this time? I'm afraid for her, she has less and less contact with reality.

SHELLEY. Reality? And what's so wonderful about reality?

MARY. It's not healthy!

Shelley, it tugs at my heart to see Claire grieve for her little girl… but, Shelley, who else was ever going to want Claire?

SHELLEY. Oh! – 'With Byron's little bastard brat hanging like a millstone round her neck?'

MARY. That is what the world is like, Shelley!

SHELLEY. A child is born with its own legacy of love. For fathers and mothers it can justly look to the whole human race.

MARY. In an ideal world, Shelley. Do you want Claire to live alone? For the rest of her life, with no one to love her?

SHELLEY. She has us.

Enter CLAIRE *with a packet.*

CLAIRE. A letter from Albé, look! I have a letter from him at last!

She tears it open, shakes out a single curl.

Empty. Empty. Empty except for a single dark curl. The lock of hair I begged him of Allegra's. But there's not a single word of her! Why doesn't he tell me she is well? My baby, I shouldn't have let her go!

MARY. Shelley had a letter too.

CLAIRE. Show it to me! Let me see it!

SHELLEY. Allegra is fine, Claire. Everything is well.

CLAIRE. What does he say about me?

SHELLEY. Nothing, Claire…

MARY. He says: 'Don't bring that damnable bitch, Madame Claire, near me. I promise to quit within the hour any town that have her in it.'

SHELLEY. Mary!

MARY. You have to be cruel to be kind, Shelley.

SHELLEY. Wrong, Mary! You have to be kind to be kind.

CLAIRE. Byron will love me again, when he sees how merry I am, and how slender I am, and how like that first summer, and how little Allegra needs her mother! Shelley says he'll take me to him. Didn't you, Shelley? You promised.

MARY. Did you? Did you promise to take her and leave me here?

MARY *doesn't believe it. Then the dawning horror.* SHELLEY *is squirming.* SHELLEY*'s eyes signal to* CLAIRE *to leave. She goes.*

SHELLEY. Just till she sets her mind at rest Allegra is safe and well. You can come too, Mary. I'm sure we can find a villa near where Byron has the child. You know you don't like it here. Bagni di Lucca is so damp and gloomy, the whole town's a dull little fever-trap this season. Once you've had time to pack and settle everything, you should follow after with the children…

He puts his arm around MARY. *She flinches.*

MARY. Leave me!

SHELLEY *takes his arm away.*

SHELLEY. You can follow, soon. With the children.

Exit SHELLEY.

Lights change. Back to widow MARY *again.*

MARY. Oh, Shelley! How could you leave us like that?

Teething. I was convinced she was only teething.

Poor little Clara.

William was suffering from the heat too. I thought: 'Go to Shelley, go to Shelley and to Claire…'

When I got to the ferry at Fusina, she seemed much worse. I summoned a doctor. Poor little innocent, she seemed to recover. There was a mix-up with the passports, they tried to delay us. Press on, to Shelley and Claire. I honestly thought the best thing to do was to press on. Once I reached there… I thought… She was only teething, there was no reason to suppose… there seemed no good reason not to travel.

Oh, Clara, oh, my baby girl…

MARY *weeps, the shadows stir, someone's there.*

CREATURE'S VOICE. This killed the child. His name was William.

The name echoes.

MARY. William!

My dearest little Willmouse! How could you die and leave me still alive? When my Clara died, I thought it was the worst pain I ever had to bear. They said to me: 'You still have William, love your little boy.' Oh, William…

While I still grieved for my baby girl, I had to watch you sicken, some fever, no one knew the cause of it. I had to watch you burn and freeze and die in my arms, only nine months after Clara! Once I was a mother. Now I was a mother no more.

Lights change. Italy, another villa, the nursery. MARY *is packing a box again.* CLAIRE *comes.*

CLAIRE. What are you doing, Mary?

MARY. I am packing up William's clothes and toys. The nuns at the convent orphanage can perhaps make some use –

CLAIRE. Oh, Mary, my dear…!

ELISE *comes.*

Elise –

ELISE. Madame, let me help you.

MARY (*coldly*). I meant exactly what I said.

ELISE (*surprised*). Yes, madame.

MARY. You have until tomorrow morning to pack up your belongings.

ELISE (*sharply*). It won't take me that long, madame.

But then ELISE *sees what* MARY *is doing, is moved to pity.*

Oh, Mrs Shelley, it's not good for you to do such a sad task alone, let me help you, please.

MARY. I don't need your help, Elise.

ELISE. I'm grieving for him too! I've been with you since he was six months old. I loved your little Willmouse. I loved Baby Clara, and I loved Willmouse. Mr Shelley, he weeps in one room and you here all alone in another. It's not good for you to be alone with such dark thoughts. You should go to him.

MARY. By tomorrow morning, please. Go.

ELISE *exits.*

CLAIRE. Oh, Mary, is it true then?

MARY. Yes.

CLAIRE. It's Paolo's, I suppose?

MARY. So it would appear. Why?

CLAIRE. A maidservant lies down in the dark with a coachman with a twinkle in his eye. I don't know I can find it in my heart to blame her. Would you condemn your sister to banishment and poverty, and all for conceiving a child out of wedlock? It's only nature, Mary.

MARY. It's for her own good, Claire. They must marry at once, and we must leave this place; it has too many unhappy memories. Now that the summer is coming we need… Florence perhaps, or Genoa. But Elise must stay here and marry her coachman, we can't afford any more gossip.

CLAIRE. Put yourself in her place, Mary.

ELISE *marches back on.*

MARY. I didn't call you, Elise.

ELISE. No, madame, I came to take my leave. I think you are a cruel and heartless woman!

MARY. How dare you?

ELISE. Easily. Now that to tell the truth costs me nothing.

MARY. Elise!

ELISE. Yes, madame. And irresponsible, and a hypocrite too!

MARY. That's enough! Go, both of you, Paolo is waiting. You'll thank me some day.

ELISE. Thank you? For what?

MARY. A child needs a father. How can you, a servant of no fortune, manage to support a child?

ELISE. So free love is not to be afforded to the working classes?

MARY. Love is never free to any woman, Elise!

ELISE. How can you be her daughter and say that?

MARY. Because I am her daughter I must say that.

ELISE. Well, I read the book too! You were always encouraging me to improve my mind, even though I was only a maidservant! Indeed, I understand it very well; *The Rights of Woman*! The marvellous Mary Wollstonecraft was very keen on freedom for woman with six hundred a year, and a mill-owning husband to support her, and a bevy of maidservants sweeping and starching and giving suck to her squalling infants, not to speak of her rutting husband!

MARY *slaps her hard.*

Don't you think we are sisters? Are we not somewhat alike?

Enter SHELLEY.

SHELLEY. Mary, Elise, what's happening?

MARY. Go with Paolo! He is your husband. He is responsible.

ELISE *looks straight at* SHELLEY.

ELISE. Oh yes! He is responsible. (*Laughs.*)

ELISE *exits.*

SHELLEY. Mary, Mary…

MARY. He must marry her. She said so herself, he is the father!

SHELLEY. Of course he is, only…

MARY. Only what?

SHELLEY. The father! Father right and paternity have been used to enslave woman since time began.

MARY. Oh, Shelley…

SHELLEY. Elise is a brave girl.

CLAIRE. And a strong one.

MARY. – And I want her to survive.

SHELLEY. But to condemn any creature to a loveless marriage! All our recent suffering mustn't be allowed to make us hard.

MARY. Hard? It has turned my heart to ice!

Lights change. Widow MARY.

Oh yes. None may know the icy region this poor heart has encircled.

Once I was a mother. Now I was a mother no more.

Percy Florence, you will never know how much you mean to me.

CREATURE'S VOICE. Frankenstein, this must love!

MARY. Today the news came.

The worst.

I think before I tore open the letter, I knew it. Anxiety. Prognostications of evil. All week I've felt it approaching. Now here it is, this is what it was.

Lord Byron is dead.

Is it possible? The only one who had the courage to bring me the news I needed from that hellish day.

BYRON *appears, ghostly.*

BYRON. Yes, we burned him. The sublime Shelley. On the beach where he was washed up. Poured quicklime on and whoosh! Trelawney snatched his heart from the funeral pyre where it was not consumed, and put it in this leather pouch for you, Mrs Shelley.

MARY. Had it always, his heart…

BYRON. I loved him. We burned him. Then I couldn't wait to tear off my clothes and swim for miles and miles like a mad thing, wash the stench of burning flesh from off my skin and out of my hair. Couldn't wait to plunge myself in the Contessa.

BYRON *disappears.*

MARY. And now you're dead.

Dead at Missolonghi, Byron, gone to fight – why? – in someone else's war. Dead fighting for Greek independence.

I think of my last dead, my dear drowned Shelley, my own.

I think of my first dead, my mother I never knew.

I think of my little firstborn, in Poland Street, Shelley's lodgings, when I was scarce more than a child myself.

I think of Italy, Baby Clara, our own beloved Willmouse… There seemed no good reason not to travel…

They died, all my babies, and left Shelley and me all alone again.

Except for Claire.

Lights change. Italy. CLAIRE *is hectic, manic, rather than truly happy.*

CLAIRE. Didn't Shelley tell you?

MARY. Tell me?

CLAIRE. I'm going away, Mary. To Russia!

MARY. Russia! But, Claire, that's…

CLAIRE. Can't you see me? Queen of a Moscow schoolroom, mother hen to a brood of little princes and princesses? Isn't it so? Every other person in Russia seems to be royal nobility. It's Princess Irina this and Prince Misha, Prince Kolya that…

MARY. But it's so far away!

CLAIRE. Exactly. So the cold wind can sweep off the Steppes and blow the last tatters of my scarlet past away. Where, in all of Italy – or all of Europe – can I find one family that's not afraid to have the infamous Claire Clairmont teach its daughters?

MARY. Oh, Claire, you don't have to leave us.

CLAIRE. I must. No, Mary, I've been your millstone sister long enough.

MARY. And Allegra?

CLAIRE. She's with her father. And his whore Contessa! She's safe, she's well, and she has every luxury money can buy. It is time. I will go to Russia.

MARY. Oh, Claire! (*Hugs her.*)

CLAIRE. My best Mary too! Oh, Mary, how can you forgive me?

MARY. Ssh… Don't –

CLAIRE. But all the things I've said, when we've quarrelled! Too much love.

MARY. Too much alike, perhaps.

CLAIRE. I could cut my tongue out afterwards. Too passionate for my own good, your papa always said so…

Oh, Mary, when I said you were glad when Harriet died and you could be the respectable Mrs Shelley, I didn't mean it, you know that.

MARY. When do you leave?

CLAIRE. On the first of next month.

MARY. Go to Shelley, sing to him.

CLAIRE. Mary, promise me you won't sit here and get gloomy amongst all these shadows!

Lights change. Back to widow MARY.

MARY. Lies! Lies and malice!

That maid Elise made up a lot of silly stories and blabbed them to some incredulous English expatriates we had been friendly with once. Of course, they were only too happy to believe them and tell the world!

But Byron should have defended us!

When the gossips talked, he should have told them it was not true. Oh, Byron, you should have been our friend.

Lights change. Back in Italy. BYRON *comes.*

BYRON. Where is Shiloh? Where is my old friend, the Snake?

MARY. Not here. He won't speak to you, Byron, and you know very well why!

BYRON. Do I?

MARY. Why, when we have never showed you anything but kindness and affection, how can you return this by –

BYRON. Telling the truth? Allowing the truth to be told? Mary Shelley, such hypocrisy from you, I should never have expected it.

Well, Mrs Shelley, I can guess why you've sent for me. You want to beg my daughter back. The answer is… no. The nuns will bring her up good and God-fearing.

MARY. Byron, listen to me, I must…

BYRON. I asked myself, reasonably enough I should have thought, whether Mademoiselle Claire Clairmont was the right person to bring up Allegra. Does a mother know best? Not, I suggest, if that mama is Claire. You see, fair Claire is most keen that Allegra be at once our little secret, and at the same time, bruited abroad as the dazzling daughter, albeit wrong side of the blanket, of a Peer of the Realm.

An impossible desire, you might think; but then, Claire Clairmont was never one to let impossibility stand in the way of her desires.

MARY. Byron, I must tell you –

BYRON. Yes, Claire does take *mange*-ing her gateau and having it to some ridiculous extremes.

MARY. You should have let us take Allegra, we would have loved her like one of our own.

BYRON. Oh yes, like one of your own!

MARY. Another slander! I heard what you said, the Hoppners told me!

'Have the Shelleys raised one? I do not want Allegra to die of starvation and green fruit and to be brought up to believe there is no Deity.'

You said that! How could you?

BYRON. So the gossipy Hoppners carried tittle-tattle! Well, I cannot eat my words, would that I could swallow them unsaid. And I should never have said them to your face, Mary, I would not have looked in your eyes and wanted to wound you.

I think you know how I grieved for you, little William too.

And your baby.

But think on it, Mary.

When our… mutual friends the Hoppners parroted out my gaudy scrap of cruel wit, who or what exactly did they wish to wound? My reputation in your eyes? Or did they wish to wound you, Mary Shelley? Ask yourself.

MARY. Shelley does not love Claire.

BYRON. Love Claire? Of course Shelley does not love Claire, even Claire has a hard job of it, loving Claire. I never pretended to love her, but if a girl of eighteen will come prancing to a man at all hours, then there is but one way!

MARY. And did you defend us? When the Hoppners wrote you that… unspeakable rumour, did you tell them it was all a lie?

BYRON. Unspeakable? Unspeakable? Don't be mim-mouthed, Mary, speak it out. If it is a lie, then look it in the face.

If you must know, Mrs Shelley, I told the Hoppners: 'Don't believe everything you hear from a dismissed servant – and if Elise says Claire Clairmont, not content with being the mother of Byron's brat, had to whelp herself on Shelley too, and was delivered of his sickly little scrap in the springtime, then I am sure it just a venomous lie, even though it would have been nine months or so from the time Shelley and Claire spent alone at my villa in Este…'

'Why, Mrs Hoppner,' I said, 'Shelley only accompanied Claire to prevail with me on her behalf.'

I said, 'Mrs Hoppner, can you believe that a man of Shelley's burning idealism could enter into a love affair with his wife's own sister – half sister, whatever – while his wife struggled alone across Europe with an ailing infant?' I said, 'There is not a word of truth in it, I swear on the head of my own Allegra.'

MARY. Well, she is dead! Your own Allegra!

BYRON *reels in shock and grief and gasps.*

The nuns wrote to us… to Claire, we've sent for her, to come home. No one could trace you, you were…

BYRON. Gadding about some spa with the Contessa. And my Allegra is dead. (*Sobs.*)

MARY. I tried to tell you, but you wouldn't listen. There has been an epidemic, it swept through the convent. Your little love child was among the first –

She goes to reach out. He shakes her off with hatred.

BYRON. No!

MARY. There is something wrong in how we all live.

BYRON. Oh yes, look in the mirror of my grief and see yourself. All men hate the wretched. That's one of yours, eh, Mary? And the wretched hate each other. We are malicious because we are miserable.

Pleasure, freedom, wine, women, song, apes, peacocks, vinegar purges, boys, opium, ocean-going, orgies – I won't give up any of it, I'll double my gluttony and double it again.

All just to kill time, eh, Mary? It will be the death of me.

MARY. But we do not live as you do.

BYRON. Oh, I forgot. The Shelleys are political! The Shelleys are principled. The Shelleys do not eat dead animals. How about dead children?

MARY. Truly you are a monster!

The worst pain a mother ever bore, to have her children die before her!

BYRON. I will live with my guilt, can you live with yours?

MARY. I loved my children! And I will never cease from grieving, even when my new child is born!

BYRON. A new baby? Congratulations! And to Shiloh too, is there to be no end to this creation? Well, better luck this time, Mary!

MARY. I lived for my children.

BYRON. Well, I have never pretended to live for anyone but myself, and there's where we differ.

Infants do benefit from travel, don't they? Florence, Venice, Padua, a bit of culture and cholera does broaden the mind.

MARY. You are a twisted person!

BYRON. Oh yes, Mary, there is something in us which is very ugly. Do you not think we are somewhat alike? We are put together all wrong.

MARY. A monster!

BYRON. Well, if I am your monster, who, or what are you, Mary Shelley?

Yes, I have read your book. Very powerful it is, too. Remarkable for a girl of… what were you? Nineteen? I'm sure I can't imagine where you got your ideas from, can you?

MARY. Damn that book! It's only a book, an idea!

BYRON. Have you read your book? Oh, I know you wrote it, have you read it, though, recently? I'm sure it's silly of me to read between the lines, though. No profit in noticing an author name a character William after her beloved Baba, blond curls and all, and then strangle him to death on page sixty-nine! Oh, not many mamas, especially not busy-fingered distracted mamas, who have not occasionally, *en passant*, wished to silence the little darling!

MARY. I'm afraid of you!

BYRON. Don't be afraid, Mary. Courage! Where's Shiloh? He wanted to see me.

Excuse me, Mrs Shelley, I'm just off to see a man about a boat!

Exit BYRON.

Lights change. Back to widow MARY.

MARY. Oh, Byron; oh, Shelley –

And, in a flash, back to Italy again.

SHELLEY *comes.*

SHELLEY. Mary, Mary darling.

MARY. I wanted to die.

SHELLEY. Doctor says wait a while, and then we'll have another.

MARY. Never! Never another!

SHELLEY. Come on. You're better, you are. No more blood. Up, for a little while. I'll wrap you up, and our precious little boy, and we'll walk, yes we will. Perciflo loves the seashore. Come, Mary, a gentle walk with your husband and your little son in the clean air by the ocean.

MARY. Shelley, leave me here alone!

SHELLEY. Come and see her.

MARY. Your new love?

SHELLEY. Come and see her…

MARY. No.

SHELLEY. New arrived from Genoa, the bonniest boat that ever sailed the seas!

MARY. *The Don Juan*.

SHELLEY. *The Ariel*! Every sail unfurled! That other name won't stick, depend on it. She's *The Ariel*. It's not to be called in Byron's honour.

MARY. Yet it sailed in, monstrous letters blazoned across the mainsail, '*The Don Juan*'!

SHELLEY. You don't seem to care how much it grieves me that you won't sail with me.

MARY. I cannot! Shelley, I won't come because I cannot! I nearly died, Shelley.

SHELLEY. Oh, Mary, it was too soon. Too soon to have another, you hadn't your strength back after little Percy.

MARY. I nearly died. I didn't care if I died. I felt… I go to no new creation, I enter under no new laws. I thought all my life-blood is drained away. No pain. I'm going to die.

SHELLEY. I saved you!

MARY. I… am… in… pain. Inside it. It is a ship, and it's bearing me away.

SHELLEY. It was pure instinct, the ice.

MARY. My element. I swim in it and I do not die.

SHELLEY. You were losing so much blood, I had never seen so much blood. I ran all the way to the Ice House. I woke Umberto, made him pack the last shard of ice into the bath. He said the shock would kill you, but I lifted you up in my arms, and I plunged you into that bath of ice, and that stopped the flow.

MARY. No baby. I have lost my last. Seven years, Shelley. I've put three tiny coffins in the earth, lost two unborn babies in the womb. Our union trails a cortège of dead infants in its wake. Who cursed us? Were we cursed by our own impossible dreams?

Never again, Shelley. Another way of making life, that's what we need.

Another way to live…

SHELLEY. We have our sweet Perciflo, he's flourishing, and when you've regained your strength, we can try again.

MARY. Never! I will never begin me another!

SHELLEY. I don't know how to make you happy!

MARY. I need a faithful mate, to be the true husband of my heart.

SHELLEY. And you have me!

MARY. Yes, I have you.

SHELLEY. That love we found, back in St Pancras Graveyard…

MARY. By my mother's grave.

SHELLEY. Yes, she died. It's a terrible thing that her child bed was her deathbed, Mary, but you didn't die.

But, oh yes! You're right, Mary. Yes, I am a man. I shall never die in childbirth. Oh no, we're a different species. Let's not try to communicate. The cracks appear. We are each on smaller and smaller islands of ice, floating away from each other, further and further away. Goodbye, Mary.

MARY. I don't want to be alone like this.

SHELLEY. Then reach out! Mary, I'll never turn from you. To turn sometimes to others isn't to turn from you.

MARY. Oh, Shelley, to live in the spirit as much as you do puts a great deal of strain on the body.

SHELLEY. Mary, darling, you're shivering. Come…

SHELLEY *tries to kiss her,* MARY *shrugs him off.*

MARY. Don't always try to kiss me when I try to talk to you!

SHELLEY. Mary, don't always talk at me when I try to kiss you.

MARY. Leave me alone, Shelley!

SHELLEY. Oh, Mary, I cannot reach you.

MARY. Sometimes, I think there's not a woman in the world that hasn't fallen in love with you, and that you haven't loved back! Oh yes, Shelley, I know 'True love differs from gold and clay. To divide is not to take away…' I'm not sixteen years old any longer! I've learned to suspect any sentiment which rhymes that easily.

SHELLEY. Back in that graveyard, you said yes! You'd sail away with me for ever. Don't turn back.

MARY. So I must make myself into the girl you saw in the graveyard?

SHELLEY. The girl I know you to be!

Exit SHELLEY. *Lights change. Back to widow* MARY.

MARY. But I could not. I disappointed him. Have I a cold heart? He turned to Jane Williams, she and Edward came over from England to join us, share the villa, share –

She was my friend, we were widowed together, we waited together all that last long week as we waited for news.

But all I really remember of that last summer as everything fell to pieces all around us, was the boat, Ned Williams singing sea shanties and Shelley, his head in pretty Jane Williams's lap, and she playing the guitar and Shelley making pretty songs for her!

Lights change. SHELLEY *comes again. Near the very end of his life. Disintegration. In a trembling state.*

SHELLEY. Such a dream… God help me, Mary, but I cannot shake it. You were in it. I was in it with you. You… got up from your sickbed and walked naked towards me, your skin all torn and tattered and bloodstained. You said, very brisk, matter of fact – 'Get up, Shelley, the sea is invading the house and it's all coming down!' I looked out on the terrace. I thought I had wakened. I dreamed I was awake and the boiling seas came pouring in. Then it changed. I saw my own self, bending over you where you were stretched out sleeping, and I was strangling you. Yesterday, I saw my own ghost walking in the garden and it called out to me –

There is movement in the shadows and a cry.

CREATURE'S VOICE. How long do you mean to be content?

Lights change. Back to widow MARY.

MARY. Not long…

They only knew him by… in his pocket they found the volume of Keats he'd been reading, bent open at the place he'd reached in it. His face, his hands, all parts of him not… protected by his clothing had been eaten away by the fishes.

I wonder what it's like to drown? Did he expect to breath easy in a brand-new element, plunge straight in, embracing it? I wouldn't put it past him. What bobbed up at him from the lone and level sands of the sea bottom?

Nymphs? Nereids? Mermaids? All the flimsy, impossible women, glittering hermaphrodites, did they tangle with him, did he clasp his sweet ideal at last? Or was he beating useless limbs, dragged down by sodden duds among the bladderwrack and nosing dogfish, fighting his way back, gulping and struggling with bursting lungs, back to his flesh and blood, Mary?

She gets together paper, quill.

I must write to Claire, tell her Lord Byron, her Albé, is dead.

Calmly, she begins to write.

Light fades.

The End.

MARY QUEEN OF SCOTS GOT HER HEAD CHOPPED OFF

For Gerry Mulgrew,
without whom not a word of this play would have been written,
and for my colleagues in the Department of Scottish Literature
at the University of Glasgow from 2006 to 2009, who taught me
properly to value this as a text in its own right, rather than
only as a blueprint for future productions.

Introduction

In the autumn of 1984 I was in Portree on the Isle of Skye doing some poetry readings for pupils in the high school. After the bell went at four, I was heading for the lonely B&B and my library book when I saw, in the butcher's window, a poster advertising Communicado Theatre Company's production of *Carmen, the Play*. Couldn't believe my luck. It was on tonight!

They were my pals too. Gerry Mulgrew had, earlier that year, played (brilliantly and all too convincingly) a talking dog in a musical touring piece I'd written for Wildcat Theatre Company called *Same Difference*. He served as both chorus and narrator, Toby Dug, complete with saxophone, talking, rapping, relating directly to us. The audience loved him, and so did I.

That spring, as we'd rehearsed, every tea break had found him reading Prosper Merimée's novel or deep in big historical tomes on the Spanish Civil War, because *his* Carmen, planned for his own burgeoning company, was to be set then, with the eponymous gypsy crossing back and forth across the lines, loyal only to her own survival and the flame of her passion for Don Jose, the Man in the Suit of Lights.

Now it was autumn and Communicado – having, that August, been the toast of the Edinburgh Festival Fringe and with sold-out weeks in the Donmar Warehouse in London and in the USA under their belts – were on tour all over Scotland. Here on Skye I easily tracked down the van outside the venue, found the company inside putting all the seats for the audience on the stage so they could play on the floor, helped them humph the minimal bits of set. And that night, as near 7.30 as was decent in the Highlands, the lights went down on one of the most thrilling pieces of theatre I've ever seen.

Two beautiful girls played the fiddle, conjuring the story out of the darkness, Alison Peebles blew the smoke from her cigarette through the slats of a Venetian blind and, with a pull of the cord and a lighting change, was revealed in a tilted beret and a raggy vintage bit of finery from a charity shop as just the sexiest, most amoral, most fascinating Carmen ever.

Stephen Jeffreys' terrific play, a radical retelling of an old story for his own purposes, remained a beacon for me later as I struggled with my version of the Mary Queen of Scots myth for Gerry and this groundbreaking company. To my enduring delight and pride it has become a Communicado – and national – landmark, joining *Carmen* and Edwin Morgan's wonderful rhyming Scots translation of Rostand's *Cyrano de Bergerac* and Mulgrew's own storytelling productions of the tinker-ish *Tall Tales for Long Dark Nights* and *Arabian Nights* and – only last month – *Tam O'Shanter.*

How I remember *Mary Queen of Scots Got Her Head Chopped Off* coming about was this: Gerry Mulgrew had the idea.

And, once his *Carmen* tour was done, he took me for a Chinese meal and said he wanted to do a Mary Queen of Scots Show and that he wanted me to write it. This must've been early in 1985, and already he was thinking forward to 1987, when it was going to be the four hundredth anniversary of Mary's decapitation at the hands of her cousin Elizabeth. With his producer's hat on, Mulgrew thought Communicado's Festival Fringe piece for that year ('If we can get the grant,' he said) ought to commemorate this. He felt that the very fact it was the anniversary of Mary's *death* rather than her birth we'd be remembering was perhaps the start of an interesting story already? 'It'll really sell, there'll be loads of attention for this subject, someone'll do that Schiller play,' I remember him saying. (The Official Festival did, indeed, with Hannah Gordon as Mary.)

It all seemed a long way ahead, more than two and a half years. I was delighted to say yes. It didn't, that night, matter that neither of us seemed to know much of anything of the history, except the blunt axe-man ending, and… oh, yes, we had both memories of a childhood game played by flicking the heads off dandelions while chanting 'Mary-Queen-of-Scots-Got-Her-Head-Chopped-Off, Mary-Queen-of-Scots-Got-Her-Head-Chopped-Off…' We were, though, already very aware that, culturally, as a Scot of Irish-Catholic descent (Gerry) and I, of solidly Lowland Scottish Presbyterian stock, had been brought up with totally different versions of the myth. The Catholic Mary is certainly a martyr and almost a saint; the Proddy version of Mary veers between limp victim and politically inept nymphomaniac devil-woman who almost scuppered Our Glorious Reformation. Of course we had long put by such childish things. Naturally, we were each at war with our own cultural biases – for example: I was as much exercised by the misogyny of John Knox, his enduring anti-feminist, anti-feminine legacy in Scottish society, as Gerry was attracted by the notion that Knox's teaching the people to read so they could read the Bible for themselves and the Protestant ideal of a direct one-to-one relationship with God, un-mediated by any clerical hierarchy, had directly led to democracy. We were both republican and anti-royalist. So it might seem odd that we would soon be so wound up in the emotions of this long-ago royal tragedy. But anyway we made a deal, Gerry would apply for a commission from the Arts Council to pay me for a script, he would get on with the next Communicado Project and, together and separately, we'd start work on the Mary Queen of Scots Show for the Edinburgh Festival Fringe, August 1987 – and then to tour.

Flash forward to June 1987 and I'm up all night, unable to go to bed as the horror unfolds and the election results come in. For the third time Margaret Thatcher gets back in to power. We can't believe it. Nobody in Scotland can believe it. We voted resoundingly against the Tories in this country and yet we are being ruled by them. Again. That Friday there is a palpable sense of gloom everywhere, and at Glasgow Queen Street I actually consider getting on the wrong train, running away, instead of boarding the train to go to that meeting in Edinburgh in Communicado's wee borrowed office to tell Gerry that we don't have a play to go into rehearsal with next month. Yes, there are scenes and fragments all over the place, we both know there are those wee bits we like, that speech of the Corbie character with the pan-Scotland overview, that sexy scene between Leicester and Elizabeth, that plotting scene where Mary, imprisoned in that castle, gets that brewer to help her get messages out to her English Catholic allies, there is mibbe something in that cruel kids' stuff but it doesn't fit with anything else… I've got a trunk-load of research material (I had increasingly spent more and more hours that spring in Glasgow's Mitchell Library doing more and more 'research' – i.e. Not Writing the Play). 'Gerry, I've got all these scenes, but we don't have a play. We go into rehearsal next month and by then I'll have to have found you a do-able one among all the literally hundreds there are about her, the library catalogues say so. I'll start reading today. I can't write the Mary Queen of Scots play you wanted. And the bloody Tories are in again.'

Gerry is amazing. He refuses, just won't release me from the job of doing this piece. No, we've promised an original world premiere of a Mary Queen of Scots Show. It doesn't have to be a proper play. (He says this like it's the last thing he'd have wanted!) He says – as a way out of this impasse – to simply tell the story as a folk tale, and then Communicado can dramatise this folk tale, in the way they did *Arabian Nights*. He says to imagine how *King Lear* would be as a fairy story. *Once upon a time there was a King who had three daughters, and he decided to divide his kingdom between them, so he called them together and…* 'Just write: once upon a time,' he says… 'What would that be? What would come next? And we'll go from there.'

So that night, back home in Glasgow, I find myself writing down – just as part of a process, that was all he'd meant it to be – 'Once upon a time there were twa queens on the wan green island.' And then realising just how well that fitted Corbie's voice…

From that point, so late in the day, the piece came to life. For a team of eight already in place – not Communicado's style to necessarily have a play written before casting it – including both Alison Peebles and also Anne Wood, one of those wonderful fiddlers from *Carmen*, and a dancer no one knew yet that Gerry really wanted to work with and the amazing Myra McFadyen we all loved for whom the chorus/narrator, and the backbone of the piece, role had initially been conceived, and long tall Anne Lacey, with her flag of long pale red hair and face from a Flemish painting, to be Mary.

Burning midnight oil, as I did just about every night from then until we opened, I was never happier.

I can remember, just a week before rehearsals began, coming up with what seemed like a good solution for how to do the murder of Riccio for this tiny cast. (In reality, more than a dozen armed men broke in and murdered Mary's secretary before her very eyes as she sat with a few trusted servants in Holyrood Palace.) Oh, but I could do it as a play-within-a-play and it could be a horrid-comical masque of Salome, which would end up with a different head on a plate… It was, for me, from now on, just simply a matter of getting on with it, and the sheer enjoyment of the rhyming and the Stanley Holloway parodying, and taking down those most passionate speeches for Mary which seemed, whiles, to almost write themselves.

When we did go into rehearsal, about three quarters of what is now here was extant. Not necessarily in the right order – I don't like to admit it but the Bairns scene was the beginning of the play, not the end. And although the first half ended properly with the wedding of Mary and Darnley, there was the wrong rhythm and build-up in the earlier scenes, which were all about the different contemporaneous circumstances and forces ranged against the queens in both Scotland and England until Elizabeth sends Darnley north, and Mary falls for him, chooses him. Her first dramatic – and disastrous – *action*.

But, at the end of the first week, as the company struggled through a stagger-run of the first half, I saw quite clearly what the structure of the whole play should be. The Bairns were a coda, Corbie the beginning and – as Colin MacNeil the designer bravely, and so rightly, held off from making any irrevocable design decisions till he saw properly what the play *was* and came up with his perfect broken circus ring and fantastic anachronistic costumes, which were all, apart from terrific actors and performers, this play needs – I set about, more midnight oil, putting the shape of it to rights, as I had to, more Corbie-glue to write too, while poor Gerry, actually playing Knox as well as directing the piece and trying to see the whole arc of the thing, was understandably going crazy waiting for the script of everything from the Murder of Darnley till the death of Mary…

We got there in the end. With the play not yet *quite* in the shape that now goes into print, but definitely in the context of a debate about the then current state of affairs between Scotland and England that the play seemed to illuminate. Margaret Thatcher is not Queen Elizabeth the First, but questions of women and power – and how to hold on to it – are always there as we consider either icon. There was at that time a real sense of frustration in Scotland, a need for us to tell our own stories and find our own language to tell it in. Communicado had a bit of a mission about that, which I was proud to share.

It was a huge success. For Communicado – I honestly did not think any other theatre company would be able to do this play or would ever want to. And yet it has had quite a life. They study it in schools and universities. I've seen many other productions, professional and student and amateur, and enjoyed most of them very much. My friend David McVicar, now a world-famous opera director, did it at the Lyceum in Edinburgh with Daniela Nardini as Mary and also in upstate New York with a tiny little Puerto Rican powerhouse of an Elizabeth. He was tough with me about the gap he perceived in the published Penguin edition of the play, sure that I hadn't finished the 'historical' story satisfactorily nor bridged it properly into the anachronistic coda. In the nineties I wrote far too long a composite scene for David's production, resolving all the characters, and including a clumsier version of the simple scene in Mary's cell the night before the execution that I am pretty sure I have now, for the first time, got right.

I'll find out tomorrow. The National Theatre of Scotland go into rehearsal with this new production of my play in this version for their *Ensemble* strand. It'll be directed by the same Alison Peebles who played Elizabeth in the original production, and who was a founder member, back in 1983, of Communicado Theatre Company. We'll be looking at the model for the set and she'll be handing out scripts, pared and considered and finalised scripts with a beginning, a middle and a '*The End*'. There is a generous rehearsal schedule and proper resources. So it couldn't be more different from day one of rehearsals in the long since demolished filthy old tumbledown Lyceum Studio in 1987. In a few weeks from now there will be sixteen ninety-seater performances in small venues in mainly fairly remote areas of Scotland from Shetland to Dunoon, and, if it is a successful production, we are assured the National Theatre of Scotland will think again whether or not to give the production a further life in bigger venues in the major urban centres.

Which'll depend on the play finding a new context. Depend on there being a demand for it. When I look at it now it is clearly fundamentally about Mary and Elizabeth, the passion of these women to have sex and love and marriage – or not – for can they, without losing power? How do you have a full life as a woman and your full independence? All these things women are still struggling with. It's not as if these issues have been solved, or ever could be. It is, it seems to me, an eternal conflict. And so it remains a great story.

Communicado and Gerry Mulgrew still struggle from project to project trying to find funding for what they want to do, usually being turned down despite their past triumphs and their many long unpaid hours filling up forms and applications, such is the shockingly unfair and capricious distribution of resources for theatre in this country. Gerry's wild adaptation of *Tam O'Shanter* for Perth Theatre, which we saw just after Burns' Night this year showed a company, and a man, with creativity still in full flight.

Why I find myself, tonight, thinking back on the Communicado days and how *Mary Queen of Scots Got Her Head Chopped Off* began isn't nostalgia for the good-old-bad-old-days-when-we-had-nothing-and-everything, but a desire to get my own mojo back and working. I want to remind myself that nothing will come of nothing. Everything has its spark in previous creative endeavours, and it is these that give both the impetus and the context for the new.

It must've been Gerry recalling his daft role as that talking dog of mine that made him say, way back in 1985, initiating the whole project: 'Remember in the theatre you can do absolutely anything – we can have a talking crow, anything we want.' It was also, as luck would have it, that much of 1985 for me was spent working on translating Molière's *Tartuffe* into a new rhyming version which to my surprise came out in a Scots I didn't even know I had in me. A first foray into a language that was to evolve into a rather rich and strange (or so it seems to me now) Scots flowering for *Mary*, coming next. It was certainly seeing Communicado on Skye and falling in love with their whole rough-magic, storytelling, poor-theatre, total-theatre ethos that both made me desperate to do it, and also gave me the glimmerings of a writing style and even of a possible structure for the Mary Queen of Scots Show – which was as near a working title as the project ever had until the deadline for the poster copy.

Gerry came into rehearsal and said: 'It's gone to print now and I just told the graphic designer it is called *Mary Queen of Scots Got Her Head Chopped Off*, it just suddenly came to me that was what it's called, okay?'

Apart from that title, I did, in the end, write and choose every word of the play. None of the dialogue or the scenes were improvised into being, though, God knows, the whole company tied themselves in knots trying all different ways of staging them and, especially, as is the Communicado trademark, segueing from one scene to the other.

The 'Jock Tamson's Bairns' ending of *Mary,* though, did come out of an early workshop day about a year or more before rehearsals when – and I really can't remember whose initial idea this was – we considered: could we tell the whole story, do the whole play, as a set of contemporary children forced to re-enact a tragedy we didn't understand?

Liz Lochhead
February 2009

Mary Queen of Scots Got Her Head Chopped Off was first performed at the Lyceum Studio Theatre, Edinburgh, on 10 August 1987, with the following cast:

FIDDLER	Anne Wood
LA CORBIE	Myra McFadyen
MARY	Anne Lacey
ELIZABETH	Alison Peebles
HEPBURN O'BOTHWELL	Stuart Hepburn
KNOX	Gerard Mulgrew
DANCER / RICCIO	Frank McConnell
DARNLEY / LEICESTER	John Mitchell
Director	Gerard Mulgrew
Designer	Colin MacNeil

This revised version of the play was first performed at Druimfin, Tobermory, Mull, on 18 April 2009, in a production by the National Theatre of Scotland, which subsequently toured, with the following cast:

LA CORBIE	Joyce Falconer
MARY	Jo Freer
ELIZABETH	Angela Darcy
HEPBURN O'BOTHWELL	John Kielty
KNOX	Lewis Howden
RICCIO	Marc Brew
DARNLEY	Owen Whitelaw
Director	Alison Peebles
Designer	Kenny Miller
Lighting Designer	Lizzie Powell
Composer	David Paul Jones
Musical Director	John Kielty
Choreographer	Marc Brew

Characters

LA CORBIE
MARY/MARION/MAIRN/MAREE
ELIZABETH/BESSIE/LEEZIE/WEE BETTY
HEPBURN O'BOTHWELL
KNOX
RICCIO
DARNLEY

and others

Note

Mary, when she speaks, has a unique voice. She's a Frenchwoman speaking totally fluently, Braid Scots vocabulary and all, in Scots, not English – but with a French accent.

Elizabeth has a robust, and almost parodic version of slightly antique (think forties black-and-white films), very patrician RP.

ACT ONE

Scene One

Scotland, Whit Like?

Music. An eldritch tune on an auld fiddle, wild and sad.

Alone, our chorus, LA CORBIE. *An interesting, ragged, ambiguous creature in her cold spotlight.*

CORBIE. Country: Scotland. Whit like is it?

It's a peatbog, it's a daurk forest.

It's a cauldron o lye, a saltpan or a coal mine.

If you're gey lucky it's a bonny, bricht bere meadow or a park o kye.

Or mibbe… it's a field o stanes.

It's a tenement or a merchant's ha.

It's a hure hoose or a humble cot. Princes Street or Paddy's Merkit.

It's a fistfu o fish or a pickle o oatmeal.

It's a queen's banquet o roast meats and junkets.

It depends. It depends…

Ah dinna ken whit like *your* Scotland is. Here's mines.

National flower: the thistle.

National pastime: nostalgia.

National weather: smirr, haar, drizzle, snaw!

National bird: the crow, the corbie, la corbeille, le corbeau, moi!

How me? Eh? Eh? Eh? Voice like a choked laugh. Ragbag o a burd in ma black duds, aw angles and elbows and broken oxter feathers, black beady een in ma executioner's hood. No braw, but Ah think Ah hae a sort of black glamour?

Do I no put ye in mind of a skating minister, or on the other fit, the parish priest, the durty beast?

My nest's a rickle o sticks.

I live on lamb's eyes and road accidents.

Oh, see, after the battle, after the battle, man, it's a pure feast – ma eyes are ower big even for *my* belly, in lean years o peace, my belly thinks my throat's been cut.

CORBIE *laughs and is suddenly surrounded by the whole* COMPANY *who mill and circle, stop and pose, striking attitudes, looking the audience in the eye – one moment confrontationally, another suspiciously, then the next with the frank and open curiousity of children. Now* CORBIE *takes, from out of their ranks, the twa queens by the hand, parades them like a ringmaster or a barker would a pair of his carnival acts or a cabaret emcee his star burlesque strippers, showing them off.*

Once upon a time there were twa queens on the wan green island, and the wan green island was split intae twa kingdoms. But no equal kingdoms, naebody in their richt mind would insist on that.

For the northern kingdom was cauld and sma. And the people were low-statured and ignorant and feart o their lords and poor? They were starvin! And their queen was beautiful and tall and fair and… Frenchified.

The other kingdom in the island was large, and prosperous, with wheat and barley and fat kye in the fields o her yeoman fermers, and wool in her looms, and beer in her barrels and, at the mouth of her greatest river, a great port, a glistening city that sucked all wealth to its centre – which was a palace and a court of a queen. She was a cousin, a clever cousin, a wee bit aulder, and mibbe no sae braw as the other queen, but a queen nevertheless.

Queen o a country wi an army, an a navy and dominion over many lands.

Quick burst of a sad or ironic jig.

Twa queens. Wan green island. And ambassadors and courtiers came from many lands to seek their hauns…

Scene Two

The Suitors

CORBIE, *watching, listening – as she does all the action of the play, always – is scornful and sceptical of the suitability of every proposed match for either queen. Nevertheless she is, always and quite openly, partial. On* MARY*'s, not* ELIZABETH*'s, side.* MARY *and* ELIZABETH *are passed from pillar to post between the entire* COMPANY, *now a motley of* AMBASSADORS, COURTIERS *or* COMMONERS, *with the dizzy queens whirled through their motions by all and sundry. A dance, a mad tango, to music.*

AMBASSADOR 1 (*to* ELIZABETH). To the most esteemed royal court of Her Majesty Queen Elizabeth of England from His Majesty King Philip of Spain, whose hand in marriage –

CORBIE. King Philip of Spain?

ELIZABETH. Our bloody dead sister's widower? We think *not*, Cecil…

ENGLISH COMMONER 1. I 'ates the bastern Spanish Spanish bastards!

ENGLISH COMMONER 2. At least 'e's not bloody *French*!

ELIZABETH. A *king*! We do not think we could marry a king!

AMBASSADOR 2 (*to* MARY). Pray accept this jewelled miniature with a portrait by our esteemed limner, Sanchez Coello, of Don Carlos of Spain, whose bride perhaps…?

CORBIE. The King o Spain's son, Don Carlos?

MARY (*delighted*). A Catholic!

SCOTS COMMONER 1 (*disgusted*). A *Catholic* – well we canny hae that.

SCOTS COMMONER 2. At least he's no *French*!

ELIZABETH. … On the other hand, Cecil, do contrive to keep the ambassador dangling. Do dandle the odd demi-promise, lest Philip o Spain should try to get a nibble… elsewhere!

MARY. A Catholic! At least he is a good Catholic, even if he's not a king in his own right.

ELIZABETH. I cannot allow her to marry a powerful Catholic…

AMBASSADOR 4 (*to* MARY). Félicitations, Madame la plus belle Reine Marie d'Ecosse from Catharine de' Medici, la Reine de France, mère du roi Charles, who wishes you should consider her son *Henri de Valois*.

CORBIE. Henri de Valois?

SCOTS COMMONER 2. Ah'd raither *Spain* nor bliddy France –

MARY. My own Francis's wee brither! But he's no thirteen year aul… How could ma belle-mère think o't?

ENGLISH COMMONER 1. I'm taking bets on it. Pickering! Ten to one it's Pickering for King of England.

ENGLISH COMMONER 2. Pickering, never!

ELIZABETH (*overhearing*). We do not think we could marry a subject!

ENGLISH COMMONER 2. We know what subject *she'd* have –

ENGLISH COMMONER 1. If he hadn't a wife already!

AMBASSADOR 5 (*to* MARY). What think you of the King of Denmark?

AMBASSADOR 3 (*to* ELIZABETH). From the King of Sweden on behalf of his son, Eric –

SCOTS NOBLE 1 (*to* MARY). The Queen should mairry a Hamilton!

SCOTS NOBLE 2. No she shouldnae! She should mairry a Douglas.

SCOTS NOBLE 3. A Gordon!

SCOTS NOBLE 2. By God and she better no!

SCOTS NOBLE 3. Wha says she'll no?

SCOTS NOBLE 2. I dae!

CORBIE. A Lennox-Stewart, that's wha she should mairry!

SCOTS NOBLES 1, 2 *and* 3 *all draw their swords*.

SCOTS NOBLES 1, 2 *and* 3 (*together*). Ower ma deid body!

ELIZABETH. If we, the Queen, were to follow our own nature's inclinations it would be this: we would rather be a beggar woman and single than a queen and married.

AMBASSADOR 6 (*to* ELIZABETH). Archduke Ferdinand of Austria…?

AMBASSADOR 7 (*to* MARY). Archduke Charles of Austria?

AMBASSADOR 6 (*to* MARY). Archduke Ferdinand of Austria?

AMBASSADOR 7 (*to* ELIZABETH). Archduke Charles of Austria?

ELIZABETH. Methinks they do try to play me and my Scotch cousin off against each other. We must keep the Emperor of Austria sure that Charlie or Ferdie will land him the fat salmon, England, until it is too late for him to net the skinny brown trout of Scotland.

AMBASSADOR 2 (*to* MARY). Don Carlos of Spain!

He gives MARY *a miniature. She holds it.*

MARY. Don Carlos, certainly, to judge from his likeness, is very comely…

CORBIE. I hope they dinna tell her the truth!

Note of discord, a beat's freeze as they parody a twisted, grotesque, crippled boy.

MARY. Aye, Don Carlos looks braw… He'd be the most politik marriage…

ELIZABETH. Back to Scotland with you, and let it be clearly known by your mistress, that should she marry Don Carlos of Spain, or make any other powerful Catholic match in Europe, then we shall be forced to regard her as our enemy. We shall never recognise her or her progeny as heirs to the throne of England.

SCOTS AMBASSADOR. Your Majesty, Queen Mary has been despairing of pleasing you by her choice of husband, or of you ever granting her right of succession.

ELIZABETH. Despair! Such a mean, unqueenly emotion. Methinks she doth give up hope too easily. Although it might be thought that to ask a monarch to name her own successor were to ask her to embroider her own winding sheet.

SCOTS COMMONER 1. They say Don Carlos isnae a there.

SCOTS COMMONER 2. Neither was her first wan, the Frenchy.

CORBIE. Naw, wi him it wis his baws never drapped! This yin is a pair stutterin slaiverin waggin baw-faced dafty that takes blackoots, and that they hae to chain up when the mune's oot, or e'en the scullery boys are no safe.

MARY. I shall marry Don Carlos of Spain!

ALL. Olé!

Tango ends. Now there are only the two queens left – and CORBIE.

ELIZABETH. Do not really wish to marry? I?

I will marry. I have said so. I hope to have children, otherwise I shall never marry.

MARY *and* ELIZABETH *come together on stage but without seeing the other, each in her own separate and different world.*

MARY. Indeed I wish that Elizabeth was a man and I would willingly marry her! And wouldn't that make an end of all debates!

CORBIE. But she isny. Naw, she isny.

There are two queens on wan island, both o the wan language – mair or less. Baith young… mair or less. Baith mair or less beautiful. Each the ither's nearest kinswoman on earth. And baith queens. Caw. Caw. Caw.

Scene Three

Queens and Maids

CORBIE.

Ony queen has an army o ladies and maids
That she juist snaps her fingers tae summon.
And yet… I ask you, when's a queen a queen
And when's a queen juist a wummin?

CORBIE *snaps her fingers,* ELIZABETH *bobs a curtsy, immediately becoming* BESSIE.

MARY. Bessie, do you think she'll meet me?

BESSIE. Aye, Your Majesty, she'll meet wi ye face to face at York, and, you're richt, gin ye talk thegither it'll aw be soarted oot. If ye hunt aw they courtiers an politicians an *men* awa!

CORBIE. She shall never meet you face to face.

MARY. They say she wears my portrait I sent her in that wee jewelled case hangin fae her girdle. And she sent me an emerald.

CORBIE. Oh aye…!

MARY. I'm shivering… Maytime, and it's cauld enough to gie me *chair de poule*! Ah dinna think Ah'll ever understand this country o mine.

BESSIE. The doctor says we have to mak shair you dinna get aw melancholick, Your Majesty.

MARY. Three years! I mind me and the maries oot on deck chitterin in oor fine French frocks, peerin through the glaur o the air for ae glimpse o my kingdom. Three years and I havena seen it yet!

BESSIE. Naw, naw, ye've never seen your country! You've never made your many progresses through the length and breadth o the land!

MARY. The stour o the air clears, then, sherp, a kafuffle atween a Lennox an a Hamilton, a Hamilton and a Douglas…

Haar fae the sea… Cauld… rebecks and chanters, a pretty masque and a goldhaired bairn presents me wi a filigree hert that's fu o golden coins, new minted. Clouds. A flytin fae Knox. Daurkness. A mad poet tries to mak a hoor o me. Wisps… A revel! Smoke… A banquet for the Ambassador new fae Spain. Fog. A bricht affray in the Canongate, a bloody clash at the Butter Tron, a murdered bairn in the Grassmarket, sunshine, and a ragged, starvin crowd o cheerin, cheerin weans jostle to touch ma velvet goon as I go by. My kingdom. Alternately brutal and boring. And I canny mak sense o it at aw.

BESSIE. It's the weather… It's yir sair side. Doctor says we'll hae to gie ye duck eggs whiskit up in wine tae keep the mist o yir melancholia awa.

MARY. It's daein nothin, Bess! The Queen. And I hae nae power tae mak my country flourish.

I want to marry, Bessie, I want to marry and begin my reign at last.

BESSIE. In good time. A guid man in guid time, madam.

CORBIE. Aye, gie her a guid man, she'll gie him a guid time!

And with another snap of her fingers: all change, and BESSIE *is* ELIZABETH, *proud queen, preening, as* MARY *becomes, in that instant, modest and wary* MARIAN, ELIZABETH*'s gentlewoman.*

ELIZABETH. Marian, what do they say she is like?

MARIAN. I don't know, madam.

ELIZABETH. Is she fairer than me? What do they say?

MARIAN. They say she is the fairest queen in Scotland, and you are the fairest queen in England, madam.

ELIZABETH *pinches* MARIAN*'s cheek and laughs.*

ELIZABETH. And how do you know this?

MARIAN (*laughing nervously*).... Because I heard you ask her envoy, Melville.

ELIZABETH. And what did he say – when I pressed him?

MARIAN. That *you* were the whiter, their queen 'very lusome'.

ELIZABETH. And who is the higher?

MARIAN. She is...

ELIZABETH. Then she is too high.

MARIAN. You told him!

ELIZABETH. What are her other amusements?

MARIAN. She writes poems apparently...

ELIZABETH. Poems? In English?

MARIAN. In French. And... 'in Scots'.

A burst of scornful laughter from both at the very idea.

ELIZABETH. What else?

MARIAN. She… plays on the lute and the virginals.

ELIZABETH. And does she play well?

MARIAN. 'Tolerably well. For a queen.'

They laugh together.

ELIZABETH. And does she dance?

MARIAN. She dances. She dances, though not so high or so disposedly as you, Your Majesty.

They laugh again. A beat's pause.

(*Emboldened.*) Madam, you know I love you well.

ELIZABETH. Yes, Marian, like all good subjects, I hope.

MARIAN. Then, madam, I beg you marry the Earl of Leicester, for there is such scandal, a babble getting louder and louder all the time.

ELIZABETH. They say what, Marian?

MARIAN. Madam, I think you know right well.

ELIZABETH. I cannot imagine what they would say about Us.

MARIAN. Just that… you behave together as if you were married already.

ELIZABETH. We do love him right well, indeed.

MARIAN. And he you – madam, I do not think much heed is paid to the bad things some people say, and if you married…

ELIZABETH. I have always said I shall marry – if I marry – as Queen and not as Elizabeth. You think because my subjects love me as their queen they'll have me marry where I will?

MARIAN. Madam, I know so. Marry my Lord Leicester, and live in happiness, that England shall be a peaceable kingdom.

ELIZABETH *holds her breath for a beat. Then smiles.*

CORBIE.

Och, when a queen wad wed,
Or tak a man tae bed,
She only does whit ony maid funns chancy.
So dinna argue the toss,
Just show them wha's boss –
You're the Queen so mairry wha ye fancy.

ELIZABETH (*to herself, considering the bareness of the third finger of her own left hand*). Robert Dudley, my darling, my Lord Leicester… my love…?

CORBIE.

Aye, in England there's a wild floo'erin love,
That the saicret daurkness nourishes.
But in Scotlan – in the braid daylicht! –
The daurk bloom o *hatred* flourishes.

Scene Four

Knox and Mary

KNOX, *in bowler hat and with umbrella, marching. Two members of the* COMPANY, *stamping, sway a banner behind him, and all the* COMPANY *swagger with exaggerated Orangemen's gait. Flute music and hoochs and ugly skirls.*

KNOX. I, John Knox, do preach the evangel of Jesus Christ Crucified, by repentance and faith. And justification by faith alone. Moved by my God and in humble obedience to Him wha is abune us aw, I hae been commandit to blaw the first blast o the trumpet against the monstrous regiment o women, an abomination against nature and before God; and to disclose unto this, my realm, the vanity and iniquity of the papistical religion and all its pestilent manifestations in Sodom priesthooses and poxetten nunneries.

A roll of bread is placed upon a bare table. MARY *and* KNOX *sit with the fact of it between them. Others fall back, listen, watch – and move their lips in prayer.*

MARY. John Knox, mair nor three years I hae borne wi you in aw your rigorous manners o speakin oot, baith against masel and ma French uncles. And yit I hae socht your favour by aw possible means.

KNOX. When it shall please God to deliver you frae that bondage of darkness and error into the one true religion, Your Majesty shall find the liberty o my tongue as a soothing balm unto ye. For, inside the preaching place, madam, I am not master of myself but the mere instrument of Him wha commands me to speak plain and flatter no flesh upon the face of the earth, nor wait on the courts o princes or the chaummers o ladies.

MARY. But what have ye to do with my marriage? What are ye in this commonwealth?

KNOX. A subject born within the same. Albeit I be neither earl, lord nor baron within it. But, however low and abject I am in your eyes, it is ma duty no less to forewarn of what I foresee hurtin it than I were o the nobility.

And gin the nobility should consent ye marry ony husband wha isna o the one true faith then they do as muckle as lies within their power to renounce Christ, to betray the freedom of the realm – and, in the end, to do small comfort to yourself.

CORBIE. Corbie says, by the bones of your beloved mother you must destroy this man! Knox, nox as black as nicht, nox lik a the bitter pousons, nox lik three fearfu chaps at the door, did ding her doon! Knox did lead the rebels. Knox did break yer mither's hert and Knox did laugh when she did dee.

Hark at him: 'The Guid Lord says – and I agree wi him!' Ach! Hark. Cark!

MARY. Maister Knox, I see in you yin wha is convincit he be moved by love of God, but is in truth fired raither by hatred o mankind.

CORBIE. Cark! Aye, tell him!

KNOX. There is yin abune us aw, madam, wha is the best judge, the only.

MARY. You raised up a part of this nation – ma subjects – against ma mither, and against me, their prince, anointed by God. You hae written a treasonous treatise o a book against ma just authority. You have been the cause of great sedition and greater slaughter in England –

KNOX. By the richt worshipping of God, men learn from their hearts to obey their just princes.

MARY. But ye think that I hae nae just authority?

KNOX. Your Majesty, if this realm finds no inconveniency in the regiment o a woman, then that which they approve I shall not further disallow.

MARY. Except within your own heart and breast?

KNOX. My heart is God's. But I shall be as weill content to live under ye as Paul was tae live under Nero.

MARY. Sae ye will gie to *Caesar-ina* whit is Caesar-ina's?

KNOX. I see madam kens her scriptures.

MARY. I ken ma scriptures. I hae baith heard and read. (*Pause.*) Maister Knox, because I am by nature douce, and queyet, dinna think I hae nae convictions or beliefs locked in ma silent heart – though I dae not *trumpet* them abroad.

KNOX. Well! If I did blaw the first blast of the trumpet, madam, against the monstrous regiment o women – this blast was neither against your person or your regiment, but against that bloody Jezebel o England!

MARY. I am shair my guid cousin Elizabeth would be maist disconcertit to ken Maister Knox, wha doth profess the same faith as she, cried her a Jezebel!

KNOX. The Jezebel is Bloody Mary before her, as weel you ken! Wha did practise murderous and several slaughter amang the hedgerows, till the vera weans o the serfs o the loyal lords wha did profess the true faith, did lie wi their guts aw skailt oot amang the stubble o the field, while the air was stinkan and corruptit wi the thick smoke fae the fires o burning martyrs and ministers o the truth.

Madam, open yir heart to God's truth –

MARY. – And you will bid my subjects obey me?

KNOX. Madam, I will.

MARY. Then they shall obey you and not me. Their lawful prince. Like I say, Maister Knox, I hae heard and read.

KNOX. So, madam, did the Jews wha crucified Christ Jesus read both the law and the prophets – and interpretit them as suitit themsels.

MARY. And do ye no interpret as suits you?

KNOX. I believe only what God plainly speaks in His word.

MARY. And yet the same words sound vera different to my ears.

KNOX, *during next, takes the bread, crumbles it, scorns it, desecrates it in* MARY*'s eyes.*

KNOX. For instance: the Mass.

A God of Bread. A god o breid, it is idolatory! Nay, I say that it is *mair* idolatory tae mak a god of breid than when the heathens in their daurkness made fause idols. Consider a god o wood or a god o stane – well, a god o bread is mair miserable… This god will putrify in a single season. The rain or snow can mak saps o sicc a god. Ony durty maid in a scullery can mak a god tae rise in a warm an yeasty corner! Rats and mice will require nae better dinner than roon white gods enough! Show me in the Bible whaur Christ Jesus at His Last Supper did command the Mass? – I tell you, nae mention is made o sicc in aw the scripture.

MARY. Ye are ower sair for me!

She breaks down sobbing. He is astonished, even sorry.

KNOX. Madam, in God's presence I swear that I never delightit in the weeping of ony o God's creatures. As I can scarcely staun the tears o my ain wife or ma ain young sons when ma ain haund is forcit to correct them, faur less can I rejoice in the greetin and howlin and bawlin o Yir Majesty.

He goes to touch her. She recoils.

But I hae tae thole your saut tears, rather than I betray my God or nation by my silence.

MARY. Yet will I in my realm and in ma heart silently defend the Kirk o Rome. And I will marry wha I please. Ye will grant to me guid tolerance – as I hae *aye* granted to you and your Reformit Kirk.

KNOX. Madam, I shall never be seduced by the Siren song o Toleration. I fear you dinnae understaun this country ye are queen o.

KNOX *goes to bow out, having said enough. But –*

MARY. Nevertheless, I will marry wha I please!

KNOX *has to have the Last Word.*

KNOX. I pray God grant you the wisdom of Deborah among the Israelites.

Exit KNOX. MARY, *shaking, is left alone on her knees, praying.*

CORBIE. Gin ye want to gag Maister Knox you will hae tae abolish the Mass and embrace his cauld kirk.

MARY. And is there nae comfort in his kerque?

CORBIE. Aye. Cauld comfort. But there are those wha say it aw the better suits the climate.

MARY. And you think gin I sat on St Giles's hard pews on a Sunday I'd sit surer oan ma ain throne aw week lang?

CORBIE. Nae doot aboot that!

He has cowped the Queen o Heaven so how could he worry aboot cowpin a mere earthly queen?

MARY. Then the Protestants dinnae love oor Blessed Virgin?

CORBIE. Knox has torn the Mother of God from oot the sky o Scotland and has trampit her celestial blue goon amang the muck and mire and has blotted oot every name by which ye praise her – Stella Maris, Star of the Sea, Holy Mother, Notre Dame, Oor Lady o Perpetual Succour.

MARY. But, if he hae torn her frae the blue sky, what has he left in her place?

CORBIE. A black hole, a jaggit gash, *naethin.*

MARY. But how should I live without Our Lady?

CORBIE. Easy. You hae livit withoot yir earthly mother, sae ye can live without your heavenly yin.

MARY *considers this for a moment, but – defiantly – back at* CORBIE*:*

MARY. I will marry wha I can love!

CORBIE *turns to the audience. She gives up, she really does.*

CORBIE. Oh, in the name o the Wee Man…

In the name of the Faither, the Son, the Power and the Glory,
I wish to Christ I could tell yez a Different Story!

Scene Five

Repressed Loves (The First)

CORBIE.

Sae oor queen, wha'd 'rule by gentleness',
Is but a pair fendless craiture –
An in Englan the Lass-Wha-Was-Born-To-Be-King
Maun dowse her womanische nature.

ELIZABETH *is alone, lying down, asleep, dreaming. She rolls over, moaning and murmuring, then wakes up with a scream –*

ELIZABETH. Robert!

Awake, sobbing and crying. Enter MARIAN*, running.*

MARIAN. Bad dreams. Bad dreams again, Your Majesty, hush…

ELIZABETH. Mum was… Dad was… Dad was there, I was only tiny and… my… dolly's head… fell off. Then it changed the way it does in dreams and Leicester, well, we were just two little children playing in the woods, but I knew the way you do that it was really I and my Robert and… then long empty corridors I was all alone and a crown rolling…

She cries again.

MARIAN. Hush! Hot milk and honey, I'll –

But ELIZABETH *detains her, cries some more, then calms.*

ELIZABETH. I couldn't have married him, Marian.

MARIAN. Well… no, madam. Perhaps not.

ELIZABETH. I told him! I said, 'Leicester, if I married you and we lay down together as King and Queen, then we should wake as plain Mister and Mistress Dudley. The Nation would not have it.'

MARIAN. Surely the scandal would have died down? Can't you marry him secretly and –

ELIZABETH. She trumped us. His bloody wife. Why couldn't she let him decently divorce her? Oh no, she has to commit suicide.

Now everyone is sure he murdered her. If he'd bloody murdered her, he'd have done it a lot better than that. Made quite sure it looked as though she took her own life.

MARIAN. Marry him secretly! In six months… a year… everyone will have forgotten she ever lived.

ELIZABETH. Too late! I've told him I want him to marry Madam o Scots.

MARIAN.… Who?

ELIZABETH. Queen Mary, and take him off to Edinburgh.

MARIAN. Madam!

ELIZABETH. Why not? I hear she is very attractive, though I've yet to set eyes on her.

MARIAN. But, madam –

ELIZABETH. Oh yes! Bit on the tall side, of course, and hair that reddish colour that makes the complexion sickly-looking – oh, and a virgin too, although she has been married. Altogether doing it exactly the wrong way round for my taste, but still, she is a queen after all, so –

MARIAN. – He loves you!

ELIZABETH. I'm sure she'll make him happy, that'll shut all their mouths and we'll have a loyal Englishman – I think we may depend on him to remain a loyal Englishman? – In her bed. Well, we really cannot have her married in France again, else the French King can straddle England with one foot in Calais, the other in Edinburgh, and piss down on us all fire, brimstone and poison. Besides, I have already broached it with the Scotch Ambassador.

MARIAN *looks on her with amazement.* ELIZABETH *suddenly crumbles and she is sobbing again. Taking her life in her hands,* MARIAN *holds her, hushes her tentatively.*

No more. What shall it profit a woman if she can rule a whole kingdom but cannot quell her own rebellious heart?

Robert, you were more dangerous to me than a thousand, thousand Northern Catholics, poised and armed. I am not proud I love him – but I am proud that, loving him, still I would not let him master me.

Repressed Loves (The Second)

CORBIE. Aye, very good, Queen Bess! Thon's a quine wi her heid screwed oan. An Mary…? Well, I've said it afore an I'll say it again:

When a queen wud wed,
Or tak a man tae bed,
She only does whit *ony* maid funns chancy.
Dinnae argue the toss,
Juist show them wha's boss –
You're the Queen so mairry wha ye fancy.

Enter BOTHWELL, *bowing, cap in hand.*

MARY. Alison Craik, Earl Bothwell!

BOTHWELL. Wha?

CORBIE. He kens her!

MARY. You ken her!

BOTHWELL. Dae I?

MARY. I ken you dae.

BOTHWELL. Well, Your Majesty, you ken, I dinna ken aw the lassies I ken. So mibbe you ken mair than I dae…

MARY. Alison Craik is the dochter of thon respectable Edinburgh merchant, whase hoose near the Saut Tron ye did rudely invade and enter, ye and ma pair auld uncle d'Elboeuf aw fired up wi drink and his brains addled.

BOTHWELL. Oh, *that* Alison…

MARY. Ma pair gyte auld uncle, Bothwell!

BOTHWELL. Aye, his auld hurdies werena fit to gang whaur his new-youthfu and fair French-style fancies would have led him tae lie…

CORBIE. Caw! Caw!

MARY. Ye led him to wickedness, Bothwell! Drunkenness and rapine, Ah'll no hae it!

BOTHWELL. Ah dinna expect ye'll get offert it vera often. No in your station in life.

CORBIE. Caw! Caw canny.

MARY. *Nobody* speaks to the Queen like that!

BOTHWELL. An that's juist wha Ah am. Naebody. Ah widnae let naebody bother you, Your Majesty.

MARY. Apparently you are naebody. Naebody to be chidit by the Kirk Assembly. The excellent Protestants were vera quick tae complain and denounced fae the pulpit ma pair auld uncle wha couldna go whaur you didna lead him. And did they chide you?

BOTHWELL. Noo, wha are you worrit aboot – your auld uncle or… the fair Alison.

MARY. I want, in my realm, Maister Hepburn O'Bothwell, that women should sleep sound in their beds.

CORBIE. You tell him!

BOTHWELL. Because dinna, you ken. Worry aboot Alison. She's juist a tail.

MARY *gasps*.

A brass nail, a hure, a daw, a penny-jo. (*Pause*.) Oh, a pricey penny-jo, her faither is a city merchant. (*Pause*.) Sleepin sound isny lik Alison, if aw I've heard be true… Though, mind, she sleeps the sleep o the just. The just-keistit that is.

No that I've a bad word for ony lass that is an honest hure. But Alison Craik is the Earl o Arran's hure. And the Earl o Arran is a bloody Hamilton… So I had her.

She wisna unwilling.

She wisna unwilling, but yir auld uncle d'Elboeuf wisna able… Sae the Kirk Assembly are makkin a mountain oot o a mowdie-hill. At least in nuncle d'Elby-boeuf's case…

MARY (*wearily*). 'Because he is a Hamilton!' Ah'll no have you nobles o this yin nation aye at each ither's throats lik terriers.

BOTHWELL. Well, madam, I fear you are queen o the wrang kintra. Terriers we are, it is our nature. Be a while afore ye make kittocky kittlin-cats o us, or wee saft-moothed spaniels to stick oor heids in yer lap and fawn ower each ither while we wait for yir favours.

MARY. I'm your queen. And in three years in this country I canna depend on any o ye to show me royal respect as I am due, although in every way I try – (*Dissolves into shaming tears.*)

CORBIE. Don't greet!

BOTHWELL. Madam: I hae the greatest respect for my anointed queen, whase grace and beauty gladdens my heart and whase gentleness and clemency does tame my savagery.

CORBIE. Aye well, there's mibbe somethin tae be said for weepin...

BOTHWELL. – And whase courage and swiftness in the chase does quicken my spirit and speed my ain steed in pursuivance of the quarry.

MARY. I didna ken ye took such pleasure in hunting.

BOTHWELL. In the chase? Aye. When there's a fine white hind dancin afore me through the trees, and I glisk it, then lose it again, glisk it, lose it... but my hound, my pointing hound, doth throw back his liver-coloured chops and bay. Because my hound and I can smell it. Glintin through the trees in the gloamin daurk.

Hunting? Aye. When I am honoured to be in the Queen's party.

Hae we no shared minny's an exhaustin day's sport, Your Majesty? And yet ye turned me doon.

I humbled masel but still you widna mairry me...

A long beat between them.

MARY. Nae mair Alison Craiks!

BOTHWELL (*bowing*). Your Majesty.

MARY. Nae mair tiltin at Hamiltons.

BOTHWELL. – But, Your Majesty, there is a history to this dispute!

MARY. I dinna want to hear your history!

Doom. A drumbeat.

Bothwell, as well as Queen, I am widow. And maiden. And I would hae all unprotectit women in my realm honoured in their privacy!

BOTHWELL. I ken. You are heart-sorry for Alison Craik.

MARY. And I tell you, if there is any mair of this I will be forcit to outlaw you, to put you to the horn!

CORBIE. Caw!

BOTHWELL Put me to the horn would you, my leddy? I tell you, Ah'll pit you to the horn and you'd be gled to rin outlawed wi me.

MARY. Bothwell! –

BOTHWELL. Nae mair tiltin at Alison Craik. Nor at Arran the Hamilton gin he gree no tae tilt at me.

MARY. Go then. And keep the peace, James Hepburn, I charge you, keep peace.

He bows out. BESSIE, *as she comes in, passes him, bristles.*

Bessie! Bessie, do you think it's true he is a warlock?

BESSIE. A warlock, Your Majesty, why?

MARY. He frichtens me.

BESSIE. Aye, madam, but Ah dinna think there is anythin eldritch or extraordinar in that...

MARY. But how then would he hae the power tae disturb me so?

BESSIE *thinks better of trying to reply.*

CORBIE (*a mutter*). Well, Bessie, ma lass, there's nae answer tae that, eh?

Scene Six

Elizabeth Stirs It Up

CORBIE, *in a 'let's get a move on' fashion, snaps her fingers in her shape-changing, scene-changing way.* BESSIE *becomes proud Queen* ELIZABETH *again, and* MARY *maid* MARIAN.

CORBIE.

Aye, a man he is a tasty dish,
But mairriage is a kettle o fish...

Twa queens, ae nicht, push their plates awa,
When they sit doon tae sup.
Yin doesnae ken whit's steerin her –
Yin doesnae ken whit tae steer up!

ELIZABETH *is speaking to* MARIAN *in a conspiratorial whisper.*

ELIZABETH. He is here, Marian?

MARIAN. Yes, madam.

ELIZABETH. And none saw him who could carry tales to my Lord Leicester?

MARIAN. I think not, madam...

ELIZABETH. Go then, send him in...

DARNLEY, *young and nervous, enters, kneels.*

Cousin!

DARNLEY. Your Majesty.

ELIZABETH. Do get up, let me look at you. Well, I haven't seen you since you were but a beardless boy – and now you are grown such a fine long lad. How old are you?

DARNLEY. Nineteen, madam, almost –

ELIZABETH. Old enough, eh? Cousin, the Scotch Ambassador and I have been discussing you lately, wondering whether we are to allow you to take yourself off to Bonnie Scotland. What think you?

DARNLEY. Madam, I don't know what to say, you surprise me so!

ELIZABETH. Oh nonsense! You know how your Mama Lennox has been two-three years a-wheedling at me. 'Will I – pretty-please will I, oh Your Maj – help her to restore your father and your sire to his rightful lands and estate in Scotland?'

What do you suppose your mother really wants?

DARNLEY. Madam, I know she desires nothing more than justice for my father, an end to his banishment from his own homeland. He's an old man, Your Majesty.

ELIZABETH. Oh, we're all old to you, Henry.

DARNLEY. Twenty years! Since before I was even born. Exiled, unfairly stripped of his lands by the Scottish Crown.

ELIZABETH. Yes, yes, and of course your mam wants him to die happy and be buried on his own soil. Commendable, such uxoriousness.

He doesn't understand.

That means nice-little-wifeyness, Henry. Do sit down, Henry!

Henry, your mama and I are both grandchildren of Henry the Seventh of England. You are aware of that?

DARNLEY. Yes, of course, ma'am.

ELIZABETH. There are even some who say she has a close claim to succeed me.

DARNLEY. Madam, I think you know my mother is your most loyal and most humble subject.

ELIZABETH (*too quickly*). Even though she is a Catholic like the Scotch bitch! (*Recovers.*) Perhaps.

Oh, Henry, some of my advisers and statesmen are very suspicious sorts of people, you know I really cannot keep up with them! They try to convince me your mother has big ambitions for her little son, and before Queen Mary's poor wee French runt had begun to rot in his coffin, Mum had sent you and your brother off on French holidays, a-commiserating with the young widow.

DARNLEY. I was but a child then!

ELIZABETH. So was she, Henry, but you're both all growed up now.

But I know, dear, you would never think to marry a lady so much older than you.

DARNLEY. – Only three years!

ELIZABETH. Ah yes, but, Henry, when the difference is the wrong way round and the maid is older than the man, it puts the balance out of kilter. Don't think of it! You are a right loyal subject of England, Henry Darnley?

DARNLEY. Madam, you know I am.

ELIZABETH. Exactly. I will tell my ministers so! I'll explain it all to them – the old dad, et cetera. I think you may depend on it, we will allow you to go.

DARNLEY. My father will be –

ELIZABETH. Except –

DARNLEY. Ma'am?

ELIZABETH. Well… can I trust you to keep a confidence? Maybe I shouldn't tell you this but… you see, negotiations are well advanced with the Scotch Ambassador that Queen Mary will marry my Lord Leicester.

DARNLEY. Leicester, but he is your…

ELIZABETH. My favourite! Yes. Well, do they say so? Perhaps. But wise monarchs should keep no favourites. I am determined there shall be no other English rival to Leicester for the hand of the Queen of Scots. And it's been troubling me a little, just in case – no fault of your own – but what if the Scotch Queen should take it into her head to prefer *you*, being there, to *him*, being here? You do see my little difficulty? Remember, when you are in Scotland you'll be beyond my power. Why, you could pretend to be a Catholic yourself and woo her, and me not able to stop you! Honestly, were I not so confident of your loyalty, I could not let you go.

It slowly sinks in that she is saying yes.

DARNLEY. May I?

ELIZABETH. I've signed the paper already. You may go. And… you may go!

DARNLEY. Your Majesty. (*Bowing, he begins to leave.*)

ELIZABETH. Young Henry, be careful, I hear it's a cold, dire, rough place. Worse than Yorkshire.

Scene Seven

Mary Queen of Scots' Progress, The Bairns, and John Knox's Shame

CORBIE *shivers. In the cold, and more than that. Shakes herself though, to drive her story forward, as she must.*

CORBIE.

Though the wind blaws snell doon the Canongate the day,
There's ne'er an honest bairn nor a rogue less,
As through the toun, in fine processioun,
Comes the Queen, and her cooncil, in progress.

Bright processional music. The COMPANY *are now a ragamuffin, shilpit, poor-looking selection of the Edinburgh common people; gadges, bairns, dafties and auld folk. They might join in with* CORBIE*'s next verse –*

Gaberlunzies in duds and pair drabs in their rags,
Can feast their een on hoo the Queen and the court dress,
Though wir teeth micht chitter we dinna feel bitter –
Naw, we cheer at *Queen Mary's progress*!

They do, raucously. MARY *is now* MAIRN, *a wee poor Scottish beggar lass, and* ELIZABETH *is* LEEZIE, *her tarty wee companion. All are cheering and watching the* (*to us*) *invisible progess as it passes them.*

MAIRN. The Queen! The Queen! She's comin.

LEEZIE. Aw, she's beautiful, eh, Mairn?

MAIRN. Lovely.

LEEZIE. Mind you, we'd be braw in braw claes…

MAIRN. Ah don't think Ah could lukk lik the Queen, Leezie…

LEEZIE. Aye ye could, if yer frock wis French flamin velvet wi a siller-lace collar.

Suddenly a shower of small coins – like those thrown by custom to the local kids at a Scots wedding as the bridal car leaves.

ALL. Scrammle! It's a scrammle! Haw, it's mines! (*Etc.*)

– and they are squabbling and fighting over every last round coin of it.

KNOX *looks on in disgust.*

KNOX. And thus are oor pair, fair bairns o Scotland reduced to fechtin ower trashy scraps o glisterin tin coins that French hoor scatters fae her progress. By smilin an dauncin does she steal the people's hearts away from the true priests and the true religion. Starvin. The people are starvin. But inasmuch as they hunger for earthly sustenance, a hundredfold were they famisht for the spiritual food of true redemption. Till the Lord God did deliver them.

Everybody except KNOX, LEEZIE *and* MAIRN *disappears.* LEEZIE *and* MAIRN *are rolling on the ground among the dirt, laughing. Under* LEEZIE*'s bold prompting and nudging,* MAIRN *is soon staring at* KNOX.

LEEZIE. He wis. He wis starin. Gaun. Ask him, Mairn!

MAIRN. Dinna, Leezie, dinna. Ah canny.

LEEZIE. Starin ett ye. He'll ken ye the next time, honestly. Haw! Lukks lik he's juist back frae a funeral! He'll be definitely wantin a wee bit rumplefyke then… (*Shouts.*) Haw, maister, ma pal wants tae ken if ye want tae go wi her?

MAIRN. Come awa, Leezie…

KNOX. Awa tae hell wi ye, ya jauds!

MAIRN. Leezie! Leezie, yon's… John Knox! Ow-ah!

LEEZIE. Maister, buy us wir denner…?

KNOX. Awa and pray the Lord tae forgive ye. You're nobbut weans!

LEEZIE. Well, yon's no whit ye said last week!

She runs off, wild coarse laughter, a rude sign, a flashed bum, a bent arm. KNOX *is right at scared wee* MAIRN, *facing her down and everything freezes.* LEEZIE *is far off from them, frozen in her cheeky running away;* MAIRN *suddenly straight and tall, suddenly totally* MARY *the Queen in* KNOX*'s eyes – as he chides a cheeky wee harlot on the cauld Canongate.*

KNOX*'s hand is raised in anger but stayed in awe.*

KNOX. By Christ. Ah'll tan yir arse fur ye, ya wee hoor o Babylon. Lukk at ye! Wi yir lang hair lik a flag in the wind, an advertisement o lust tae honest men. An, ach, they big roon een lik a dumb animal, slinkan alang the road wi yir hurdies hingin oot yir sark, an yon smell aff ye, ya durty wee fork-arsed bitch, ye.

Nae wunder it is written in the Guid Book that your kind are the very gate and port o the devil – Ah'll leave the rid mark o ma haun on your white flesh afore Ah –

By an effort of pure will, that moment of lust, madness and ambiguity passes and KNOX *is back in control of himself.*

Awa and behave! Pray God forgive you and sin nae mair.

CORBIE (*singing*).
In papische days wi evil ways,
The sinner sins and then he pays.
The blind bishop –

ALL (*joining in*).
– The blind bishop he canna preach,
For playin wi the lasses.
The friar flatters aw in reach,
For alms that they possesses.
The curate his creed, he canna read –
But noo we are reformit.
Hoo shall the meenister creesh his palms,
Or his cauld bed be warmit?

BOTHWELL *comes now, urgently, to* KNOX.

BOTHWELL. A wee burd tells me the Queen isna pleased wi you! Well, you arena feart, ma freen, speakin oot lik yon!

KNOX. The marriage o our queen is in all men's mouths, Bothwell, sae it is ma duty to denounce France and decry Spain and to preach against allowin her a papish marriage. For by the same act o takkin a man tae her bed, she maks a king tae a people.

We, the people, should choose a husband fur a lassie raither than a silly wee furrin lassie should choose a king for a people.

BOTHWELL. Well, you tell her! You arena feart…

KNOX. Why should the pleasin face o a gentlewoman affray me? I hae lookit in the faces o many angry men and no been afraid, no above measure.

BOTHWELL. Well, Ah'm mair feart o a pleasin female face nor an angry male yin ony day. No that I'd ever let a quine ken it. They're lik dugs – show them fear and they are forcit tae bite ye.

KNOX. She's only a silly spilte wee French lassie, Bothwell.

BOTHWELL. Only a silly spilte wee French lassie wha could cowp the kirk and cut your heid aff, John Knox.

KNOX. She's only a queen.

BOTHWELL (*as they begin to exit*). And what's a queen?

KNOX. Juist a silly, spilte wee lassie.

Scene Eight

Darnley and a Fever

CORBIE.

Yestreen the Queen was wyce enough,
To forswear all desire,
From love, and the keist-and-rummle o love,
She flinched, as at fire.

But noo… the Queen and Lord Darnley!
Close-closeted thegither,
Young Lord Darnley's on his sickbed –
But baith o them hae a fever!

DARNLEY *in bed,* MARY *by his bedside with a bowl of soup.*

DARNLEY. Your Majesty, is it you?

MARY. Yes, it's me. It's Mary.

DARNLEY. This is humiliating.

MARY. Wheesht!

DARNLEY. Measles! A childhood complaint, it's –

MARY. I had it in France when I was a wee, wee girl!

DARNLEY. You poor little thing, so far away from your mother too.

MARY. Aye. I grat full sore for her.

DARNLEY. I don't know how she could have sent you away. You must have been such a pretty child.

MARY. I dinna ken boot that. But I missed her.

She had to dae it though, to keep me safe an soond. There were plenty plots to steal the infant Queen and rule in her stead.

If I had a child though… oh, I dinna think I could send ma ain bairn awa.

DARNLEY. Poor Mary!

MARY. Oot on the deck, ready tae embark, an Ah wis sae excitit – I'm a great sailor, ye ken, I wis the only wan no seeck aw the wey tae France – but, ma mither, she wis greetin an roarin and stitchin wee medals o the Blessed Virgin intae ma claes tae keep me safe…

I didna ken whit was the maitter. I didna realise hoo lang it'd be ere I'd see her again.

DARNLEY. My mother's a Catholic too!

MARY. Is she?

DARNLEY. Oh yes.

I can't imagine my mother ever sending me away!

MARY. No even for your ain guid?

DARNLEY. I don't think so. (*Laughing*.) I'm glad she's not here now, she'd be rushing around with junkets and milk jellies and broth to get my strength back up!

MARY. I brocht you some broth! I forgot! That wis why I came! It'll be cauld noo, I'll go get some mair.

DARNLEY. Mary, don't – I'm not hungry!

MARY. Do ye not want onything?

DARNLEY. No. Just… stay with me, Mary.

Long beat. They look deep into each other's eyes.

CORBIE. Ach, here we go…

A burst of ironic music segues into –

ELIZABETH. And really it has proved remarkably simple. All we had to do was keep it nice and complicated. Well, once Philip withdrew Don Carlos – although clearly the boy was an idiot, even Mary couldn't have married him – well, we pushed for Leicester, hinted we might be about to ratify on the succession question, if we got her married to an Englishman and a Protestant… but, alack, our heart was not in it.

A weakness of course, must be a bit of the old *dad* in me, must cut it out.

But, secretly, we were somewhat relieved when the old religion bit was a little too much for Mary to swallow. Well, we might have got somewhere if Master Knox could have been persuaded to be a little less confrontational – really there is no *moderation* in the man – but, truth to tell, I was glad really when she would have none of my Robert.

Then the measles! What a stroke of luck, poor Darnley all flushed and fevered, and Queen Mary playing nursemaid, brought out her tender feelings, most affecting… And now they are to be married. All it took was for me to *expressly* forbid it and he was irresistible.

Which should keep her busy at home sorting out the snarls and quarrels that lad'll cause among her nobility! Too busy to indulge in any mischief among *my* Disenchanted Catholics.

And it does let my Lord Leicester off the hook. Pity, really. There were no more *piquant* nights than those ones he were never sure if he were off to the *Tower* or to *Scotland* in the morning.

Scene Nine

A Wedding

Music. Solemn and processional. Celebratory. Erotic.

As MARY *and* DARNLEY *enter, robed for their wedding –*

CORBIE (*singing*).
Oor queen has mairrit her a knight,
His curls are fair as ony child,
Sma is his mooth and his manner douce,
His eyes are meek and mild.

Oor queen has mairrit her a knight,
She fondles him an he were her pet,
He moves sae spry and his voice sae high –
Yon long lad he is a-growin yet…

Oor queen has mairrit her a knight,
His cheek as saft as ony baby boy,
Soon may she declare a son and heir,
To be oor nation's joy.

COMPANY *all join in with the song and the ceremony.*

ALL. And we hae made to them a bed.
We made it large and wide,
That Mary oor queen and the Lord Darnley,
Micht lay doon side by side.

MARY. And each o ye draw oot a pin,
A pin frae oot ma mournin gear,
Alas, alack, in weeds o black,
To show I hae a widow been,
And ever sin I hae been wrapped in,
Ma mournin gear, ma mournin gear,
For many a long and weary year.

And I shall loose ma lang rid hair,
Ungimp ma girdles o the plaited silk,
Slip frae ma sark and in the dark,
Ma bodie will gleam as white as milk.

And I shall be dressed in nakedness,
My briests twa aiples o desire,
And you shall hae the brichtest jewel,
That nestles in my brooch o red-gowd wire.

MARY *and* DARNLEY *kiss*.

Blackout.

End of Act One.

ACT TWO

Scene One

Seigneur Riccio, a Fortune, a Baby, and a Big Baby

The clattering noise of an old typewriter. Lights come up to reveal RICCIO, *typing away efficiently, with* MARY *pacing, dictating. Fast, secretive, well-established hard work.* RICCIO *has a slight hunchback, is small and slight, but with a face both beautiful and gentle in his twisted body.* CORBIE *snaps her fingers.*

MARY. Twa copies, Seigneur Davy, yin tae the Papal Nuncio, yin tae the Cardinal o Lorraine – ssh! Carefu, carefu, no a word tae naebody, no tae the King, no even tae Bothwell.

RICCIO *puts his fingers to his lips, smiles.*

RICCIO. Puoi avere fiducia in me, Davy Riccio!

He goes back to typing. MARY *sits down and looks at her belly.*

MARY. Please mak it be true, mak it a richt enough. And mak it a boy – for your ain sake.

RICCIO *looks at her, shakes his head and wags his finger, goes on typing.*

CORBIE. And is that what we'd expect to see, no three month eftir yir weddin? Whaur's yir bonny young groom? Eh? Eh?

RICCIO *rips out the sheet of paper, takes it over to* MARY, *who plucks a feather out of* CORBIE*'s coat sleeve and signs flamboyantly.*

MARY. And you hae the stamp we hae made up o the King's signature?

RICCIO *produces it with a flourish and rubber-stamps each paper with a thump.*

Aye… oan the richt-hand side, o coorse. Mine must aye hae the pride o place, because it is the name you read first! On the left. (*Pause.*) Oh, Riccio, Riccio, you dinnae think it was… petty o me to withdraw the silver ryal?

RICCIO *comes and starts massaging her temples.*

Na, I dinna think so, there was nae choice, Davy. I couldna allow it as a coin o the realm.

CORBIE *does a trick, conjures up one of these very coins.*

CORBIE. The silver ryal, a commemorative coin worth thirty shillings, Scots, to celebrate the love of King Henry for Queen Mary –

CORBIE *bites the coin, testing the metal.*

– Is it genuine?

MARY. The damnable cheek of it – *Henricus* et Maria, Deo Gratia *Rex* et Regina Scotorum! Wrang order.

CORBIE. Whom God hath jined together let nae man cast asunder.

And the coin is turned by a trick magically into two.

MARY. I wish Henry widna harp and carp aboot the crown matrimonial aw the time, for it widna be politick to grant him it.

CORBIE. Even if you wanted tae.

MARY. So, Henry Darnley, you hae nae richt to ma throne eftir ma death – even if it werena for *you*, ma son.

If you *are* a son. Och, I widna wish for ye to be a lassie. Whit think ye, Davy Riccio, boy or girl?

RICCIO *shuts* MARY*'s eyes, leans her back, takes a ring on a ribbon from his pocket and swings it like a pendulum above her belly.*

CORBIE. Whit is't then? Widdershins an it's a boy!

RICCIO *waits as the ring swings and stops, then cheekily makes a wee wiggling baby's penis of his crooked little finger at his crotch.*

RICCIO. Ragazzo!

MARY. Thank God, a son.

CORBIE. Funny! Yesterday it went the *other* wey and *still* ye said, oh aye it wis a laddie! Dowsers an diviners an fortune-tellers, ever noticed how they aw tell ye whit they think ye want to hear?

MARY. Make him strang! (*Pause.*) Davy Riccio – tell ma fortune!

CORBIE. Ta-rocco!

Tarot cards, outsize, appear. RICCIO *spreads them in a circle.*

MARY. Only you, Davy, only you said I wis richt to marry Henry Darnley. You cast ma cairts for me – an you chartit ma birth staurs – time an again we turnt up the same cairt…

RICCIO (*turning it up, announcing it yet again*). Gli Amanti!

MARY. The lovers. Numero six. 'A choice.' Except there wis nae choice at aw, you kennt that! Though even *ye* couldna hae fortellt the anger o ma nobles! Damn them aw! Damn England for harbouring the bloody rebels, I'll depend on France and Spain afore England, I'll show them aw I was richt tae follow ma destiny an marry the man I loved.

CORBIE. Lov-*ed*. Note the past tense.

MARY. Noo, Davy, we hae tae cast three, is that no richt?

First card.

MARY and RICCIO. Il diavolo!

Second card.

RICCIO. Numero tredici –

MARY (*shivering*). The unnamed card…

RICCIO. La morte.

MARY *tries to laugh it off.*

MARY. Ah ken that's supposed to be a lucky caird, dinna cairds aye mean the opposite? But it frichts me aw the same!

CORBIE. A skeleton wi a grin as wide his ain scythe. Airms and legs in the broken earth. A crowned head, cut aff, in the boattom corner. Only a picture! Colourt in ower crudely by some Admon Kadmon trickster at a tally fair! La morte!

MARY *and* RICCIO (*as the third card goes down*). Justizia!

MARY. Justice, well yon's a lucky caird, eh, Davy?

CORBIE. Oh aye, an – lik chance – it'd be a fine thing.

RICCIO *smiles, soothes, massages her feet and ankles, the original reflexologist.*

CORBIE *picks up the rest of the pack. She fans them.*

An whit else is in here? There's… the world, il mondo; la ruota, the wheel o fortune; the ruined tower; the wummin pope; the hangin man; il pazzo, the fool –

On the very word 'fool', DARNLEY, *bottle in hand, appears, staggers.*

– Zero. The King – nay, the knave, the knave o cups!

And CORBIE *shows us that very card.*

DARNLEY *is now supported by* BOTHWELL *and* BESSIE. *Drunk as he is,* DARNLEY *registers* RICCIO *with* MARY*'s bare foot in his hands, on his lap.*

DARNLEY. What in hell's name is going on? Leave my wife alone – I'll bloody well –

DARNLEY *makes a drunken lunge.*

CORBIE. He will!

BOTHWELL. C'moan, man, wheest…!

BOTHWELL *bows low at* MARY*'s feet, acknowledges* RICCIO *perfunctorily.*

Madam, at your service. Seigneur Davy.

MARY. Bothwell, hoo daur you let him get intae sicc a state?

BOTHWELL. Madam… Ah nivir encouraged him. Ah… did advise him that mibbe he should caw canny. But he is the King.

MARY. He's only a laddie.

BOTHWELL *shrugs, ruffles* DARNLEY*'s drunken head indulgently.*

BOTHWELL. Ah ken, Ah ken… he hasna the heid for it yet.

DARNLEY. I'll tell you where I have been. I have been making friends among your nobles. On *your behalf.* You make no attempt to understand them or make them your allies. I'll tell you where I have been. On Tuesday, after the hunt, a great day's sport, we came upon a deserted little cove… near Aberdour. Very rocky… Bothwell and I swam a race across it. All the other nobles cheered. And I won. Didn't I, Hepburn…? I won!

MARY. Bothwell, I thocht I had askit ye for your help?

BOTHWELL. Madam, I hae missed ma ain dinner and ridden fifteen lang mile tae bring him safely harne, he isna ma responsibeelity…

MARY. Maister Hepburn, I am sorry.

Bessie, tak the Earl o Bothwell doon tae the kitchens directly and wake someone, middle o the nicht or no! Somethin hot for the Earl o Bothwell.

BESSIE *curtseys,* BOTHWELL *bows and both exit.* DARNLEY *lurches up to* MARY, *breathes in her face.*

DARNLEY. Ah, Mary, Mary. I'm sorry… Give me a kiss.

She recoils.

Leave us alone, Seigneur Riccio!

MARY. Davy, stay exactly where you are!

RICCIO *stays. Begins typing fast.* DARNLEY *crumples in humiliation. Slurring –*

DARNLEY. Clack, clack, clack, like the tongues of foreigners… Italians. French… Only thing I can stand about the bloody French is the wine.

(*Singing.*) Oh – oh – Give me twelve and twelve o the good claret wine,
An twelve – and twel o the muskadine…

Mind you, the Scotch are as bloody bad. God made the Highlander out of a lump of dung… Then for the bloody Lowlander, He decided to economise on even that basic raw material.

What are you writing?

DARNLEY *pulls the sheet out of the typewriter, crumples it up, throws it away.*

Because it's too late at night. Go away, Seigneur Davy, I want to kiss my wife.

My lovely wife. My beautiful wife. D'you know she is the Queen? Therefore she must be beautiful.

She is though.

DARNLEY *touches* MARY*'s hair.*

MARY. Davy, leave us.

RICCIO *bows, goes – with palpable relief.*

The royal couple are now alone. DARNLEY *sobs like a child.*

DARNLEY. Oh, Mary, Mary, I am sorry.

MARY. Aye, Henry, aye. You aye-weys are.

DARNLEY. Mary, Mary, I love you, hold me!

She rocks him and cradles him.

MARY. Wheesht, wheesht, Henry! Ssh.

CORBIE. Yin big bairn – and yin on the wey!

Scene Two

Rumplefyke

CORBIE. Haw – somethin hoat for the Earl o Bothwell!

BOTHWELL *and* BESSIE, *dishevelled. He grabs her and kisses her lewdly.*

BESSIE. Dinna!

She bites his mouth. He jumps apart from her.

BOTHWELL. Ya jaud ye, ye are as sherp as ye are soople.

BESSIE. Wheesht! The Queen'll hear us, or *somebody'll* –

BOTHWELL. The Queen! She's likely busy daen the same –

BOTHWELL *kisses* BESSIE, *grabs at her up her skirt.*

BESSIE. I dinna think sae!

BOTHWELL. Richt enough, he's ower fou tae even pish straight.

Ah wunner if he cin still pit a smile on her face?

BESSIE. Whiles. But no vera oaften.

BOTHWELL. Hoo dae ye ken?

BESSIE. Ah ken fine! What do you want to talk aboot the Queen for?

BOTHWELL. Ah dinna!

They kiss again, get right into it. When finally they break –

BESSIE. Bothwell, ma mistress kens naethin o the happiness you hae taught me.

BOTHWELL. Ah should hope no! The difference in oor ranks! Besides, I am a married man.

BESSIE. You ken fine whit I mean. I'm sure she has never kennt it for hersel.

BOTHWELL. Whit?

BESSIE. Love.

BOTHWELL. And her mairrit tae sicc a handsome long lad?

BESSIE. Ah'm sayin naethin!

BOTHWELL. And she doesna love him?

BESSIE. Mibbe aye… mibbe hooch aye!

BOTHWELL. Pair, pair Queen! Nae wunner her an Davy Riccio are sae thick thegither.

BESSIE. Noo dinna you start ony daft –

BOTHWELL. You're no tellin me it's true that the Queen and Davy Riccio –

BESSIE. Davy Riccio is as ugly as sin… He is a humphit backt wee puggy monkey o a man!

BOTHWELL *kisses* BESSIE *lewdly.*

BOTHWELL. Does he kiss her lik this? And does he stick his haun –

BESSIE. Dinna! You're makkin me shudder.

BOTHWELL. Maks a lot of women shudder, so I've heard. Maks them shiver when they see their smooth milk skin up agin greasy, creashy, warted skin, when they run their haun ower the bone-hard gnarl o the hump –

BESSIE. Dinna!

BOTHWELL. Oh aye! There is a big attraction – beauty wad fain keist wi ugliness, its opposite!

BESSIE. Naw –

BOTHWELL. Oh aye, oh aye, ma lassie. When you ken the weys o the warld as weel as this auld tod-fox o a man, here, does –

BESSIE. Does it no occur tae ye, maybe she looes Davy Riccio because he is the only man wha has ever touched her *withoot* he wants tae tummle her?

BOTHWELL. Och! Mibbe I should stap tummlin ye and ye'd looe me aw the better…?

BESSIE. Dinna!

She reaches for him.

BOTHWELL. Awricht, mibbe Ah'll no…

Touchin her, though! Ah hae heard it said a cat cin lukk at a queen, but never that a durty wee lowborn furriner can run his hauns aw ower her. Nae wunner the King droons his pair hornit heid in his cups, an the rumours…

BESSIE. He is a healer.

BOTHWELL. Och, Ah bet!

Pause.

What was aw yon wi the bare feet then? By God, the King was bleezin…

BESSIE. It's a healin airt! (*Holds out her own bare foot.*) Ilka bit o yer feet is… lik a map o the rest o yir body – oh, I dinnae ken, but yir ankle-banes are your briests…

BOTHWELL *sucks at her ankles.* BESSIE, *arches her back cups her own breasts and runs her hands down her body.*

…and the gimp-bit is your waist – an when you touch that bit on the fit it soothes that bit o the body…

Simultaneously BOTHWELL *is running his hands over her foot and finally tickles with his thumb between her toes. She gasps and arches.*

It works!

BOTHWELL. Ah'm trickery-Riccio… Ah'm Seigneur Davy… an you're the Queen… brawer than the Queen by faur…

BESSIE. I'm no!

BOTHWELL. Oh aye. An Ah'm Riccio! Touch ma hump. Gaun. It's hard and gnarlit, but it's got a bone in it. Go an.

It's lucky… a hunchback. Touch it! Touch. (*Whispers.*) Touch.

Scene Three

Rumours, Soughs and Chatters

The whole COMPANY *in a moving motif of whispers, passing letters, espionage.*

MARY *and* RICCIO *hard at work,* MARY *speaking French fast,* RICCIO *typing fast.*

A paper aeroplane swoops and loops across in front of them and lands. Silence. MARY *looks at it.* RICCIO *looks at it.* MARY *goes and picks it up.* RICCIO *tries to stop her, but she unfolds it and reads aloud –*

MARY. 'Seigneur Davy – beware o the bastard.'

Whit does this mean?

CORBIE. The bastard? That could be awmost hauf the court!

RICCIO *takes it, screws it up into a ball and kicks it away in feigned scorn and bravado.*

RICCIO. Parole! Parole!

CORBIE. Rumours, souchs and chatters in the court, an in the streets gowsters mairch vaunty an crawlin, chauntin oot hatred tae the Catholics.

Scene Four

Knox and Bothwell

Orange-Walk style, the COMPANY *approaching, sing out their hatred and bigotry with this, 'The Good and Godly Ballad'.*

ALL *(singing quietly, distant at first).*
Up wi the hunt. Up wi the hunt,
Tis noo the perfect day,
Jesus oor King is gane hunting,
Wha likes to speid they may.

(*Louder.*) Yin cursit fox lay hid in rocks,
This lang and mony yin day,
Devouring sheep whaur he micht creep,
Nane micht him fricht away.

(*Louder still.*) It did him guid to lap the bluid,
Of young and tender lambs,
Nane could he miss for all was his,
The young yins wi their dams.

(*Crescendo.*) That cruel beast, he never ceased,
By his usurpit power,
Under dispense to get oor pence,
Oor souls to devour.

(*Stamping, getting louder than ever.*)
The hunter is Christ that hunts in haste!
The hounds are Peter and Paul,
The Pape is the fox, Rome is the rocks,
That rubs us on the gall.

KNOX *and* BOTHWELL *peel off from the rabble band.*

KNOX. I sympathise – as I am shair the Guid Lord does – wi the zeal which inspires destruction and indiscipline, although of course I condemn the act itsel.

And ye were saying…? Aboot the Queen…?

BOTHWELL. Och, I wis gey suspeecious o her tae, when she arrivit, and I hae much watcht for ony dissemblin I'd see there. And there is nane.

KNOX. You see nane?

BOTHWELL. Nane.

KNOX. Then beware o yir ain een, Bothwell. Beware of women, the charms o their hair. Beware, for adultery begins wi the eyes. Are ye mair virtuous than David? Are ye wiser than Solomon? Are ye stronger than Samson?

BOTHWELL. Ah am an ordinary man, but kinsman, I see… a wummin wha in six years in this country –

KNOX. – Has in her ain private chapel ilka Sunday heard the filthy Popish Mass.

BOTHWELL. Aye, in private. She has never heard Mass said in public. Ye ken how strang I am agin the Mass –

KNOX. Bothwell, it were mair fearfu tae me that yin Mass be heard in this realm than ten thousand men, armed and bristlin, were landed in a hundred foreign men o war upon oor shores.

BOTHWELL. And has she restored yin Scotch Catholic or yin abbey? Ye hae dingit doon the nests. The rooks *are* flown awa. Never tae return! Oh, the Queen does maintain her diplomatic contacts wi the Pope and aw Catholic Europe. Whit does it avail her? Jist words. 'Parole, Parole.'

There are three things they can send: Promises. Hard cash. Soldiers.

Hae they armed her? Hae they fattened oor skinny Scotch coffers? I say we maun maintain her safely on this throne – otherwise foreigners will be *forcit* to intervene to uphold the vera idea o sovereignty and legality.

On oor throne we hae a Catholic who has aye in word and deed affordit oor New Truth toleration.

And she is oor queen. Anointed by God.

KNOX. She says. And God says we are His, we belong to Him, justified by faith alone, and His election.

BOTHWELL. But I tell ye, Knox, there is a plan – you *ken* there is a plan – to bring doon the Queen and bring chaos to this realm.

KNOX. What wind have ye o this?

God – in His infinite mercy – aft-times does yase wicked men to punish other wicked men…

BOTHWELL. Maister Knox, stop hiding ahint your holiness just for once. I care naethin for Davy Riccio –

KNOX. Seigneur Davy is a poltroon and a vile knave.

BOTHWELL. Exactly. But I care *less* for him-that-ye-cry oor Bold Young King.

KNOX. He is a Protestant.

BOTHWELL. Is he? Oh aye, is that whit he is these days? Chynged his mind again, has he?

If aw his hums and haws were hams and haggises, the country wad be weel fed!

KNOX. – And he is the King.

BOTHWELL. The Queen's man.

KNOX. The King! And he kens he disna want to hae to rock Seigneur Davy's son in the royal cradle.

BOTHWELL. It is Henry's bairn she is big wi.

But wicked men – aye, Knox, ye dae ken wha they are and only ye can stap them – are yasin Henry Darnley's weakness as their strength.

KNOX. Hoo dae ye mak that oot?

BOTHWELL. I ask ye, the vera men wha rebelled agin the Queen when she mairrit Darnley, and wha were pit tae the horn and banisht tae Englan – they looe Darnley sae weel six months later that it is aw for advancement o him abune the Queen that they are plottin aw this mischief?

Acht! –

KNOX. I ken naethin o ony mischief.

BOTHWELL. Ye could forbid it, skail the hale thing fae the pulpit and stap it.

KNOX. I am a man o God. I care naethin for politics.

BOTHWELL. Because in this instance ye think the hail cowp will benefit ye and yir kirk.

KNOX. God's Kirk, Bothwell.

Plots and mischief? And whit benefit is there to you in stappin it? Keepin aw thing sweet for you and for her intae whase favour an influence ye hae ingratiated yoursel by crawling flattery?

BOTHWELL. I dinna think either queen nor maid ever accusit me o flattery.

KNOX. Oh aye, there is honey-flattery and there is sourrock-flattery. Such is the perverseness o women, I hear they like the sherp taste better.

BOTHWELL. As I love my kirk, and my country, so I love my queen. Nae mair.

Besides, the Crown cowps and the bliddy English will be up owerrinnin us again.

KNOX. Elizabeth is a Good Protestant…

BOTHWELL. I love the Scottish Crown.

KNOX. Oh aye. And what it will provide ye wi!

BOTHWELL. And ye wad suffer treason…?

KNOX. James Hepburn, Earl o Bothwell, kinsman, I tell you I am a man o God. My God has charged me, loud and plain, in the words o His ain Guid Book, no tae meddle wi the temporal filth o politiks. And it is my duty to obey my God. As God's kirk teaches its truth by the preachin o the word, then the spreadin o the word *demands* that all people be educated to read so that they may freely read and feed at his word, but there be nothin temporal or political in educating equally all God's subjects. If the kirk fight to feed them and claithe them it is only sae that they can maintain, on earth, God's *heavenly* kingdom.

If the word of God teaches men that all earthly palaces and power systems are robbers' caves then the punishment o wicked princes is the *duty* of their subjects.

I will leave it unto God to deal with the prince o this realm. I am shair the Good Lord will protect her, if she deserve to be protectit. Neither I, nor the yane true kirk have ony richt tae interfere. And I'd advise you no tae either, Maister Hepburn o Bothwell.

Scene Five

Mummers and Murderers

Noise of drumbeat or clattering bones. Tumbling the first of a long string of them she has been setting up all during the last, a standing chain of dominoes, CORBIE *announces flamboyantly as the last goes down –*

CORBIE. Dominoes!

A now very pregnant MARY, *with* BESSIE *and* RICCIO *by her side, all very relaxed, domestic and easy, playing said game of dominoes. Couple of plays in silence, then –*

BESSIE. Ah'm chappin.

She does so. Picks up one.

MARY. Och, kickin!

BESSIE. They do say a boay kicks mair…

CORBIE. An that's juist on the inside, wait till he gets oot!

DARNLEY *bursts in looking weird, pale and strange. He is drunk.*

MARY. King Henry… so you jine us?

DARNLEY. And you aren't pleased to see me? It's me. Your husband. To while away the night with my sovereign, my wife, and my unborn son…

MARY. Of coorse we are pleased to see ye, Henry, maist gratified you have deserted mair congenial companions for our sake.

DARNLEY.… yes, with my sovereign, my wife, my unborn child and… assorted servants and menials, of course. Do excuse me, I did not *prostrate* myself before you all in greeting.

MARY. King Henry, you are drunk.

DARNLEY. Right you are, Queen Mary!

Not drunk. No. Just merry. And wishing to share my merriment with my poor lumpen wife.

I wonder if there can be a God, He arranges things so unfairly, eh? Deed it's true enough, you women get all the pain and burden, We Men, we get all the pleasure. Isn't that so, Seigneur Riccio?

MARY. Sit doon, Henry, if ye are going to drink a loving-cup with us.

DARNLEY. A loving-cup. I will indeed.

He drinks. Sound of music approaching.

BESSIE. Whit's that? Queen Mary, dinna let –

The rest of the COMPANY, *masked and strange, now disguised as* MUMMERS, *burst in;* MUMMERS 1, 2 *and* 3.

DARNLEY. Only a troop of travelling players. Here to entertain us.

CORBIE (*seeing trouble*). Mm-hm!

The MUMMERS *stand like stookies.*

DARNLEY. What are you going to perform for us tonight then?

CORBIE. Ah wonder…

They stand.

DARNLEY. Ha! Dumbshow… haha…!

Suddenly the MUMMERS *move.*

MUMMERS. Tara!

MUMMER 1 (*clears throat and announces*). The Mummers' *Masque of Salome*! –

MUMMER 2.

A mellow-drama that entails
Sex and lust at the court of King Herod –
Plus the Dance of the Seven Veils!

A rude fart noise on a Harpo Marx horn.

CORBIE. Oh goody, the Bible! Ah love a story with a bit of blood and guts in it.

MUMMER 3 *pulls out a cushion with a very cardboard, or crudely improvised crown on it.* MUMMERS 1 *and* 2 *put exaggerated hands in the air and 'Ooh…!'*

MARY. Wha the hell are you?

DARNLEY. Just mumbling mummers, poor travelling players…

The MUMMERS *offer* DARNLEY *the crown.*

…Not at all! The crown does not fit me!

DARNLEY *places it with exaggerated ceremony on* MARY*'s head.*

Tara! Hail the King!

MUMMER 2.
The King, he was called *Herod* –
He was King of all the Jews –
And he fell in love with his brother's wife –
Which was: Exceeding Bad News.

MUMMER 1.
Because a man called *John the Baptist* –

MUMMER 2.
Said: 'Herod! Upon my life,
It is written in the Law of the Prophets
Thou shalt not (*Parps horn.*) – Thy Brother's Wife.'

MUMMER 1.
Herod looked at John the Baptist,
And his face turned deathly pale –

MUMMER 2.
Said: 'I'm the one that gives the bleeding orders',
And he clapped the poor prophet in gaol.

MUMMER 1.
Herod said –

MUMMER 2.
'A king can mairry wha he likes
Holy Joes like you can wheesht their din!'
And he promptly turned back to his feastin,
And got boozin and beastin in.

MUMMER 1.
To assuage his Foul Lust, nothing for it but he must
(*Bleep.*) – The brother's wife in an adulterous lee-aison,
Then he done in the brother,
So they could marry one another –

MUMMER 2.

Acht! For murder, och! It's aye the silly see-aison!

MUMMER 1.

Noo the honeymoon's *been* for the *King* and *New Queen*,
And they are back to auld claes and parridge.
And the palace is the home y them and Salome –

MUMMER 2.

That's the new Queen's dochter by her first marriage.

DARNLEY *has been thrown a crude Salome-kit costume, and he dons yashmak/falsies, etc. and begins lumbering grossly and drunkenly.*

DARNLEY. Salome! That's moi!

MUMMER 1 *skelps him, he quietens down, suddenly shocked to find himself their puppet.*

MUMMER 1.

Now, Herod was throwin a wee stag night,
For some visiting pot-entates.
Says the Queen –

MUMMER 2.

'Haw, ony chance… o Salome daen a wee dance
For the entertainment, like, o you and yir mates?'

And they lead out DARNLEY *as a gross Salome.*

MUMMER 1.

Now Salome had always been… big for her age,
Sortae… lamb dressed up as mutton.
Buxom and pretty wi a tassel on each titty,
And a jewel in her belly button.

And DARNLEY *as Salome begins to clumsily dance sand-dance and mock striptease.*

So Salome done the seven veils
– At furst it wis jist fur a laugh –
She hooched, shimmied and skirled,
Shook, shoogled and birled,
Till they shouted, 'Get them aff!'

MUMMER 2.

Salome's mammy's look said, 'Go for it!'
So she didnae mess aboot –

MUMMER 1.
An soon – sweet sixteen wi slanty een –
She stood in her Birthday Suit.
Herod said –

And they force a bit of paper on MARY *– she's to read Herod's part. More forcefully –*

Herod said – !

And, finally, out of time, bullied and flustered, but trying to pretend she's taking it as a joke –

MARY.
'Och, Good Lord! Lassie, name your reward,
Ask for anything – yon wis great!'

DARNLEY (*as Salome, to* MARY *as Herod*).
'Give me the head of John the Baptist –
With some parsley, on a plate!'

And DARNLEY *points right at* RICCIO. *All three* MUMMERS *rush at him, pull him to the ground, knives out and he screams and clutches at* MARY*'s skirt.*

RICCIO. Justizia! Justizia! Sauvez ma vie! Justizia!

They stab him viciously and drag him off.

MARY, DARNLEY *and* BESSIE *are left. And* CORBIE.

MARY *glares her hatred at* DARNLEY, *who has crumbled completely at the sight of the real and actual violence. When he begins to sob,* MARY *runs at him.*

MARY. Kill me! Go on. Kill me tae. Kill me an your ain bairn. Go an, ye micht as well. Plunge the knife in. Tear yin ain bairn oot o ma tripes an strangle him wi yir ain hauns. Because if you dinna he will grow up tae be revenged on ye.

Kill me. Kill me. Kill me!

MUMMER 1 *grabs* DARNLEY*'s wrist very hard, holds it there.* MUMMER 2 *draws his sword against* DARNLEY*'s throat.*

MUMMER 1. Naw, I wouldna dae that, young Henry…

MUMMER 2 (*tuts*). Regicide, that is.

MUMMER 1. Killing a king! Very nasty…

MUMMER 2. That's no hoo we dae things here in Scotland.

MUMMER 1. Never been heard of!

MUMMER 2. Not all through history…

MUMMER 1. *I've* never heard of it, have you, Jimmy?

MUMMER 2. Naw, Jock!

He sucks his teeth.

Not nice to kill a member of the fair sex either.

MUMMER 1. Not nice at the best of times but to kill wan that's thon wey wi a bairn…?

MUMMER 2. We couldnae hae it, Tam!

MUMMER 1. Neither we could, Wullie.

He hawks and spits. Bows.

Even though we are at your service, King Henry.

MUMMER 2. Behind you all the way, King Henry, we're your men, yes sir, oh aye!

MUMMER 1. Aren't we, Rab?

MUMMER 2. Aw the wey, Geordie.

DARNLEY. Is he dead?

MUMMERS *chuckle softly.*

MARY. Wha are ye? Wha are ye an wha did this?

CORBIE *goes circling and drumming herself up with this list and litany to a quiet frenzy.*

CORBIE.

There's Ruthven and Morton and Lindsay and Lethington,
Ormiston, Brunstane, Haughton and Lochlinnie,
There's Kerr o Fa'donside, Scott, and Yair and Elphinstone,
There's Ballantin and Douglas,
There's Ruthven and Morton…

She continues over the next, repeating this, becoming sotto voce.

MUMMER 1. King Henry, we need ye a wee minute, don't we, Jake?

MUMMER 2. We dae that, Eck. (*To* DARNLEY.) Ye see, sur… some o the townspeople are clamourin at the windaes –

MUMMER 1. There's been a wee bit o a disturbance an they're wonderin if the Queen's awricht.

They go, DARNLEY *flanked by* MUMMERS. MUMMER 1 *suddenly wheels back.*

(*At* MARY.) There's nae windaes in here, an Ah warn ye: there's ten big strang men staunin by that door wi the twa-handit sword and if ye try and get oot they will cut ye intae collops!

He exits. MARY, CORBIE, BESSIE, *alone and still. Silence.*

CORBIE. Blood!

MARY. He has killed oor maist special servant wha I looed richt well. I hate him.

CORBIE. Aye, hatred can be got in an instant, lik a bairn is, fattens faster in the wame an is, whiles, a lot langer in the nursin o it.

MARY (*to her unborn child*). So much are ye yir faither's bairn I fear for ye in the future.

CORBIE. A bairn's bairns are ill tae prosper!

Blood. Whit does that cry oot for?

MARY. Nae mair tears. I will think o a revenge. Bessie… Bessie, when they send ye for claes for me – I'm gonnae pretend ma labour has sterted, they'll hae to get me a midwife… we maun somehow get haud o ma black box wi Davy's foreign correspondence and somehow smuggle a message tae somebody…

Bothwell!

Tae onybody wha will help us!

Scene Six

Sweet Baby James, News for His Auntie Elizabeth, and a Gey Sore Sickbed for Darnley This Time

CORBIE *wheels on baby in a pram. She sings a sinister wee song, a familiar Scottish lullaby.*

CORBIE (*singing*).

Wee chookie burdie,
Tol-a-lol-a-lol,
Laid an egg on the windae sole,
The windae sole it began to crack,
And wee chookie burdie roared and grat.

CORBIE *wheels the pram.*

ELIZABETH *has a letter with a Polaroid snapshot of a baby in it.*

ELIZABETH. And so she has a son and heir.

They do say he is perfect. (*Looks at photo.*)

Well, 'James of Scotland', are you going to end up my heir for want of a better or a nearer?

Surely not…

CORBIE *wheels the pram.*

CORBIE. Wee Jamie, eh? Born tae be King James the Saxt o Scotland. Some day. If ye live sae lang… An awfy big name for sicc a wee rid-faced scrawny shilpit wee scrap o humanity, eh?

Dinna greet. Aye, wha's the lucky laddie tae have made it this faur, eh? Eh?

ELIZABETH *with a hand mirror. She looks in it.*

ELIZABETH. A son and heir… and I am of but barren stock. 'The Virgin Queen.' Too old to whelp now at any rate.

CORBIE. Wheest, wheest, does your mammy love yir daddy, eh? Eh? Does she no? Ach well, son, you'll no be the first bairn i the warld conceivit in love and born intae hate.

DARNLEY *in his surgical mask lying on sickbed,* MARY *once again with that bowl of something, spoon-feeding him.*

DARNLEY. Love me, Mary.

MARY. Sup this up, Henry…

DARNLEY. But you will love me again, Mary…? When I'm better?

MARY. Aye, Henry… when you're better.

DARNLEY. Doctor said he didn't think it'd mark my face. You don't think I'll be marked for ever? Surely smallpox doesn't always –

MARY. Likely no, Henry.

DARNLEY. It's disgusting to you, isn't it? What if I'm all pocked… Mary, could you ever let me back into your bed again, with my face all –

MARY. It'll leave nae mark, Henry.

DARNLEY. Want to come back to your bed, be a proper husband again, Mary.

MARY. Eat. You're weak.

DARNLEY. Don't say that word. It's been a taunt at me ever since I was a boy.

MARY. You're still but a boy, Henry.

DARNLEY. And God help me but it's true! I'm weak. Wicked men used me, you were right, they would have killed me too. They used my weakness, my – Is loving you a weakness?

They made me jealous, I was a mad person, not myself, it wasn't…

Jealousy! It was a poison, it filled me up, they manipulated me, it wasn't my fault.

MARY. Wheesht. Eat.

DARNLEY. It was my fault.

MARY. Aye, but it wisna aw your faut, Henry. You're… only young yet, I tellt you.

DARNLEY. It's a long time ago now, Mary. I've changed. Honestly I'm not the same person! And our fine son is growing, eh?

MARY. Fat and bonny.

DARNLEY. I tell you, this last year… ever since that terrible night –

MARY *shrugs.*

MARY. We hae ither secretaries.

ELIZABETH *lets out an incoherent cry and crumples letter and photo.*

ELIZABETH. I do think it's hard to think of her so happy and me not! Dark deeds, bloody murders, plots against her life and throne, and she wins out again and again. All those involved just scatter when Darnley deserts them, most of the original rebels are pardoned and back in favour in Edinburgh, such is the wheel of fortune, and she is – if my spies tell me true – quite sweetly reconciled with the child-husband.

All her people love her, she has a husband and a fine healthy son.

Such is the wheel of fortune!… '*Oh, madam, you never wanted to marry!*'…

How the hell do any of them know what I wanted?! Shut up! Shut up!

I don't know what I wanted.

She looks at herself in the mirror.

Lord! Grey hairs. Pluck them out!

CORBIE. Aye, King James the Saxt. Some day. And mair, mair than that, shall be. Some day. Wheesht. But watch ma lambie, watch!

Listen, once upon a time, aye, aye, oot on the open moor, caw, caw, an there was a moose thocht it was lord o the heather, and there was a foumart's den an it lay toom and empty. Sae the wee moose moved in and thocht it wis in heaven.

Till the foumart cam back an ett it fur its supper.

CORBIE *wheels the pram.*

DARNLEY *and* MARY *at his sickbed again.*

DARNLEY. We'll be happy again, you'll see.

MARY. Aye, Henry.

DARNLEY. And I can come to your bed again?

MARY. Once… once you're better o the smallpox, aye.

DARNLEY. I wish I could come back to the palace.

MARY. Soon.

DARNLEY. But you will stay here?

MARY. Aye. Downstairs. Richt ablow ye. I'm your wife.

DARNLEY. Will you come and sit with me tonight? We could have music.

MARY. No, no the nicht, Henry. I hae tae gang tae a weddin – ma best page is tae be merrit at the palace and I canny no go to the feast o ma favourite, it widnae be lucky.

DARNLEY. Don't go.

MARY. I must. Fasten ma necklace, Henry.

She bares the nape of her neck, hair forward and he fastens clasp of her necklace and kisses her neck, burying his face in her hair.

DARNLEY. You smell beautiful. Amber, isn't it? I wish it could drown out all the camphor of this sickroom, I wish, I wish –

MARY *bursts out suddenly –*

MARY. Henry, come with me to the wedding! Get up, Henry Darnley! Quick! Now! Come and dance wi me!

DARNLEY. Mary, you know I'm sick, I can't go out of doors.

MARY. Of course you canna. Guidnicht, Henry.

DARNLEY. Kiss me?

She does. Goes calmly from him. Straight to where BOTHWELL *is waiting for her. She goes into his arms. They dance.*

MARY. To hell in a white petticoat wi you, Bothwell. Aye, I will go. I maun go.

BOTHWELL. Ah only hud tae bide ma time…

They dance.

MARY. An thegither we shall hae justice!

MARY *and* BOTHWELL *kiss, sink together down to the floor, rolling over and over.*

Drums are building up to a crescendo. DARNLEY, *where* MARY *left him on his sickbed, stirs in his sleep, murmurs her name.*

DARNLEY. Mary…?

MARY. Justice!

An enormous explosion happens as, at Kirk o'Field, DARNLEY *and the house go up in flames.*

As smoke clears MARY *and* BOTHWELL *lie, still in each other's arms, on the floor. The rest of the* COMPANY *begin the accusatory chant. It builds.*

ALL. Burn the hoor! Burn the hoor! Burn the hoor!

And BOTHWELL *gets to his feet and runs off one way,* MARY *in another. The* COMPANY *go viciously, murderously after them. They are separated and exit on opposite sides.*

CORBIE, *alone among the clearing smoke, sings her devoid-of-pity lament for Lord Darnley in this, her version of the old ballad, 'The Twa Corbies'.*

CORBIE (*singing*).
Twa weet black corbies in the snaw,
Wi naethin in oor wames ataw,
Tae the other yin Ah did say,
'Whaur sall we gang and dine the day?'

In ahint yon auld fail dyke,
I ken there lies a new slain knight,
And naebody kens,
Naw, naebody kens,
That he lies there,
But his hawk and his hound and his lady fair.

His hound is to the hunting gane,
His hawk to fetch the wildfowl hame,
His lady has taen another mate,
And we may freely mak our dinner sweet.

Ye'll sit on his white hause-bane,
And I will pike oot his braw blue een,
And wi wan lock of his gowden hair,
We shall theek oor nest when it grows bare.

And ower his white banes when they are bare,
The wind shall blaw for ever mair.

The wind starts up, blowing around what snow and rose petals might still be strewn about the stage. CORBIE *can't speak, is no longer controlling things, or driving them forward; rather she is compelled to watch – and there's a sense of is compelled to watch all over again – the last act of the tragedy.*

Scene Seven

Aw Thing Smashed and Skailt For Ever

ELIZABETH. Why me? Why? Why help her? Why does she come here, throwing herself on my mercy? Merciful God, I cannot *afford* to be merciful.

ADVISER 1. Kill her now.

ADVISER 2. It were a kindness.

ELIZABETH. I cannot welcome her here at court. I cannot help restore her to her throne in Scotland. I cannot be seen to condone rebellion against a rightful prince.

ADVISER 2. Exactly.

ADVISER 1. And you cannot keep her in prison indefinitely.

ELIZABETH. She is my honoured guest.

ADVISER 1. Yes, and some day she'll escape.

ADVISER 2. The focus of every Catholic hope, of every anti-Elizabeth faction in England.

ELIZABETH. Is she a witch?

ADVISERS 1 *and* 2. Ask the Scotch.

They fall back into the shadows, leaving her isolated and alone.

ELIZABETH. They split her from her Bothwell, drive him from their shores, they seize her infant son, strip her of her crown, lock her in a castle in the middle of an island and throw away the key.

And still she can charm some man into helping her escape.

God help me, why does she come to England when she could have sailed to bloody France!

ADVISERS *advance again, mill around* ELIZABETH –

ADVISER 2. Three years…

ADVISER 1. You really cannot keep her in prison indefinitely.

Seven… Eight…

ADVISER 2. – And some day she'll escape… thirteen, fift–

– and then, audibly counting the passing years, they fall back again into the shadows.

With steely determination –

ELIZABETH. My subjects love me! I am the Virgin Queen! I love my good cousin Queen Mary and will continue to keep her my most honoured guest in all luxury in the lavish hospitality of my proudest castle. For her own safety.

And my so-called 'wise advisers' would have to trick me before I would consent to sign a warrant for her death.

Would have to trick me. Trick me. Trick me!

Her manic repetitions increase in volume, turn into obvious instructions. Thus summoned, ADVISERS *reappear by her side complete with a document. Without looking at it or them, she signs it. One of these absolutely impassive* ADVISERS *blots it, picks it up and blows on the signature.*

Careful! We do not want a blot!

The ADVISER *puts it inside his jacket. Both of them melt away.* ELIZABETH *stands alone, breathing, then exits in the other direction.*

A loud hammering. Noise gets louder and louder, stops.

MARY. Whit's that noise, Bessie?

BESSIE. It's nobbut the men, madam. It's jist thae bliddy men an their tools!

MARY. Is it ma scaffolding they are building? I ken it. Nineteen lang year…

Bessie, I am to die tomorrow.

BESSIE. Wheesht!

MARY. Last nicht I dreamed the strangest dream…

BESSIE. Wheesht!

MARY. I havena spared sae much as a thocht for him in years, yit… in my dream, large as life… larger! Bothwell.

BESSIE. Bothwell?

MARY. Aye. I ken… I ken… He's deid. A lang time deid. Mair nor a dizzen year. He dee'ed doublit up wud mad in a Danish jile. (*Long beat.*) You are greetan, Bess.

BESSIE. Greetin for us aw, madam.

MARY. Don't greet. I dinna.

I said: 'To Hell in a white petticoat wi you, Bothwell, oh aye, I will go. I maun go.'

Wis it love? No, no what you think, Jamie Hepburn. Oh aye, ye were richt, I did – aye did… lust for ye. Wis that whit it wis? At the time I was ower innocent to ken whit wis steerin me? But I ken noo, Bothwell, I ken noo.

Dinna think it was lichtsomely or in love that I lay me doon wi ye, in the daurk. Naw, it wis in despair. Oh and wi a kind of black joy I reachit oot for ye to cover me and smother me and for yin moment snuff oot the hale birlin world in stillness. And ilka dawn I woke up wi ye, I saw disaster aw mapped oot for me, clear as my Davy's magic cairds. The ruined tower, the hangin man, the Empress on her Throne, Judgement…

And aw thing smashed and skailt for ever, tummeling aw aroon.

BESSIE. Madam, listen, wheesht, you maun…

MARY. – Call for ma confessor? Och, I ken what you are thinkin, Bessie!

BESSIE. Madam, dinna –

MARY. Your thinkan… that Ah'm thinkan…

MARY *shakes her head – 'Oh no, I'm not' – and manages the strangest wee laugh.*

Pair deid Darnley.

Violet velvet, Henry Darnley. Furs and pelts, baith civet and the genet. A press for you to keep your perfumes. A jewelled pomander. A bolt of cloth of gold, so much did I love you. Blue bonnets for your fools. Myself. That's what I gave you on oor wedding day.

And what did you ever give me, Henry Darnley?

A son. Wha will not lift a hand to save his mother. King of Scotland. Thus far. And even Auntie Elizabeth canna last for ever…

Poor Elizabeth. Tonight you dance in my dream. Tomorrow and ever after I will dance in yours.

Bessie, bind my een in silk! Ne criez point pour moi. J'ai promis pour vous!

One beat of absolute blackout and the terrible, final noise of the axeman's single heavy blow. Lights come back up and CORBIE, *exhausted, devastated, has her hands over her ears and her eyes shut, blocking it out.*

Elsewhere, KNOX *is alone, on his knees with a scrubbing brush and a pail of soapy water. Scrubs harder and harder still at that indelible stain.*

CORBIE *opens her eyes. There is nothing more to say. She hears the noise of* KNOX*'s scrubbing, goes and looks at what he's doing. He doesn't see her or acknowledge her. Still silenced, she watches, bewildered, as all the rest of the* COMPANY, *except* MARY, *emerge transformed to seemingly bewitched and compelled brand-new-looking modern-day children, all now playing roles they have not chosen and scarcely seem to understand. As they come there could be weird slow playground bursts of leapfrog, peever, bools, fivestones. There are* WEE BETTY (ELIZABETH), WEE HENRY (DARNLEY), WEE RICHIE (RICCIO), *and* JAMES

HEPBURN (BOTHWELL), *a playground bully, who runs up and kicks over* KNOX*'s bucket with a clang and a spill.* KNOX *gets up to his feet as if to challenge, but instead is transformed back to childhood too, into* SMELLY WEE KNOXXY, *who shrivels and whinges, puts up 'Keys', conceding victory, cringing, scared.* JAMES HEPBURN *pokes him viciously in the ribs then moves on laughing.* SMELLY WEE KNOXXY *rights the pail, then turns it upside down, sits down on it, 'Oor Wullie style', an iconic Scottish picture of childhood. Once more he puts the 'Keys' up, he's not playing…*

CORBIE, *shocked from her silence and her fugue state by the noise of the spilt pail, watches, sorrowing, as the others set up in slow motion a silent game of skipping ropes.*

CORBIE.

Bricht days, dull days, toom days, full days…
Mair nor fower hunder years o Scotlan's historie –
Aye, mair nor tongue can tell, sin that fell blow fell –
Hae birled by, like the wind in the dark.
An still we see Jock Tamson's bairns –
Nobbut a wheen o loast weans in the park.

Scene Eight

Jock Tamson's Bairns

CORBIE *watches the slow-motion skipping ropes turn and, exasperated – as if 'Hell, if we've got to play this bloody game again, then let's get on with it' – calls out –*

CORBIE. Caw!

So they spring to full life, turn the ropes in real time, singing –

GIRLS (*singing*).

Queen Mary, Queen Mary,
My age is *sixteen*.
My faither's a wino on *Glesca* green.
He's drank the Broo-money should dress me up braw.
Och, will nae bonny laddie come tak me awa?
A! B! C! D! E!

MAREE (MARY) *appears, all by herself, very prominent, an outsider. She stands silent. Others nudge each other and look at her, hostile. Singing continues, tune changing to –*

On a mountain
Stands a lady.
Who she is I do not know.
All she wants is
Power and glory.
All she wants is a fine young man.

WEE BETTY *wolf-whistles.*

WEE BETTY. Get her!

ANOTHER. Get swanky!

WEE BETTY. Big banana feet and legs long and lanky!

JAMES HEPBURN *wolf-whistles.*

JAMES HEPBURN. Hello, stranger!

WEE BETTY *and* ANOTHER *play a clapping game.*

Hiya, stranger!
I hope yir maw
Thinks you're braw!
Naw, naw,
Nae chance! Nae danger!

WEE RICHIE. That's a sin. She's a wee orphan.

WEE BETTY. Little Orphan Annie! Show us your fanny.

ALL (*shocked*). Ow-ah!

– except WEE BETTY *and* JAMES HEPBURN *who guffaw like the lewdest of children.*

WEE BETTY. What's your name anyway?

MAREE. Maree.

WEE BETTY. Maree?? Whit school do you go to?

JAMES HEPBURN. She means urr ye a left-fitter? Haw, stranger, d'you eat fish oan a Friday?

WEE BETTY. You a Tim?

JAMES HEPBURN. You a Fenian?

WEE BETTY. Are you a Pape?

MAREE. I'm a Catholic. Ih-hih.

WEE BETTY. Ih-hih? How you mean 'uh-huh'?

MAREE. Just…

She shrugs, trying not to rock the boat.

WEE BETTY. Well, away and get converted! Go an get born again. Away an jine the Bandy Hope, get tae the Tabernacle and go on a Crusade up the Tent Hall tin hut and get saved or somethin – Away and get saved for a sweetie!

They turn on SMELLY WEE KNOXXY. *They begin to torment him.*

WEE BETTY, JAMES HEPBURN, WEE HENRY *and* WEE RICHIE.

Wee Johnny Knox
Peed in the jawbox
When he thought his mammy wisnae lookin.
She hit it with a ladle
That was lying on the table,
Walloped him, and gied his heid a dooking!

SMELLY WEE KNOXXY (*singing*).

I'm H. A. P. P. Y.
I'm H. A. P. P. Y.
I know I am, I'm sure I am,
I'm H. A. P. P. Y.

I'm S. A. V. E. D.
I'm S. A. V. E. D.
I know I am, I'm sure I am,
I'm S. A. V. E. D.

JAMES HEPBURN. Haw! Get Smelly Wee Knoxxy!

Some grab SMELLY WEE KNOXXY, *some* MAREE.

WEE BETTY. Stick his heid up her skurt!

And they all shove SMELLY WEE KNOXXY*'s head up* MAREE*'s skirt, holding both of their struggling victims.* SMELLY WEE KNOXXY *is crying in real terror and distress.* MAREE *too.*

THE REST.

A queen cried Mary hud a canary
Up the leg o her drawers!

SMELLY WEE KNOXXY. Yuck it, youse! Yuck it. Dinnae! Ah doan't like lassies… Ma faither says I'm no tae play wi lassies!

WEE BETTY. Goan then! Get tae! Away an play wi yoursel then, stinky!

JAMES HEPBURN. Aye, git!

WEE BETTY. Skoosh!

RICHIE. Skeddaddle.

WEE BETTY. See you later, alligator!

She performs some sudden, physical, spiteful action on MAREE. *This is too much for* JAMES HEPBURN, *who's been, up to now, no slouch at being one of the torturers himself. He grabs* MAREE, *runs with her, crying out –*

JAMES HEPBURN. Leave the lassie alane!

All turn on the two of them, including SMELLY WEE KNOXXY, *who can see now how to taunt back.*

SMELLY WEE KNOXXY. Haw, Hepburn! Ah think you love her.

WEE BETTY. So do I, I think you love her! You gonny marry her?

JAMES HEPBURN. Nuh!

WEE BETTY. Aye, you urr! James Hepburn loves Maree Stewart!

THE REST. James Hepburn loves Maree Stewart! James Hepburn loves Maree Stewart!

JAMES HEPBURN. Ah jist says: (*Beat.*) Lea the Lassie Alane!

Freed, MAREE *looks right into his eyes, he into hers. She spits right in his face.*

Right!

THE REST. Fight! Fight! Fight! Fight! Fight!

JAMES HEPBURN. I am the axeman.

THE REST. Kiss the axe.

SMELLY WEE KNOXXY. Pardon the executioner.

THE REST. And kiss the axe!

ALL.

Mary Queen of Scots got her head chopped off.
Mary Queen of Scots got her head chopped off!

WEE BETTY. And eftir you're deid, we'll share oot yir froacks and pu aw the stones oot yir brooches and gie yir golden slippers aw away to the Salvation Army, and we'll gie the Saint Vincent de Paul –

JAMES HEPBURN. – Sweet fuck all!

WEE BETTY.

And eftir you're deid,
We'll pick up your heid,
Up aff the flair,
By the long rid hair –

JAMES HEPBURN. Wallop!

WEE HENRY. Haw-haw! It was just a wig! (*Beat.*) Yir heid goes –

JAMES HEPBURN. Wallop!

And it stoats alang the flair like a great big… Tumshie!

ALL. Wallop! Bum… bum… bum… bum.

WEE HENRY. Skoosh!

ALL. SPLAT!!!

Pause.

WEE BETTY (*mock-tearful*).

And her wee dug…
Oh, her lovely wee dug…

Her lovely wee dug wi the big brown eyes that loved her *sooooo* much…

Comes scooshing oot fae under her crimson skirts where it has been hiding –

And skites aboot among the blood-rid *blood*, barking and shiting itself!

Shriek of laughter from WEE BETTY, *totally wild and hysterical, scaring herself as much as it does* MAREE. *Silence.*

CORBIE *plays, with a marigold on its stalk, the old childhood game –*

CORBIE (*very quietly*).
Mary Queen of Scots got her head chopped off.
Mary Queen of Scots got her… head… chopped… off!

– And CORBIE *flicks the golden flower-head off.*

All the rest of the COMPANY *suddenly around* MAREE/MARY *and, at the word 'Off!', they grab up at her throat. And all freeze in a tableau.*

Blackout.

The End.

QUELQUES FLEURS

Quelques Fleurs – in a slightly different form from the text here printed – was first produced by Nippy Sweeties Theatre Company at the Assembly Rooms, Edinburgh Festival Fringe, on 10 August 1991. The cast was as follows:

VERENA	Liz Lochhead
DEREK	Stuart Hepburn
GUARD (*voice recording*)	Billy Riddoch

Characters

VERENA
DEREK

Note

The set for this play is two isolated spots, one containing an armchair, rug and coffee table bearing, initially, a small imitation silver Christmas tree (Verena's home); the other a double InterCity seat and table (Derek's 'Rattler' train). Verena's costume changes indicate her passing year. Verena's scenes span from 24 December 1990 till 23 December 1991, the date of Derek's single journey – shown backwards from drunk till sober and measured by a dwindling mountain of beer cans – from his Aberdeen home to Glasgow.

Scene One 24th December 1990

At home, VERENA *on Christmas Eve.*

VERENA. His Mother's a problem. Always has been. I don't know what she wants. (*Pause.*)

Take last year, racked my brains, no help from Him as per usual, left to Him we'd end up getting a bottle of Baileys, a gift voucher and a petted lip all through Christmas dinner! Anyway I done my best, lovely wee lambswool cardi, sortofa mauvish, a *blu*eish mauvey no pinkish, nothing too roary, not my taste but then I'm not seventy-four in February. Self-covered buttons, none of your made-in-Hong-Kongs. So. I goes into the top drawer of her tallboy looking for clean guest towels for her toilet and there it is. Still done up in the blinking glitterwrap the following November! Says she's keeping it for a special occasion. I felt like saying Where do you think you're going, your age, crippled with arthritis? But I bit my tongue.

Thing is too, only the week before – well, He was home at the time, you know, one of His weeks off – and we'd went to the bother of driving over there, and we'd picked her up in the car and we'd took her along with us to our Stephen's engagement party – aye, My Mother's losing her baby at last – well, anyway we thought His Mother would be company for My Mother while the young ones discoed. Plus it would be a wee night out for her. And naturally it was an occasion for the glad rags, Big Night for The Wee Brother exetra – even Our Joy had made somewhat of an effort. Good appearance, my sister, I'll admit that. If she bothered. I says to her: Listen, Joy, I hope you have not bankrupted yourself paying through the nose to get that wee costume on tick, I says (because it's a false economy yon Provident cheques and whatnot, you know!). I says: Joy, I'm sure I could've gave you a loan of something perfectly acceptable to put on. Because I've got the odd silky trouser and matching top, several dressy wee frocks jist hinging there since the last time I wis down at ten-below-target…

Anyway I was telling you about His Mother: we get there, she takes her coat off and, honest-to-God, I could of *wept*.

I says to her, I says: What's up wi your wee lambswool cardigan, wee brooch on the collar and you'd have been gorgeous? She says: Och I thought I'd let my hair down, you're only young once, and she winks at Him. I says to Him afterwards I says: Your Mother. What was she like? Telling you, talk about mutton dressed as lamb? Crimplene trousers. Thon stretchy efforts with the underfoot stirrups. And this sortofa over-blouse affair that quite frankly lukked like it came from Whateverrys. Big blooming Dallassy shoulder pads, hectic pattren, *lurex* thread through it, sent away for it out Myna-Wylie-Next-Door's catalogue, cheap-lukkin wisnae the word for it. I was quite affronted, you'd think we never bought her anything decent. I caught our Stephen's fiancée's mother looking at her, eyebrows raised. Although what right *she's* got to be so blinking snobbish, all *she* was was a manageress in Robertson's Rainwear… Aye, I think my young brother'll no have his troubles to seek dealing with that one! Looked to be the type that likes to *control* everything, get everybody dancing to *her* tune. (*Pause.*) Fiancée seemed to be a nice enough lassie. Pageboy. Good bone structure, but. Suited it.

I mean, you want to give, but – basically – you want to give something *acceptable*… So. Our Stephen's no problem for once, something-for-the-house, naturally. Well, they're both *modren* so the electric wok seemed the obvious thing. *My* Mother's easy pleased, she's had nothing all her life, give her a good thing she's delighted. With His Mother I give up. Designer thermals. At least I'll no know if she's wearing them or not! For Him *this* – (*Holds up a men's dressing gown.*) plus the exact same golfing sweater Moira-McVitie-round-the-crescent-in-the-cul-de-sac got for her man Malcolm last Christmas. Well, *He's* been threatening to take up golf for yonks and if not… well it would always do for lounging around the house. When *He's* home. Plus, I've got some stocking fillers for Him, nice wee items in the novelty-line hid away for months up the back of my night-dresses. Well, the July sales can be a very good time for Christmas shopping. Particularly in the discontinued toiletries.

Actually I got Moira's wee minding then as well. We just tend to exchange a wee token thing, just to be neighbourly, nothing pricey – well what with her Malcolm only being on a teacher's salary I think Moira was frankly quite relieved when I suggested putting a ceiling on it. Because the whole thing can get out of hand. Over-commercialised. Which is a pity.

I hope I done right. I asked Him when He was last home, I said: Country Diary of An Edwardian Lady Drawer Liners, does that say Moira McVitie to you? He goes: *Drawer liners?* I said: *Don't* start, you know fine well it's for fragrant clothes storage. He says that sounds like Moira to me. Defin*ate*ly.

Big sigh. Several beats.

So, basically, that just leaves me with the recurring nightmare of Our Joy and family. Because recently I've frequently had the feeling I just cannot say or do anything right as far as my sister is concerned.

I blame My Mother. I mean to her my man's God Almighty. Fair enough. He is a Good Provider, unlike some.

I said to My Mother though, I said: Fair enough you worshipping Him, *fine* you being over the moon we've a new shagpile but, Mum, I said, there's no need to rub Our Joy's nose in it! Causes resentment. (*Shakes head.*) I said: Mum, think about it. Use your imagination.

Families, eh? This is the pretty one. This is the clever one… (*Shrug.*) Basically Our Joy's always been jealous. Don't like to think that about my own sister but I'm afraid it's true.

Naturally, we're good to the kids. Me and Him. Having the none of a family ourselves. Although Simeon's getting to be a wee shite! Semi-adolescence I suppose… Kellymarie, and Kimberley, and that wee monkey Charlene are gorgeous all the same. Easy! Money, record tokens, clothes, merr money… (*Big sigh.*) My Little Pony…

But that wee new one! Now he *is* a sweetheart. I could *eat him up*, so I could! Went to yon designer-baby shop in Princes Square, yon, you know, that imports everything from Milan and France exetra. Well, I'd got him this, you know, down-filled mini-ski-suit, arm-and-a-leg-time, still it's not every day you become a godmother, all the thanks I got from Our Joy was her sneering at the make: and turning her nose up at the pattren, which was of Babar the Elephant skiing down a hill saying French things in a bubble. Goes: Oh, a *ski-suit, very* handy in Easterhouse! My, that must've cost your Auntie Verena a not-so-small fortune! (*Pause.*) Which I don't think was a very pleasant remark.

Consequently I've restrained myself Christmas-wise with regard to the baby. *Well*, that was the master plan, just the matching hat-and-pawkies to complete his ski rig-out… *Until* the girl says to me: Have you seen our wee Italian dungarees? Just in. I says: That's his *name,* she goes: What? I says: *Justin*, my new wee nephew. (*Beat.*) Fatal. (*Beat.*) Born to shop, that's me! Honest to God if Magnus Magnusson done a *Mastermind* on Brand Names and Merchandise of the House of Fraser I'd be champion, no question. I can resist everything but temptation I'm afraid, so basically I'll just have to reconcile myself in advance to another slap-in-the-face from my sister…

Her man's no bother. Bottle of Bell's and he's happy, wee Tommy. Pleasant enough, mind. Basically a nonentity. Hate to say it about my own sister's husband, but she could've done one helluva lot better for herself than yon. Chances she had. *Her* looks! And smart! All brains, nae bloody common sense…

So. Five weans. Man that's no worked since nineteen-canteen. Steys in a three-up in Easterhoose that's that bogging damp the paper's curling aff the walls, has to humph that pram doon three flights past pish, broken glass, auld hypodermics and Alsatian shite. Excuse my French. (*Beat.*) Anyway I thought I'd get her something nice. Something-nice-for-herself… Upshot, I splashed out over-the-odds at Arnotts, got her a jumbo gift basket. Matching cologne, talc, perfume-creme and body lotion. Gorgeous. 'Quelques Fleurs.'

Scene Two 23rd December 1991

Between Springburn and arrival at Glasgow Queen Street.

On the Rattler, the Aberdeen to Glasgow train, DEREK *by the end of his journey, is very, very drunk and giving it laldy. Although it will only be apparent by the end of the play, it is one year later. He sings the third part of 'Winter Wonderland' by Felix Bernard and Richard B. Smith.*

He breaks off his singing, speaks out.

DEREK. My wife is a dog. Merry Christmas.

He is interrupted by the two blows into the intercom and the pre-recorded voice of the GUARD *announcing –*

GUARD'S VOICE. This train is about to arrive in Queen Street Station where this train will terminate. This is the sixteen thirty train from Aberdeen to Glasgow Queen Street. Would all customers please check that they have all luggage and personal belongings with them before they de-train. We hope you will travel with British Rail again soon.

Halfway through, DEREK *lurches to his feet, gets himself drunkenly together and exits belting out his version of –*

DEREK. C'mon over to my place,
Hey girl! We're having a party.
We'll be swining,
Dancing and singing,
C'mon over tonight.

He remembers he has forgotten a small white teddy with a Christmas hat, goes back for it, picks it up.

Oh, fuck! (*Shakes teddy, its bell jingles.*)

Scene Three 6th January 1991

Twelfth Night. VERENA *takes down the tree, talks.*

VERENA. Of course, one year we dispensed with the tree entirely. Tried something I seen in a magazine. Just this barren branch flat-whited with emulsion, *very* sparingly glittered up, you know, just where the twigs forked and just... very, very sparsely hung with just – mibbe five or six, maximum seven – giant silver mirror-balls. Sort of monochro*matic*. Quite effective, but. (*Pause.*) Depressed me. It wisnae the same.

Moira McVitie came round this morning for a cappuccino. Phoned up and said: Is that your man away back? I says: Uh-huh footloose and fancy free that's me! She says: Yes I *thought* so. Saw you both getting into the car together and I thought that's unusual. I suppose that'll be her driving into Queen Street for the Aberdeen train? I says: Do you fancy coming round? Sample my new Beverage-Master? Because it even foams the milk. Of course, in the event I spoke too soon and we were reduced to Marvel because I could tell Him till I was blue in the face, but he will be over-lavish with milk in his cereal. Moira can talk though. I've had more black instant than I've had hot dinners round at her house.

So round she came. Wee Scott in tow. I think she's lonely. Says she gets bored, nothing but a two-year-old's conversation all day. I mean he's *lovely*, but he can be quite wearing. Will of his own as well! I said: Do you miss the staffroom? She says: Well… I do and I don't. The *banter,* uh-huh…

Usual from her: *I've* got a beautiful house… *I've* got marvellous taste… *hers* is like a *bomb*site but what's the point with young Genghis Khan scattering his Duplo all over the shop? Plus apparently he's felt-tipped all over her anaglypta… says the seven-year-old is *worse*, if anything! Face like a wee angel as well. Goes to ballet…

Course, my tree was much admired. I do try and stick to a different theme every Christmas. Obviously this year I'd stuck to the cherub motif only. Nothing gaudy, no baubles, no fairy lights. Nothing.

Less is more. We had an English teacher at the school was always saying that. (*Pause.*) I think it's true.

Course, wee Scotty was into everything what with me being in the middle of dismantling the decorations. Ever noticed how fond mothers tend to just content themselves with the odd Don't-son and basically just let the wee buggers run riot?

Moira says to me: I'm full of admiration, she says. See if it was me I doubt I'd bother to go the effort of a tree. Not if it wasnae for the weans. (*Pause.*)

I don't think that's the attitude. Course I couldny be doing wi pine needles. Clogs your tube.

Moira says: Different story from last year! Mind how your sister was quite the celebrity. The big TV star! I says: Don't start me. She says: I think she was excellent. Very articulate.

Oh she's that all right. Always was. Never short of some bloody thing to say, Our Joy…

This was yon 1990 TV special. Channel 4, *Contrasts… A Tale of Two Cities*. Joy had to swap wi some other wummin they'd found born the exact same time as her in a private ward in Guy's Hospital, Honourable Felicity something and they put them through a full twenty-four hours of each other's lives – well, with *limits*, they didnae go the lengths of making them shack up wi each other's *husbands* nor nothing!

Anyway, at the time thon TV programme took quite a trick with the world and his wife. *Evening Times* called Our Joy 'a passionate spokesman for the unemployed, the poor, the poll-tax rebels'. Said she'd of brought a lump to the throat of the most hardened Tory. They called her a 'bonny fechter'. Practically know it off by heart because everybody wis stuffing that blinking cutting down my throat till I was sick-fed-up looking at it – Him, Moira McVitie, Our Stephen, Isobel Hislop at the checkout round the delicatessen...

Thing is, Our Joy's obsessed with poverty. Makes a meal of it. I mean, I was embarrassed for My Mother. Dragging us up she had nothing, because my feyther – God forgive me speaking ill of the dead – but he'd have took drink through a shitty cloot. She kept the three of us beautiful, nobody knew the heartache when wan of us grew out our shoes just when she had the Co dividend earmarked for something else... Nae money in her purse to give us our dinner money she'd say: Tell your teacher you've got sangwidges because your mum doesn't have change of a five-pound note! That's My Mother.

And when I seen Our Joy sat there on that television on the Honourable Felicity's horse in Dorset done up in the breeches, the riding hat, describing day to day in Easterhouse, how you're at the mercy of the medical profession, the social workers, the social security... Rhyming it all off. No shame. I mean, how did she think My Mother would of felt, watching that?

Funny programme. Not what you'd call festive. Actually it was on the night before Hugmanay among all yon kinna gloomy programmes, you know, résumé of the eighties, lukkin back on all the disasters exetra. Lockerbie. Piper Alpha. (*Sigh.*) You tried to switch channels but they were all at it...

Funny thing is, Joy says she was sorry for that Honourable Felicity, would not cheynge places wi her for all the tea in China. Man's a bad yin, never there, leaving her languishing in the sticks, up at his London flat all week, getting up to all sorts, palling about wi MPs exetra. (*Beat.*) Stepson a heroin addick.

Course, that'll be how they tracked Joy down for their programme. Be that Mothers Against Drug Abuse thing that Joy is so involved with in Easterhouse. Aye, she's a volunteer at the Community Flat place, aye campaigning against dampness, sticking up for tenants' rights exetra, single-handed she actually fought through the Rid Tape and won some grant off the EEC only the shortfall had to be made up by the Housing Department and they said their hands were tied. Blamed Central Government. Anyway, Our Joy was up to ninety about the whole thing at the time. Like I said, she's obsessed.

Pause of several beats shaking head over perverseness of her sister.

Moira McVitie was asking would I like to join her Book Group seeing I was all on my ownio? Just a few folk she's knew since the uni, couple of lassies she taught with and three like-minded types she met at the playgroup. They all read the same paperback every fortnight, meet in each other's houses to discuss it and not be cabbages. Turns out it's at Moira's this Thursday that's why she thought of asking me. Left me a loan of the book they've been reading. I took a wee peek at it over my lunch, but I couldny really be bothered. *Woman at the Edge of Time* or some damp thing…

Anyway, that's Him away back this morning. So that's me. Auld claes and parritch! Never really slept right last night, well, you don't, do you? (*Pause.*)

Och, I hope that's not me heading for another dose of yon honeymoon cystitis…

Scene Four 23rd December 1991

Somewhere between Perth and Stirling.

Continuation, moving backwards in time of DEREK*'s single journey.* DEREK *is much less pissed. That many less cans cover the table. He speaks to an (invisible) person opposite, trying hard.*

DEREK. Good book, eh? Good book? Like reading? Engrossed, eh? I used to be a big reader. Aye wance upon a time but I've gave it up. 'M I annoying you? Interrupting your concentration? Because I wouldnae like to think I was disturbing you. I've seen it often, guys on the Rattler, pestering women, making right tits of theirselves forcing theirselves on innocent fellow travellers with their sob stories. A liberty. You from Perth yourself? Going to Glasgow? Stirling? You stay in Stirling? Going home for Christmas?

Danielle Steele, eh? Is that a love or a murder?

Nothing but cowboys. Nothing but cowboys and science fiction in the liberry up therr on the rig, and nine times out of ten you get to the lass page and some bastard's torn it out. I mean, imagine a whodunit. Whodunit? Don't ask me, pal, the lass page is missing. I don't understand the mentality. See, what some folk love more than anything else is to destroy other folk's pleasure. Do you like happy endings? I like happy endings, I'm a simple sort of guy. You look like a happy-ending kinda person. Lovely smile. Whit's your name? That's lovely. Lorraine, eh? When I marry sweet Lorraine. Nice song. Derek. But I'll answer to anything.

Naw, you look like a happy-ending person. I think women generally are, eh? Unless it's a weepie yiz want. Yiz like that. Aye ye dae, don't come it. I canny greet. Wish I could. Sometimes I wish I could kinna… get it out my system.

Yeah, yeah, that's right, Lorraine. Offshore. For my sins. Oh aye two weeks on two weeks aff – well, for the roughnecks and the roustabouts and that, my line of work it's four and four, Lorraine. Want a can? Want a wee gin and tonic well? Lorraine?

Sure? You're sure you're sure? Just to be seasonable. It's nice to be nice. You don't mind if I do? That's right. That's right, up therr's totally tee-total. Funny thing is you don't miss it. You really don't. That's the amazing thing. Or the fags. No, because I'm not allowed to smoke, no in my line of work. Diver. Yeah, yeah up to a point it is dangerous, but they certainly pay us for it. Have to! Yeah the other guys up there they hate us, but they've got it dead cushy compared wi us.

Okay. It's nae teddy berrs' picnic the twelve hours on twelve hours aff, but they've the rec room and the videos, even a wee blaw of the wacky-baccy noo and again on the fly, try to make up for the lack of bevvy. But in sat it's a different story. Even your meals come in through a err-lock… 'Slike outer space. Walkin aboot in your woollyberr… Makes you talk like Donal Duck… the *helium*, you know…

Naw, it's borin doon therr and bloody dangerous but I wouldnae say you get used to it. The dive is the dive. Thank fuck for your umbilical, eh? You just get yoursel out the bottom, five hunner feet of black watter above you, you climb to the tap of the bell and you dive…

Well, thing is obviously up therr you've got all this stuff deep deep down below the surface on the seabed. Needing maintenance. Well, say your concrete casing gets damaged, say by dragging anchors of mibbe fishing boats or something and the installations need to be inspected constantly so you're continually cleanin up the welds to bright metal. Particle inspection exetra. I don't want to get too technical…

Back to the book? Eh, eh? Ut a good bit? Seen in a book wance… wis reading this book, know, quite interessin… on the history o oil. Here there wis this guy used to hink the earth wis this shuge creature, the waters wis its blood, the rocks its bones, the grass and trees its hair, the hills were pimples on its face and Vesuvius and Mount St Helens 'n' 'at wur boils and big pussy abscess-hings erupting all over its skin and all you had to do to get oil was to bore through the skin intae the stinkin blubber of this huge animal. Whit do you think of that? Eh? Plus zis bam minister or sumphn… Texas… says that oil was the oil that kepp the Fires of Hell burning, and the Fires of Hell wid go oot if… eh… petroleum kepp getting sooked oot tae the surface for, lik, Profane Purposes. And then wherr would we be, Lorraine? Withoot the Fires of Hell!

Aye, we've to live doon therr.

In saturation…

He abruptly switches from the glittering-eye approach and the horror story back to the bragging.

But it's all down to us. The Divers. Headbangers the lot of us, darlin, you don't have to be crazy to work here but it helps!

Aye the high cost of oil, right enough. In shuman terms. Well I think that's wan thing – you interested in politics? – that Gulf cerryoan showed up didn't it? Wir priorities. A lot of folk up therr that time were scared nae doot aboot it. Theory wis Saddam Hussein would take out a rig or two in the North Sea nae bother. A possibility. Could of. Safety up therr the best of times's a joke… Joke: J.R. has this big blow-out at one of his oil wells. Flames everywhere, it's costing him billions every day, a disaster. He says to his right-hand man: Get me Red Adair, his man gets on the phone and gets back to him, says: If you want Red Adair it'll cost five billion and you'll huv to wait eight months, he says: Red Adair's very busy puttin oot the fires of Kuwait. But the good news is I can get you Green Adair, he's willing to come the morra and it'll cost you twenty-five thousand. J.R. goes: Get me Green Adair then. Well, so the next day this big Hercules Transport comes fleeing in, big shamrock painted on the side of it and it comes screamin intae land in this airfield right next to the fire, back door of the plane flees open and this Jeep comes fleein oot hits the tarmac and goes fleein intae the heart of the fire, four guys in welly boots and donkey jackets come leapin oot start stampin and jiggin and jumpin all over fuck on the flames stampin them out. Here it's oot in nae time, they walk back oot aw black, kinna coughin a bit. J.R. goes up to them goes: Guys, that is fantastic you've earned every cent, now what are you gonna do with your twenty-five K? Green Adair goes: Well the first thing Ah'm gonny do is get the brakes mended on that fuckin Jeep!

Disappointed with the response to his joke, he tries yet another tack.

Tell you a *true* story, well. Guy I came over wi on the Chinook therr. Wee Eddie, A berr.

First wife wis a cracker! When Eddie went offshore she used to wave him tata, take the train tae Edinburgh, book into a B&B and go on the streets down near Leith Docks. Never knew a thing about it. Not for years. Eventually, well he's no Epstein, but even Wee Eddie got suspicious, he'd rang up jist wance or twice too often and naebody therr so he gets the idea she's having an affair. Asks her. She denies it, naturally, he gets a private detective and the whole story emerges. Waved her bank book in his face. She's only amassed a small fortune!... Eddie's shattered.

Ma Big Mate, Big Malk jist goes: Listen, Eddie son, how should it worry you? What you don't see disnae hurt you. She disnae see you covered in muck, grease and snotters clamping pipe on the drilling flair and spitting intae the hole for good luck. So how no jist let her screw on regardless? On the wan condition she makes it a joint account, like. And he winked at us. Christ, I thought Wee Eddie was gonnae murder him, midget or no.

Big Malk, but... Jist recently therr got hisself hitched to Mrs Malk Mark Three. Nuther sunbed kid. No three-month merrit an he's flashing photaes of her topless all over the module... Wee

Eddie but, Eddie… Kinna guy Eddie is: this is years later, right – he's married again, lovely girl, primary-school teacher, she's expecting their second, Eddie's on his way home, meets this burd on the Rattler, lassie fae Dundee, jist gets aff wi her. Gets aff the train and gets aff wi her. Twenty-four-hours-from-Tulsa style. Shacks up with her for six or seven month afore she chucks him out on his ear and nae wonder. I mean, nae herm to the guy but some of his personal habits…

Quite unconsciously DEREK *scratches himself.*

Men kin be horrible, hen. Watch yirsel.

DEREK *is by now getting desperate. He's tried the chat-up, the smarm. The offer of a drink, the brag, the impress-you-with-technology, the gothic-horror approach, the political discussion, the stand-up comedy act, the true stories with a sleazy hint of sex, the avuncular watch-yirsel… Now his self-dramatisation just goes for broke, he's inventing wildly, on the hoof, he'll try anything.*

Spain. Yup. Yup. That's wherr I live. Aye, aye right enough naw I huvnae much of a tan… Naw. I havenae been back there recently. No since the tragedy.

Aye, few years ago we decided what's the point the four weeks off, the money I was making, as well travelling hame to Spain as somewhere in Scotland or England, eh? How no? Sold up, Costa del Sol. Costa del Crime as it's widely known, several of the neighbours well-known wide boys from gangland and that. Used to drink wi that Barbara Windsor's ex-husband… To drink with, many of them the nicest guys you could ever meet…

Aye we couldnae of been happier… the wife, the kids, everybody brown as berries and happy as the day was long. Beautiful lassie my wife. Ex-model. Former Miss Scotland in fact. Gorgeous nature as well, Claudette. A angel. Everybody loved her. Accident on her motorbike. Head on. Her and a juggernaut. No chance. Mangled.

Got the news and I was in sat. Well, that's you. You're scuppered. No way of getting back to the surface. Beam me up, Scotty, but they canny… They lifted that hatch four days later and I was a crazy man. Insane. Three years later think I was still in shock. I still didny know what hit me. All I could think of was Claudine, ma Claudine.

My wee daughter and the wee filla they were my whole life after their mother died. No that I can have been that much use to them state I was in, thanks to the drink.

That's what kills you… it's the regrets, it's the regrets that get you, isn't it?

I can just see that wee lassie, the herr in bunches, doing wheelies on her BMX and the wee filla wi his waterwings on jumping into the pool. The image of his maw, the blond curls, a wee cherub. Burnt to death the baith o them in a fire in the basement while that bitch of a nanny was oot by the pool chatting up the Spanish gardener… (*Pause.*) Roy Orbison? Roy *fuckin Orbison*?????

GUARD'S VOICE. We are now approaching Stirling Station. Stirling…

DEREK. Aye. Aye well screw you, sweetheart, sorry I spoke.

Aye, well this is where I get aff as well, darlin.

Only spoke to you because I was sorry for you, you're that pigging ugly, Merry Christmas.

He breaks away completely, in disgust. Closes down, not even registering her departure. He sits. Silence. When he speaks, it's with a total switch to a lonely attempt to look at the truth.

If sixteen year of this life have taught me wan thing it's this: you're better aff cutting your life into two weeks on, two weeks off and never the twain shall meet. I mean: hauf your life is hauf the time in a force-ten gale and hauf the time in a four-bunk boax in ablow a guy that never cheynges his soaks or wyes in a hale fortnight.

Opposite you is the yap whose wan topic of conversation is how his daughter used to winch the Yorkshire Ripper.

As-nice-a-filla-as-you'd-ever-want-to-meet, big-Peter, his-lorry-was-never-out-the-layby-along-the-road-he-was-that-daft-aboot-oor-thingwy, used-to-sleep-in-the-house-but-never-shacked-up-wi-her-or-nothing, coorse-me-and-her-mammy-wouldnae-huv-allowed-it-but-he-always treated-the-lassie-like-a-lady. Say-whit-you-like-but-I-ayeways-thought-Sutcliffe wis-a-great-block.

And you're thinkin to yirsel: out of five hunner blocks on the flotel how come yet again you've ended up wi Ma-Daughter-

Almost-Married-A-Monster and how come he canny mind how often he's telt you the same fuckin story?

Gets so you think you're gonnae lam the other poor bastard that never says boo, the big silent cheuchter type, jist a laddie, the wan that's no botherin emdy, jist lyin on his back on the bunk whistlin through his teeth while he works his way through a big pile of fishin magazines and old Fiestas.

You know you've been up therr too long when even the dogs in the Fiesta begin to lukk attractive…

I *am* morbid wi the offshore carry-on. Up to here wi it.

Big Derek Jimmison forty-two, failed fitter. Correction, it wis the fittin that failed me… So offshore.

Supposed to be short-term mizzure. Jist till the economy takes a wee upswing. Jist till we get a few bob thegither, get a wee start. Jist till we get the hoose up to Ags's standards and I'd start my ain business. Ha. Ha. Then it would be no longer the roughneck. Tata the Rattler. I wish.

Sixteen fuckin year. Young man's gemme as well, definately.

So's fatherhood, son. As you are just about to find out…

Scene Five March 1991

VERENA. Course, I'm used to it now, after all these years, never give it a thought. Since ever He first went up there on the rigs it's been much better. Definately. Well, financially speaking anyway, I mean see before, with his other job, before, on shore… honest to God the mortgage was a millstone.

Him away, the diet is a piece of cake. I mean, you've no dis*tract*ions. Well, until he bought me this blinking Easter egg! Plus a big bunch of flowers! Wonder what he's feeling guilty about!

And I am out a lot.

Och just round to My Mother's basically, just to get out of the house. An Ann Summers the night, round my mum's next-door neighbour's. Although I hope their lingerie's better quality than yon Pippa Dee party. Set of French knickers you could spit peas through.

Telling you though, He is that jealous, always was, vernear divorce proceedings he phones up and I'm no in!

Although as I try to tell my mother and Our Joy, I'm convinced it's with us having the none of a family ourselves I've adjusted so well. (*Pause*.) Means I'm a free agent. (*Pause*.) Moira was just asking me when I was round there the other day, she says: Did you never think to *investigate* it, if that's no too cheeky a question…

I says, No, I don't mind telling you I says, it was a *night*mare, Moira, I says you know nothing about indignity if you've never had your tubes blown.

Doctors! Och it was into the ins-and-outs of everything.

Could find nothing wrong. Nothing wrong with either of the two of us. Not that they could put their finger on. Suggested we might simply be missing the moment, what with the two weeks on, two weeks off, mibbe he should think of changing his job, or something?

But och, it's security isn't it…

And is a kid compatible with an off-white fitted carpet, that's the question…?

Because I gave Moira a wee tinkle this morning, asked her round, she said she would love to if it was just her, but wee Scotty was having one helluva hiccup with his toilet training. (*Pause*.) Hope she wasn't offended I body-swerved her Book Group…

Scene Six Between Montrose and Dundee

DEREK. The first I mind of noticing Joy – well, apart from her being Ags's young sister – was funnily enough the night Dixie and me were arranging my stag. There was this pub, the Dagwood Bar, near wherr I grew up, bit of a dump it was in many ways but they had this upsterrs room they let out for like meetings, clubs, twenty-fursts, and me and Dixie, he was my best man, huvny seen him in years, imigrated to South Africa, anyway, we'd went to the Dagwood to book it for the Wensday before the wedding. Because no way was I gonny be daft enough no to leave the two or three days recovery time before the Saturday. I've seen too many grooms green about the gills. Foolish…

Anyway, fair enough, we'd fixed it up, we're just ordering up a pint and Dixie spies through the alcove in the lounge this burd. Dixie was always spotting burds. He goes: You know who that was, Big Man? I go naw. He goes: Big Gwynneth. Big Gwynneth Thingwy. I says: Gwynneth Inglis, Big Gwynneth that was at the school with us? I says: I very much doubt it, last I heard of her she was living down in Macclesfield. He goes: I tell you, that was Big Gwynneth in therr. Big Gwynneth that used to wear the *nylons*.

Oh aye! The diamond-mesh nylons. With the wee rips stopped with the wee dabs of nail varnish. Big Gwynneth had a stoatin perra pins, no skinny, dead shapely wi good firm muscles an that, she used to be great at the PT, a runner as well… Wore high heels even at the school, all the old-bag wummin teachers used to go crazy, big spike stilletos, thirteen-year-aul… Likely all the men teachers used to go crazy an all. That wee hollow in behind Big Gwynneth's knees… She was a right big ride goes Dixie. Although that used to be what we said about everybody. A mixture of wishful thinkin and pure resentment of the fact when we were fifteen she wouldny even have looked at us. I mean ever looked recently at a school photo of back when you were fifteen? I mean there's just all these big women, some of them look about forty, the bouffongs, the perms, the big pointy tits, and guys? – ther's always this wan neanderthal type with eyebrows that meet in the middle and black hair curling out the neck of his shurt – and then aw these Wee Boays… A joke! Dixie goes: Mibbe we should go in and buy the lassie a drink for old times' sake. But mind, Big Man, you're a married man as near as dammit he says. I'm like that… I says next month, Dixie, next month anyway I'm not interested. I'll believe you, thousands wouldny says Dixie and anyway mibbe she's got a pal with her, mibbe I'll be well in therr or mibbe she's in wi a block or her mother in which case I don't like the wan you're getting.

So through we goes. Ben the lounge. Usual shite from the barman about how it's couples only through therr, you need to be in with a partner and anyway it's waitress service so you're no allowed to take your pint in from the public or everybody would be doing it because it's threepence cheaper. So ends up Dixie slapping ten pee on the bar and telling him we're meeting somebody and in we go.

And who should Gwynneth be sitting with but Joy. I was amazed. Because Joy is out the house at this time, her father and her have had one of their famous fa-outs. Every hoose is different I suppose but, Jeezus, in Ags's family the Third World War was never mair than a nasty remark away. Well, Joy and her da had had a big falling out, he'd threatened to put her out the door and here she'd upped and went just to spite him. Nobody knew where she was, she'd left the college, mibbe that was what the fight had been about in the first place, nobody had seen hide nor hair of her for about three weeks or somethin. And there she is, sitting wi Big Gwynneth. Aw naw, goes Joy. I goes: Well hello stranger, your Ags is up to ninety about you, you've missed about three fittings for your bridesmaid's thingwy. She says: Gwynneth, you don't know thame do you? Of old, says Gwynneth, worse luck. Joy says: Well, you can tell our Agnes Verena – from me – that apple green is a bogging colour. I go: Joy, Joy, it's Ags's big day, c'mon noo, I'm gonny be all done up like a dish o fish in the Moss Bros masel, the brown tuxedo, the cumberbund I don't know all what. Well, says Joy, I wish you health to werr it.

Turns out she's working beside Big Gwynneth. In a bookies. And she's sharing a flat with her over the South Side somewhere. Talk about the odd couple! I mean Gwynneth's got to be my age at least! Twinty-four or five. This is – whit? – the middle seventies, and she's in a time warp. Froze in the kinna style she hud at fifteen. Dusty Springfield. That kinna sketch. The pale pale pink lipstick, the two black eyes like burnt holes in a blanket...

And Joy, she's seventeen or eighteen but looks about fifteen or somethin. Dead young for her age. That wis Ags's theory anyway. Easy led. But there she is, a pint of Guinness in front of her, a pint, in a pint mug, the freckles, the fork and knife herrcut. The bib-front dungarees.

Dixie's like that. I hate to see that, he says, a wummin wi a pint tumbler. I thought you'd chucked the yoonie. Joy just makes a face and says nothing. Him and Gwynneth seem to be getting on just dandy, although I notice he's elevated himself to a draughtsman...

I mean why do guys do that? Pub in the Torry docks, Union Street disco, the guy's a K.P. in the caterin, he tells the burd he's a roughneck, roughneck's a mud-engineer, mud-engineer's a diver, diver's a chopper pilot. I mean burds aw know that. He knows they know that. Mibbe he's feart he says he's a roughneck she'll think he's only a bender kitchen porter.

Anyway that night...

Course in the finish-up we go round there to their flat wi a carry-out. Well I know for fact Joy wasnae very pleased but she never says nothing. Well it was Big Gwynneth's flat originally. Few cans, some Carlsberg Specials, a quarter bottle of Bacardi for them, a quarter bottle of whisky for us and a boattle o ginger. Flat was basically just the wan big room. Gwynneth goes dancing over to the settee picks up a perr y tights wi the knickers still in them rolls them up into a ball and chucks them over this partition along a bit from the fireplace. There was a partition hing normal wall height that didnae go right up to the high ceiling – that cut a corner out the room, took a big bite out of it. Dixie goes: That your bedroom in therr? Wouldn't you like to know goes Gwynneth. I sat on the settee and picked up a woman's magazine. As if I was interested. What to do if he wants oral sex and you don't. The usual.

Dixie makes a beeline for the record player and starts slagging the record collection. Amazing sound system, Gwynneth. The hi-fi Dansette, haveny seen wan y these for dunkey's and geez oh, some ell pees! Dave Dee Dozy Beaky Mick and Titch, Wayne Fontana! Bob Dylan? Whit's he dane here? That's my album, says Joy. Oh *album*, sorry I spoke says Dixie, have yous nothing good? How about some of the late great Jimi Hendrix or somethin?

This is what I'm thinkin when I'm sittin on the settee with the magazine. I'm thinkin *burds' flats*...

The wee frilly bags of rollers lying about the place, the inside-out jerseys drying over towels on the backs of chairs, the durty coffee mugs on the ironing board, wan of they big paper lantern hings, slightly tore, the light blue Tampax box among all the make-up and stuff on the dressing table. Burds' flats...

Of course I've been up in plenty burds' flats over the years. Several. But no enough. No really. And I'm thinking about the room and kitchen Ags and me have been dane up for about three month, the silk-finish woodwork, the breakfast bar I'd aw the bother wi the rawlplugs for…

Later on I come back in from having a slash. And there's no sign of Gwynneth or Dixie. Just Joy… I go: Where urr they? But Joy just shrugs. She just sits there on the settee hunched up round her cup of coffee singing along to the Bob Dylan record, and when she turns it over she ups the volume a wee bit, but nothing too obvious. Otherwise – it's ridiculous – but we just sit there completely ignoring the noises from the other side of the partition while Dixie and Big Gwynneth get down to it and do the business. I mean I'm thinkin this is my burd's wee sister here. She's starin down into that coffee cup as if it's got the answer to somethin in it and mouthing along to 'Positively 4th Street'.

Eventually – everything's quietened down a bit through there by this time – she looks up at me. Light clear eyes she hus. She says to me: One thing I just don't understand about guys she says. What's that? says I. She says: Why is it some guy's called Deans everybody's got to call him Dixie?

The next mornin, Joy's got this mark on her face from where she's been lyin all night on my corduroy jacket. It's imprintit. I touch her face and I can feel it. The wee ridges, the grooves. I kiss her and say it's gonny stay like that, wee pal. And she just smiles at us. She says: Gonny no tell Verena or my ma or my da or anybody where I am? I say: Don't worry…

Course in the event at the wedding three weeks later it's all blew over. Like most of the big dramas in their family. Joy's there, in the identical-same bridesmaid dress as wee fat Alma, Ags's pal fae work. Just the way Ags wanted it. End of story.

GUARD'S VOICE. Will all passengers who boarded the train at Stonehaven or Montrose please have their tickets ready for inspection…

DEREK. Nothing actually happened, but…

Scene Seven July 1991

VERENA. Hired a sunbed. Well, you don't want to give yourself a ridneck turning up totally paleface at the beach day one, do you? Although possibly we'll generally use the pool at the hotel, because – if you can trust the brochure – it looks immaculate. Kinna kidney-shape. Although if it's anything like Portugal there'll be a shortage of sunloungers.

So I was saying to Moira if she wanted to come round, because I've the six weeks' hire of the blinking thing, and there might as well be somebody using it. It's not as if I can just lie there all day toasting myself. Over thirty and your skin can get yon leathery way. Not attractive.

But she's no turned up. So far. Shame because it'd help her acne.

I suppose we'd better enjoy this holiday, Him and me, because it'll be our last fling before the joys of parenthood. (*Pause.*)

Aye it'll be changed days. Funny how it's all worked out. It was in the March or April there, just around Easter anyway, Moira and I went along to see yon Destinastra.

Moira had said to me Scotty's wee pal Chloe at the playgroup's mother was having a night in the house where she was getting in a clairvoyant and she was looking for one or two to bring up her numbers. Because with Destinastra it's minimum a dozen before you can get her to come out to you. Moira says apparently she's excellent, prophesied Pauline Patullo would be crossing water for profit in connection with a Leo with the initial R. And here, her husband's boss – *Roy* – turned down the promotion he'd been offered (and had at that point in time accepted!) at head office in Florida because his wife's mother took Parkinson's – so her Harry got it and him and Pauline were sold up and off in jigtime. I mean how could she have *knew*?

So we went. Top whack, she reads your palm, does the crystal ball and gives you a choice of either the cards or the tarot.

She takes my hand and she says: I see here a secret sadness. I says: I don't think so. I says: I tend to be quite content with my lot, anyway I don't go around with a long face moaning about things. Unlike some.

She says: No, I can see that you are self-effacing, tendency to sacrifice yourself for others – and was I Taurus? I says: No – Gemini – but funnily enough I am frequently taken for one and mibbe it's because I am on the cusp. Anyway, she says, I see a Big Joy in your life and it's in connection with the patter of tiny feet. Could it be a sister, or someone close because it's not actually in your own personal house of happiness, but it's a very very close-run thing, and it will deeply affect you? You *and* a partner, but I'm not getting him very clearly, is he fairish, anyway that's all very shadowy, am I right to get water, and a brownish car? She said complete change of lifestyle coming within a nine.

Amazing. And to think that it was only a coupla month before I so much as got wind of Joy's Big News.

Although – and here's where I think you have to believe in something, call it fate, call it what you like, but – Well, this day Moira had been going down the shops and she said can I bring you back anything? I says och, mibbe the *Woman*. If you're passing. Upshot she brings a *Woman's Own* because turns out they'd ran out – and is there not this big article about surrogate mothers? It's very big in Australia apparently, and they'd two or three case histories, one woman it was her own egg and you know yon in-vitrio fertilisation with her own husband's sperm and her sister – I think it was mibbe her twin – carried it for her, because there was some blockage or something in her fallopiums and a badly tilted uterus. Another case, the woman didn't ovulate herself, so her sister (who actually had a grown-up family of her own) had a baby for her by artificial insemination off the woman's husband. Own husband didny mind, thought it was just a case of womb-leasing, a favour one woman could do for another, sister or not and nobody's business but their own.

So I had been reading that on the Tuesday. Yet when – this was the Wensday – Joy let the cat out of the bag by no means did the penny instantly drop.

Well, she was looking hellish, but I didn't think anything of it. Well, I knew she was worried about the poll tax. I mean it was all very well, but when push comes to shove and the chickens come home to roost they'll seize your television as soon as look at you. Politicians. I mean it's folk like Our Joy are going to suffer.

Plus Joy runs herself ragged all that volunteering and social activating and whatnot she does locally. Newsletters. So it's not unusual to see her looking kinda peely-wally and washed out.

Of course, you've guessed it, it was quite the reverse and she was pregnant! Up to high-doh she was, I mean the baby's only what? Nine or ten month old, wee Justin, and when she fell she must've been actually still breast feeding. I says: Could you not persuade that man of yours to get a job so the time doesny hang so heavy on his hands so to speak? She says: Very funny. Turns out according to my mother he'd actually hud the vasectomy, but they were still waiting for it actually to be finalised, because it takes a month or two before you can be certain that they're firing blanks, as her GP put it… So it was rotten luck.

I mean obviously they'd the five kids already, and Justin, gorgeous as he is, was a mistake.

But, although the GP said he'd put her in for a termination no question, say the word – thing is, she said, I'm *torn*.

Mibbe it was the fact that – vasectomy exetra – it felt like slamming the door on her last chance, mibbe it was just that whatever her head thought about it – because definitely they couldn't *have* it – her heart thought different.

My Mother was surprising. She said: Jesus Christ, Joy, get rid of it or you'll never get out the bit.

Joy just sighs and says: I know, Mammy, I know, you're right, okay.

Pause.

It was driving the car home later that it came to me. Thing is He was due home the next day and I knew I could put it to Him. Discuss it.

Course in the event the money that we're actually giving her isn't a payment. How could it be, between sisters?

And it's as old as the hills this kind of arrangement, sister for sister, servant for mistress, all through history. Since Bible Days. A lot longer than test tubes or USA palimony lawyers that's for sure!

No, a friendly arrangement, enough to keep her comfortable while she's carrying – because obviously it's hard work, blossoming or not blossoming! Plus a wee nest egg for the rest…

Scene Eight Aberdeen to Montrose

GUARD'S VOICE. This is the sixteen thirty-three InterCity train from Aberdeen to Glasgow Queen Street stopping at Stonehaven, Montrose, Arbroath, Dundee, Perth, Dunblane, Stirling and Glasgow Queen Street. This train is about to depart so would anyone not wishing to travel please leave the train immediately.

DEREK. I do admit I am somewhat of a settee spud. At home, the tendency to turn into quite the couch potato and I freely admit it.

Has caused problems in the past. The way Ags is as well, she's very unlikely to come straight out with something, could be something schunnered her the last time I wis hame and – since then – it's been sorta simmering? A possibility!

Ach, who am I trying to kid? The way she lit into us on the phone last night, I doubt it was about me forgetting to flush the toilet…

Queued up, queued up the regulation three quarters of an oor waiting on the phone, nae answer. I gies up, tries again later, nothing. Thurd time, thurd time lucky she picks up the phone. I goes: Fuck you been? She says… (*Shakes his head.*)

I mean: What was all that aboot?

I hope to fuck nothing has happened.

I hope naebody has said nothing.

No with this wean due in a coupla weeks.

I don't think so.

Surely no… Nah.

Christmas fuckin Eve, eh?

Alang Union Street therr lukkin for a jeweller's. Get Ags a eternity ring. For her Christmas… Ended up wi eighteen-carat set wi zircons and synthetic sapphire… Bar that I've a coupla bottla scent out the Bond. Obsession. Better be the right thing. Big Malk says wan thing each and every wan of his wives wanted that wis a eternity ring.

Sometimes I think I'm the only person offshore that has been married jist the wance. To the wan lassie.

I don't think I'd ever split up wi Ags. No at this stage in the gemme.

I've been off the drink as well. Off the drink for vernear nine month. So what has induced you to start the night, son? Ach, I dunno… Perhaps it is the Christmas spirit. Cheers! Gaun yirsel!

See when oor Ags comes oot wi the suggestion we should adopt Joy's wean. Out of the blue. Joy's wean… I'm like, eh? Joy's pregnant? You have got to be fuckin jokin? I thought I was gonny burst a blood vessel. I'm like that… Ags goes: You are as white as a sheet. I go naw, it's jist the shock of this adoption caper. I thought we'd thought about that and thought that it wasnae for us.

This wis what? – three-four years after we got married, round about the time of all those tests and everything, when she was desperate to start a family and we were never away from yon Southern General. I couldnae love a stranger's wean, Ags said, could you? I goes: I don't know. The consultant suggested for starters mibbe Ags should give up her work, relax, let nature take its course so she did. Nothin.

Now this about us adopting Joy and Tam's wean!

Well, I'm out of there and down the pub and I phone up Joy. I goes: Get out of there, get a taxi, meet us in the city centre, I'll meet you upstairs at Sloan's. She goes: Whit am I gonnae yase for money? I goes: I'll pey it, just get there. Whit the fuck is going on?

It was only the wan night. Well, no the night, the efternin. Out of the blue an all. It was April. April Fools' Day. I'm no kidding, I wish I wis. Wan y my weeks aff. Hitting the heavy bevvy at that time an all. You don't notice, creeps up on ye. Anyway, I'd put away two-three Superlagers, I'm lying aboot on the settee in my stoakin soles watching a video I've seen umpteen times already. When the doorbell goes. It's Joy. I goes: Well hello stranger. Because I hadnae seen hide nor hair of any of them for donkey's. Anyway, there she is, on the doorstep. In a right state an all. She goes: Oh you're home urr ye, where's my sister? I says: Come in, come in, you've no long missed her, away intae the shoaps wi yon Moira McVitie. She says: When will she be back? I says: Well, as a matter of fact I'm no expecting her, no till later on the night because she was talking about going on to some fortune-teller or something. Girls' Night Out. And you know what they're like. Nuh, goes Joy. And I suppose she doesnae.

Anyway she's up to ninety, anybody can see that. Shaking. Eventually – oot it comes – she's just – oot the blue – had a wee visit from the mammy of the wee fourteen-year-aul lassie that lukks aftir the weans for her while she's oot at the Tenants' Association and the Community Council and whatnot. Babysitter's mammy has found condoms in the lassie's bag and read the riot act and here has it no emerged that she's been kerryin oan wi Tam. Who is auld enough to be her faither and merr than auld enough tae huv a loat merr bloody sense. Shiting on his ain doorstep like that. I canny believe it. I tell her that. I says: Whit did he say? But she's no confrontit him yet. Lassie's mammy's jist away and Joy's come running ower here in case she stabs the bastard wi the breid knife when he comes in the door fae the Job Centre.

Gies her a drink. To calm her doon. There's a bottle of Bezique in the sideboard been lying there since Christmas. Normally she is fanatically anti. Guzzles the loat y it this time, but, state she's in.

Don't really know how it happened. Wan minute I'm cuddling her, patting her on the back, trying tae get her to stop greeting…

First thing I mind is coming to on the carpet. Nae Joy. In she staggers wi' the basin and the disinfectant, white as a sheet, says: Get up, get up, we'll huv tae clean up this mess. Huv you ever tried to clean a carpet when somebody's boaked up a boattle y Bezique?

Course ever since then I'm waiting for seventeen shades of shite tae hit the fan. Two weeks on. Nothing. Two weeks aff. Nothing. Ags never mentions her sister, nor her sister's marital problems, nothing. Until – this is June – Joy's-pregnant-and-I-want-us-tae-adopt-the-wean. Hullo?

Well when Joy turns up at Sloan's that night she is very quick to disabuse me of any notion that it is my child. No way. A wummin knows these things. The dates don't tally, forget it. She is adamant. So that's that.

Thank fuck. I suppose.

Never really done it right we were that drunk.

Anyway, turns oot there was no truth whatsoever in the business about Tam and the babysitter either. Naw, it was Simeon – thirteen-year-aul! – Simeon and the babysitter had been mucking aboot, and when the lassie's mother fun the packet of three, lassie just panicked and blamed Tam, because she knew she would get nothing but sympathy fur getting abused by an adult whereas if they fun oot it was wee Simeon *she* would get a tanking for leading *him* on. Which she did. Joy says: I don't know what gets into the young wans…

Listen, says Joy, I feel terrible about thon day, I don't know how I could have done that to my man and my sister. She says: If you ever tell anybody what happened I will kill you, because a lot of people would get hurt, including my kids, and nobody hurts my kids. She says she's thought about this surrogate business and she's thought about her sister and she's going to go through with it. I go: Let her have our wean?

She goes: It's Tam's. Can't you get that into your thick skull?

Do you know the funny thing? I tellt her. I tellt her how I'd felt ever since yon night up at thon flat. Her and Big Gwynneth. And she couldnae remember it. At first I thought she was acting it. But she wasnae. She couldnae remember.

Ags is ecstatic aboot this wean. Place is like Mothercare.

I don't think she cares whether it's a boy or a lassie. Well, nane of the two of us do, really.

Beryl, Beatrice, Claire, Mabel, Maureen, Renee. Brent if it's a boy? Mibbe Ninian…

Scene Nine December 1991

VERENA – *dull-eyed, dirty, barefooted and rat's-nest hair – slumped.*

VERENA. Bought a big bunch of flowers, got myself over there, says where's the labour ward, where do you find the women that have just had their babies, they said Thirteen B upstairs. Think I knew alreadys, my heart was hammering, tried to tell myself it was just I was just dying to see her. Seven pounds nine ounces. Perfect.

But I knew.

Knew ever since the phone went that morning. Out of the blue. No warning. Everything great. I'm driving over there every day feeding the rest of them. Getting mucked in. Three-and-a-half weeks to go. Her totally serene. Blossoming. First thing I knew, he phones me. Her man. Eleven o'clock in the morning and I'm just about to go over for the three girls coming home from the primary when he phones me. Says don't bother because he's gave them their dinner money. Thing is Joy went into labour last night at six o'clock and had a wee girl at quarter past midnight. My heart stopped. Says: Why didn't you phone me? Supposed to let me know. I wanted to be there. He says: I know. I know that. Obviously. Just Joy wanted to be on her own. Didny even want *him* there… Scratched his face and fought like an animal, doctor hud to ask him to leave because it was upsetting her. I says: I'm going in there, he says no, no the now, she's sleeping. Joy is exhausted.

He goes: Verena, surely embdy's entitled to a change of heart?

Christmas. No bloody Christmas. Never be Christmas again.

He can go to His Mother's. Go wherever the hell he likes.
No use to me. Never has been. Never. I-know-it's-a-shock. Big-heartbreak-but-you'll-have-to-snap-out-of-it-
sweetheart. Life Must Go On. Can just hear the pish he will come out wi…

Don't care if I never set eyes on him again. He can drill a big, big, black hole for himself deep at the bottom of the big black North Sea.

And My Mother. Coming round here greeting, saying she's sure Our Joy will see sense. Don't want her. Don't want our Stephen or that pass-remarkable smart-arse tart he's shacking up with. Fostering. Adoption. Know fuck all about anything. Any of them.

And I told Moira McVitie where to go and take her fat brat with her.

Her. Our Joy. Joy! Coming round here crying. Saying she's sorry. Bringing that envelope full of money. I told her I don't care. Tore it up in front of her face. Crying! Trying to touch me, reaching out…

Asking me please will I be the godmother. Please. Felicity. Felicity Verena.

Our Joy thinks of nobody but herself. Selfish to the core. God forgive her, because I never will.

Slow fade to black.

The End.

PERFECT DAYS

Perfect Days was first performed at the Traverse Theatre, Edinburgh, on 7 August 1998, with the following cast:

BARBS MARSHALL	Siobhan Redmond
ALICE INGLIS	Anne Kidd
SADIE KIRKWOOD	Ann Scott-Jones
BRENDAN BOYLE	John Kazek
DAVIE MARSHALL	Vincent Friell
GRANT STEEL	Enzo Cilenti
Director	John Tiffany
Designer	Georgia Sion
Lighting Designer	Chahine Yavroyan
Sound Designer	John Harris

The play was revived at the Hampstead Theatre, London, on 6 January 1999.

Characters

BARBS MARSHALL, *thirty-nine, a Glasgow celebrity hairdresser*
ALICE INGLIS, *forty-four, Barbs's oldest friend*
SADIE KIRKWOOD, *sixty-two, Barbs's mother*
BRENDAN BOYLE, *twenty-seven to thirty-seven, Barbs's best friend*
DAVIE MARSHALL, *forty-two, Barbs's estranged husband*
GRANT STEEL, *twenty-six, an attractive stranger*

The action of this play is all set in the same large and very stylish Merchant City loft in Glasgow, Barbs Marshall's home.

The scenes take place consecutively on nine different days in Barbs's life. They span from Scene One, a week or so before her thirty-ninth birthday, till Scene Ten, about eighteen months later.

ACT ONE

Scene One

Music – it's Dusty Springfield singing 'I'm Going Back' – the end of the second verse. It fades out as the lights go up.

ALICE INGLIS, *a handsome and pleasant-looking woman in her early forties, sits in her clean M&S slip on a chair in the middle of this large space. A trendy loft. To one side, off, is the kitchen, to the other, off, bathroom/bedroom. There is a loft bed or mezzanine above part of this living space. Centre back, there is a large door into the public hallway, the outside world.*

BARBS MARSHALL, *a very flamboyantly attractive woman in her late thirties, is just finishing cutting* ALICE*'s hair. The last two snips and she picks up the newspaper on which the fall of clippings is caught and pours it into the waste bin.*

Around them, piled on the sofa, are some expensive and chic clothes.

BARBS. So, Alice, I was telling you, we get to Glasgow airport, guy on the desk recognises me, we get an upgrade, very nice, thank you very much, first class practically empty, great, spread out a bit, relax, the champagne cocktails, the blue blue sky, the white fluffy clouds beneath us… I'm feeling: okay maybe he's not got the highest IQ in the world but he does have a gorgeous profile and at least he's not wearing that fucking awful jumper that he turned up in wan night, tucked into his trousers can you believe, and gave me a red neck in front of Brendan from work.

I mean true and everlasting love it is not, but he's a nice guy and all that, own teeth, daft about me, well so far, it's only been three or four weeks, defin-ately dead keen, or so I've been led to believe by the dinners, the phone calls, the nipping my heid off about Paris – how he used to live there how there are all these sweet wee dinky little special places he knows that he'd like to take me, so there we are, we get to the hotel and here they've overbooked so this time we get an automatic upgrade to the four-star no problem, it's gorgeous, the corner room, the fruitbowl, the flowers, the complementary chocolates, the half-bottle of champagne, the big king-size bed all turned down at the corner… And – now, to let you know, Alice – back home in Glasgow I've been avoiding it, by the way, because truth to tell I do not really fancy him, at least I do not fancy him when I am actually *with* him, I've been, frankly, postponing the inevitable for this weekend where I have calculated, quite correctly according to my Predictor Kit, I will be *ovulating* – and he says to me he can't sleep with me because he's Met Someone and he's fallen in love! No, correction, he can *sleep* with me, but we can't have sex because that would be him being unfaithful to his new wee dolly inamorata.

I'm like: What? I'm like: What are we doing here? And Why? He's like: Well, it's a fantastic city, and I'm his best friend – best friend! – and he wants to show me it and he didn't want to disappoint me!

Chin*ese*!

ALICE. Men! Eh? What a fucking wanker!

BARBS. I'm like… naah, he won't be able to last out, *but* we go for dinner, we walk along the Seine in the moonlight, we have a couple of brandies, and yet, no, quite oblivious to me and all my brand-new extortionate La Perla flimsies bought special, nope – bedtime, he pecks me chastely on the cheek and falls fast and instantly asleep, snoring away like billy-o while I am lying there wide awake and just bloody raging.

Because, apart from the galling fact that one of my dwindling supply of eggs is up there, yet again going to waste for want of the Sparky Sperm the Tadpole with its name on it, now that I can't have him do I not start to fancy him something chronic? Torture.

ALICE. Mental!

BARBS. So much for the Romantic fucking Winter-break Valentine Special Weekend in Paris. I mean you lower your standards to minus zero, decide you'll settle for fuck all and even that is denied one.

ALICE *laughs*. BARBS *is taken aback then joins in*.

Well I guess I'll always have Paris… (*Beat.*) Product!

BARBS *applies a scoosh of mousse to* ALICE*'s hair.*

ALICE. Barbs, this is helluva good of you, pal, but don't go to a lot of bother.

BARBS. Nearly done… Wur Own Make. Softstyle shinegel megamousse. This is *the* styling product out of the range that may well yet bankrupt Razor City. However, Stefan would not be deflected from his dreams, would he? And I do have to admit it is a super product. Among a market chock-a-block jam-packed hoaching with super products…

Don't move.

ALICE. Ach, as long as I'm neat and tidy…

BARBS. Alice, you get your hair cut. By me. At my home. Which is something I have never done for *anybody* since 1978 –

ALICE. I'm sorry, I'm sorry, I know, I know, I didny mean it like that… yes, I'm an ungrateful bitch, so I am. I know. I mean, here am urr getting styled by The Stylist that every single person on *Morningtime Makeover* fights over –

BARBS. Exactly. Doing your hair for you in the privacy of her own home so that tonight you will look *fabulous*. Neat and tidy your arse, Alice!

So – Paris – you'd think that was bad enough. That was me. Humiliated. Following month I'm like forget it. Month after that same. Then the next month, unexpectedly, something presents itself…

ALICE. Barbs, excuse me, but can you not get that artificial insemination stuff?

BARBS. Yes, Alice, you can, but something about it does not appeal to me. Maybe I do not like to think of having to tell my baby its daddy is a wanker…

They both laugh.

Na, for some reason… Maybe it's aesthetic, maybe it's pride…

ALICE. You could always go back to our Davie!

BARBS. Aye right!

ALICE. He's crazy about you, Barbs, he's never ever got over you.

BARBS. Aye right, aye! *Anyway* Howard next door –

ALICE. The dishy one?

BARBS. P – G – L.

ALICE. Eh?

BARBS. Pointless Good Looks… Computers. Anyway, he's always been after me. My Midnight Caller. He wished. But I've always knocked him back. Well, obviously he's never come out with it in so many words, it's just been a matter of my not taking him on, never giving him any encouragement, nipping it in the bud sort of thing, you know what I mean?

ALICE. No really.

BARBS. *Aye* you do. Well, turns out Howard is moving out, going to Singapore on a three-year contract, has sold the loft, this is him in for a nightcap saying cheeritata for ever, one thing leads to another, I realise it's Mid-Cycle… *As* you say Howard is nice looking, is obviously highly intelligent, good bet genetically, I mean the missing bits I can put down to bad conditioning which no way would I be guilty of, and best of all he is leaving. For good. Well, one thing leads to yet another, I tell him no need for precautions I've got a coil, which is a lie but he doesn't know that, he says it's okay anyway because before he left his marriage he got an eternity-ring vasectomy!

ALICE. A what?

BARBS. Common phenomenon. Big article about it in the *Marie Claire*. Middle-aged marriage begins to show cracks, man has affair, wife finds out, goes mental, threatens suicide or that he'll never see the kids again, husband shits himself, dumps dolly bird, promises wife never again, very sorry, totally into marriage and this family *and*, to demonstrate one hundred and ten per cent commitment to the status quo, from now on *he* will do the contraception and Have Vasectomy as family teenage and complete. But nevertheless marriage breaks down anyway as fucked, basically, inevitable, and ends up with man in new relationship with much younger woman who is deprived of her own children because his vasectomy turns out to be irreversible.

ALICE. What happens to the wife?

BARBS. How do I know what happens to the wife? She moves to the Borders with her new partner, a much younger man who is a furniture-maker or something, I don't fucking know.

ALICE. You'd think they'd tell you what happens to the wife.

BARBS. Listen, Alice, the article was in the *Marie Claire* not the bloody *Good Housekeeping*, okay?

ALICE. I didn't know Howard was married before.

BARBS. Howard's been married, he's lived with the younger woman, been dumped by her, and now he's fucked off for ever to Singapore without doing me the very small favour which it seems it's too much to ask for these days.

Plus the sex was terrible.

I mean to me, well I guess I'm just a pure product of my generation, but to me sex is about sex. Sometimes, when you are lucky, sex is about love. But sex as anything to do with pregnancy? Humping Howard was my idea of nothing to do, quite frankly.

Mibbe I'll end up at the artificial-insemination clinic yet.

Only it seems so… clinical…

Maybe I could *pay* somebody…

ALICE. Make it somebody gorgeous well!

BARBS. Naturally. A big cock and a high IQ. Anyway, Alice, I've told *you* everything, so tell. Tell. Who was he?

ALICE. Who?

BARBS. You know who. Gorgeous that you were having your lunch with in thon place in Princes Square. I saw you.

Shutters come down in ALICE. *She's clearly very taken aback.*

ALICE. I never saw you.

BARBS. Too right you never saw me. I was going to come over. I *approached*, I was coming over when just something about the two of you made me go… *naaa*.

ALICE. It was a meeting.

BARBS. How old was he anyway?

ALICE. It was a work thing.

BARBS. Nice work if you can get it. Tell!

ALICE. There's nothing to tell…

BARBS. Nothing to tell you are sat there the middle of the day the middle of the week looking fabulous, honestly you were like a girl, Alice, the *glow*, the animation, like a *lover*, do I know love when I see it? I think *so*, I could see the love-light in your eyes, sat there, Alice, with the dolliest Toyboy in the West sitting there opposite you hanging on your every word, drinking you in? What is going on?

BARBS *stares at* ALICE*, sure she'll tell.* ALICE *stares back, sure she's not going to. A beat. Finally –*

ALICE. Barbs…

BARBS. Alice!

ALICE. Listen, Barbs, you didn't need to go to all this bother.

BARBS. That's right, change the subject!

ALICE. Barbs, how long have you known me?

BARBS. Just about all my life.

ALICE. And how long have I been married to Tommy?

BARBS. Donkey's…

ALICE. Twenty-two year come November.

BARBS. You're kidding! Christ, I'd hotpants on. Davie and I had only been going wi each other about a month or something, he wasny allowed to bring us to the meal, I was only invited to the reception… Twenty-tw–

ALICE. Twenty-two years. Tommy and I. And do I strike you as the toyboy type?

BARBS. No. I can't say that has been my impression. Up till now.

ALICE. Well, then.

BARBS. How is Tommy?

ALICE. He's fine.

BARBS. And the girls?

ALICE. Thank God. Wee Andrea's got her Highers this year, so we'll just have to see how she gets on. Our Noelene could knock spots off her in the studying department…

BARBS. Give them my love.

ALICE. Course I will.

BARBS. Gorgeous kids you've got.

ALICE. They're all right. They're nice girls, I suppose. Touch wood.

Barbs, see this 'having a baby' idea that you've suddenly come out with, out the blue…?

BARBS. Out the blue nothing, Alice! Doesn't every woman want a pop at pregnancy before her womb goes pear-shape?

ALICE. I've never ever seen you as the wanting-kids type. In fact, haven't you always worked very hard to make sure that this was never ever the option? I mean if you'd wanted kids would you have split up with our Davie and put Heart Soul and Hormones into Razor City and your telly career?

Do you no think you've mibbe got romantic ideas – from where I don't know! – in your head about it all? Motherhood…

I mean it's hard work, they're not a toy –

BARBS. I know it's bloody hard work, Alice!

ALICE. But, darlin', you *don't* know.

BARBS. Don't you fucking dare mention this to anybody whatsoever!

ALICE. I won't. I wouldn't! Course not… Barbs, I'm sorry, listen, it's none of my business –

BARBS. It isn't.

ALICE. This is helluva good of you, pal, I mean I only phoned up for some advice about what to wear and that, I didn't – honestly – expect my own personal makeover.

I'd of thought you'd be busy anyway, the weekend and that…

BARBS. Aye I'd to cancel three dinner parties and a film premiere.

ALICE. It's only a daft work thing.

BARBS. At which you are going to look fan-fucking-tastic.

ALICE. For the Gartsheuch Housing Association executive committee and the deputy director of Scottish Homes?

BARBS. You won your lottery funding for your centre didn't you? So tonight you are going to look A Million Dollars. Anyway, I'm about done. Let me show you the back…

ALICE. That's neat. That's nice and neat into the back of the neck anyway.

BARBS. *Neat?* It's *fab*ulous. How I want you to do it yourself, you need product, that's *essential*, but not too much right, I'll give you this away with you, just lift with the heel of your hand, roughen it up, just to give root-lift, then either a touch of wax, or – better – the totiest drop of freeze and shine rubbed on your fingertips, then – Alice, are you actually listening to me? – see, I've just *chipped* into your fringe –

ALICE. Well, that'll go wi the *mug* underneath it! Haw, haw…

BARBS *gives her a mock clip round the ear.*

BARBS. *And* I want you to chuck out that keechy 'wash away the grey' home colorant from your bathroom cabinet! I could take years off you. Come into the salon, how many times do I have to tell you, we'll colour it, nothing roary, it'll be a really subtle mesh of lowlights and highlights –

ALICE. Och, I don't know that I'd suit dyed hair. Don't get me wrong, *you* do, but –

BARBS. Come on try this, this'll suit you, it's a wee Sara Sturgeon out of Moon –

ALICE. Barbs, my own frock will do me fine –

BARBS. Put it on. Let me see it on you. Or will I get yon Armani…?

ALICE. No!

BARBS. You could huv that, it's only Emporio.

Surveys what ALICE *has got into.*

Mmm. Maybe… That's nice and simple, but it hings well. Keep it, I never wear it anyway, I bought it during my shopholic phase when I'd put weight on, it's no me. That's better. That's much better. Perfect. You look great!

ALICE. Barbs, don't mammy me! (*Beat.*) I'm fine the way I am.

BARBS. Christ, I am as bad as my own fucking mother!

ALICE. Barbs, listen…

BARBS. Lonely. That's why I want a baby, Alice. I feel empty. I feel lonely.

ALICE. Well, children don't stop you from feeling lonely.

BARBS. Well, what does then?

ALICE. Work.

BARBS. And what exactly does my work contribute to the sum of human happiness? Sweet fuck all…

ALICE. Quite a lot I should think.

A rueful laugh –

BARBS. At least if I make an arse of it I could make somebody miserable… For months.

ALICE *is looking in the mirror. She whirls in delight.*

ALICE. Honestly, Barbs darlin', it's amazing! Total transformation! You've got me so I would hardly know myself so I wouldny! Can I borrow it? Please? I won't keep it, no, but can I get a loan of it? For the night? Please?

BARBS *shakes her head, speechless. Of course she can.*

Barbs. Listen… It wasn't my toyboy. He was my son…

Black.

Music bridge: 'Don't Make Me Over' by Dionne Warwick. ('Accept me for what I am. Accept me for the things that I do'.)

Scene Two

Semi-dark of all-day emptiness. On the middle of the table is a single 'To a Daughter' birthday card.

Door opens, BARBS *enters, slams door, sighs theatrically, walks over to coffee table, puts a pile of cards and other mail down without opening yet, picks up the birthday card, opens it and shuts it to activate the Casio-tone tinny little version of the anthem she sings along to, quite enjoying acting out the self-pity.*

BARBS. Happy birthday to me,
Happy birthday to me,
Happy birthday dear Barbs-ie,
Happy birthday to me.

She rotates her stiff neck, picks up the blue vodka bottle from the table and has a quick neat swig.

A big leather armchair swivels round. In it, an open copy of HELLO! *magazine in front of her, is* BARBS*'s mother,* SADIE.

SADIE. How much are you paying for fabric softener these days?

BARBS. Jesus, Mum –

SADIE. There was a 'two giant-size for the price of one' offer in the supermarket last week, so I brought you one over, pet.

BARBS. – I nearly shat a brick.

SADIE. Language.

BARBS. Mum, I have told you I don't want you coming here cleaning. I've got a cleaner.

SADIE. A lick and a spit. Does nothing!

BARBS. Sitting there in the bloody dark scaring me half –

SADIE. I just sat down for five minutes with the *HELLO!* while I was waiting for the kitchen floor to dry so's I could Jiffy-Wax it and here I must've went and fell –

BARBS. – I don't want my own mother working as a cleaner.

SADIE. It wasny that when it was a matter of your ballet-tap-and-highland.

BARBS. I was eight. Jesus.

It's a Tuesday.

SADIE. Your birthday.

BARBS. You always come on a Thursday.

SADIE. That's correct, the state that so-called Thingwy leaves your work surfaces in on a Wednesday just as well I pop up on a Thursday, pet. Damp disgrace. I'd do it twice as well for half the price.

BARBS. No way!

SADIE. Is that all the thanks I get? Traipsing all the way over here, waiting ver near an hour for a forty-eight, just to gie your penthouse a wee birthday hoover...

BARBS. Mum, I'm very grateful –

SADIE. Exactly. By the way, hen, here's a wee present. Happy birthday, Barbara.

BARBS *takes the present and looks at it. Apprehensive.*

SADIE. Course you'll likely no like it.

BARBS *opens the present with composed pleasure. She finds a horrific hot-pink acrylic garment with appliqued pearls. She looks at it. A beat, then –*

(*Simultaneous.*) You don't like it!

BARBS (*simultaneous*). It's lovely!

SADIE. You don't.

BARBS. I do! Gorgeous!

SADIE. Try it on.

BARBS. After... I'm sure it'll fit me...

SADIE. Come on, let me see it on you.

SADIE *won't give in till* BARBS *does.* BARBS *tries to resist her, then begins to get out of her own top and into* SADIE*'s present...*

I says to Mina next door, I says, she'll likely no like it, I says, I don't know what she *does* like. It'll likely no be dreich enough to please her. Gorgeous shade isn't it? Unusual. I've the exact same one in turquoise.

It's mohair and acrylic. I bought the wool and Mina knitted it for you. Washes like a ribbon. That's what Mina says. And she's from Hawick, knows her jumpers.

BARBS. Inside out.

SADIE. Eh?

BARBS. Nothing.

SADIE. She does, but. Presser in Pringles. Says she wouldn't give cashmere houseroom. This is softer. Brushed.

BARBS *struggles into the awful jumper.* SADIE *produces some magazines, an incongruous mix of* People's Friend *and* HELLO!

That's better. That's much better. That's a bit cheerier for your birthday. I brought you over a few *HELLO!s* and Mina sent over some old *Friends* she was finished with.

BARBS. Eh?

SADIE. Have you got them?

BARBS. No.

SADIE. No I didny think so.

BARBS. Mum –

SADIE *holds up the* HELLO! *magazine from her lap.*

SADIE. I was just reading there that thon Princess Marie Kristen of Sweden's developed an eating disorder.

BARBS. – Mum, it's my birthday, let's pop out for a wee bite and a glass of bubbly.

SADIE. Course, the *Friend* is right aul-fashioned but Mina likes it. I don't think emdy in the *People's Friend*'s ever heard of bulimia… But, och, if you don't want them yourself you can always take them into the salon, save you a few bobs' worth of glossies.

BARBS. Anyway, c'mon…

BARBS*'s hands go to the waistband as she prepares to strip off her horrific jumper.* SADIE *sees this.* BARBS *sees her seeing.*

BARBS*'s hands leave the waistband immediately, she smooths jumper down.*

C'mon, I'll wear my new jumper, you stick on a wee lick of lipstick and we'll pop over the road to the Italian Centre, nothing fancy, they do a lovely focaccia and roasted vegetables.

SADIE. Ach, where is the enjoyment for me in that?

BARBS *gives in deflated.*

So, can I get a fag? Seeing as it's your birthday…

BARBS *goes and fetches and ironically presents an ashtray.*

You never said thank you for your card.

BARBS. Thank you.

She flaps it open and shut to air the Casio-tone 'Happy Birthday' again and puts it back down on the coffee table.

SADIE. Zat all you got?

BARBS. No, there's all these.

SADIE. You've never opened them.

BARBS. I haven't had the bloody chance.

SADIE. Did Davie send you one?

BARBS. Did Davie ever send me one? In twenty years did he ever send me one? Davie phoned.

SADIE. When?

BARBS. This morning.

SADIE. What did he say?

BARBS. He said happy bloody birthday, what did you think he'd say?

SADIE. Did he?

BARBS. He did. Actually he said he was sorry he forgot to send me a card this year, doll, I said he was sorry he never sent me a card every year, he said to listen to the 'Mystic Memories' slot on Radio Clyde because he had put in a request for me when he was up at the DJ's flat selling him a Lalique lamp for his burd's birthday, I said Radio Clyde gave me the boke, I was a James Naughtie and John Thingwy fan in the morning, he said suit yoursel but gie it a wee go, but! Because he had a feeling the DJ might play it, see, and he couldnae listen to it hissel because he was on the motorway in England somewhere driving up a load of gash shoes from a fire-damaged factory in Northampton for his pal Peem then he must've drove under a motorway bridge or something because the signal on his mobile began to break up and that was about it although if I mind of anything else I'll put it down in writing for you, Mum, okay?

SADIE. You broke that boy's heart…

BARBS. I broke *his* – Mother, let's have a drink, it's my birthday, there's a bottle in the fridge.

BARBS *exits to kitchen, is back in no time ready to pop it.*

Here, look, Mummmm's, it's got your name on it.

SADIE. By the way, I was tidying up your bathroom cabinet and that old tube of spermicidal cream next to your Dutch cap was past its sell-by date. I chucked it out for you.

BARBS. Thanks…

BARBS *pops the champagne.* SADIE *sips, wrinkles up her nose.* BARBS *ignores this through gritted teeth.*

Mmmm.

She shuts her eyes and lies back.

SADIE. Anyway, pet, did you have a nice day?

BARBS. Mmm, I had a lovely day.

I had a super day, and gosh it's getting better and better as it goes on, well, there was a surprise Buck's Fizz *brunch* for me, and here had all my employees not clubbed together for the biggest bouquet you ever saw in all your puff, Stefan was utterly charming all day, *didn't* do any skiving, *never* mentioned the products problem, never nipped my head over the stupit franchising idea, never let a patronising syllable pass his lips, never managed to get up my nose at all. I had a perfect day.

SADIE. No much point sending you a card you don't even bother to open them. I suppose I should be flattered you opened mines…

BARBS. Mum, you sent yours three days early with 'do not open till the 29th' all over it, these just arrived today, presumably after I left for work, because I do have to work, you know, being the boss means you are in earlier, not later, okay? But I will certainly open them right now, and see who, if anybody, still loves me. Four people, eh, och, well that's better than nothing –

BARBS *opens one.*

Howard. Howard next door.

SADIE. He's good appearance –

BARBS. He's moved out! Fancy Howard remembering. Correction, Howard no doubt has a computer programme which remembers for him. Oh and this one is from Jane Izzard and all the production team at *Morningtime Makeover*, that's *very* personal, wonder why I don't have one from the bank, or the Taj Mahal Deliver-A-Curry, they always send me a lovely Christmas card… Oh, *Alice,* lots of love from Alice, Tommy, and family. That's nice.

SADIE. Alice? Alice Marshall?

BARBS. Alice Inglis, Alice Marshall as was, uh-huh.

SADIE. Davie's sister Alice?

BARBS. The same.

SADIE. You still see Alice?

BARBS. Ma, you know I do! We go to the aerobics. I told you I cut her hair a couple of weeks ago.

SADIE. How is she?

BARBS. Alice? Oh… Alice is fine. Fantastic, as a matter of fact. Blossoming… Anyway, Alice pal, you remembered…

BARBS *drinks then opens fourth card.*

Oh, but Noelene's sent me one anyway! No need for the 'and family', Alice, Noelene's done it herself. One from her and Andrea.

SADIE *takes the card. She doesn't get it.*

SADIE. '*Oh no I forgot to have children*'…?

BARBS. It's out the feminist bookshop.

SADIE. I don't get it.

BARBS. It's supposed to be a joke. Noelene's only seventeen.

SADIE. Aw…

She puts the card out on the table. A beat or two of silence.

I met the girl Macalinden there.

BARBS. Uh-huh…

SADIE. You mind the lassie Macalinden?

BARBS. No.

SADIE. You do.

BARBS. I don't.

SADIE. Passed on her youngest daughter's Brownie tunic to you, I was up all night unpicking the Pixies badge and sewing on the Scottish Kelpies the night before the Armistice Parade.

BARBS. Mum, I don't remember…

SADIE. Aye you do. Brown Owl said no harm to the woman, but her Melting Moments weren't a patch on mines.

BARBS. Eh…?

SADIE. This is gey wersh isn't it? The only champagne I like the taste of's Babycham.

BARBS. You mean this 'Girl Macalinden' is about sixty.

SADIE. Oh she'll be more than that! Year ahead of me at the school. Anyway she was asking for you.

BARBS. That's nice.

SADIE. Said she'd seen you on *Morningtime Makeover* and she'd thought you did wonders for that woman that was just out the jail.

BARBS. Good.

SADIE. Uh-huh, she said to me Your Barbra's never off the TV.

BARBS. I wouldn't say that…

SADIE. She says to me: Plus I see 'Barbs Marshall' was the Celebrity Starscope in the *Sunday Mail* last week, I says yes, she says big changes ahead if there's anything in it, I says our Barbra is not superstitious.

BARBS. I bloody am.

SADIE. She says to me had you a man? I said not as such. Och and anyway what would you be wanting with a man with your lifestyle. I says Barbara's got a career, I says she co-owns a salon, she's never off the telly, she's got a life of her own and four weeks in a luxury timeshare on the nice bit of the Algarve. I says our Barbra's perfectly happy.

BARBS. I'm not.

SADIE. Aye you are!

BARBS. Jesus Christ on a bike.

SADIE. She was saying to me did I not want grandchildren? I said what did I want grandchildren for? I've got grandchildren! Our Megan, Darren and Patrice.

BARBS. In New South Wales…

SADIE. Well, I've seen them. Except wee Patrice.

BARBS. Mum, I'll go into the travel agent's tomorrow and get you a ticket to Australia if that's what you want.

SADIE. Ocht no, pet. It's all barbecues. I'm not a big barbecue hand. Not at my age.

BARBS. Mum, honestly, how old are you?

SADIE. Sixty-one.

BARBS. That's not old.

SADIE. Oh is it not? Wish I'd had your chances. Career. Travel. Own home. Wish I'd done something with my life instead of just frittering it away bringing up you and Our Billy.

BARBS. Mum.

SADIE. I was a widow before I was thirty.

BARBS. Christ, Mother, I wish you wouldn't always say that: 'I was a widow before I was thirty.'

SADIE. I was. I was a widow before my thirtieth birthday.

BARBS. Okay. But… Bloody saying it like that. 'My Life Story'…

SADIE. It's not a story, it's a fact. You and Billy were my whole life.

BARBS. I know, I know...

SADIE. Not old? Sometimes I feel bloody ancient I'll tell you.

BARBS. Well, I bet you do. Cause so do I. The day for instance. Bloody ancient. But I'm not actually. I'm thirty-nine. I wish it wasn't my bloody birthday, because I can't stand thinking about the next one. I don't see how I can possibly be pushing forty when I still don't even know what I want to be when I grow up.

SADIE. Peak of your profession! Fabulous salary!

BARBS. I don't have a salary. You don't even know what a salary is do you? I have a business. I have *half* a business. That could go down the tubes, like any other business. Stefan might bulldozer me into this stupit franchise idea of his. Over my dead body, but you never know. Plus fashion is fickle, face it. The now we're the flavour of the month, next year for all we know the last place anybody will come to get their hair done is Razor City. I've seen it before. That daft horoscope could be right. Everything might change. I might meet a fabulous rich old man. I might meet a fabulous younger man. I might go and work among the slums of South America, drive a lorryful of food to Bosnia, I might buy myself silicone tits, I might do the Open University. Ach I might arse around exactly the same neither here nor there from one wee mini-crisis to the next. Or I might do *something*.

I might decide to have a baby on my own –

SADIE. – Don't be stupid –

BARBS. – I might do *something*. I might be happy. I might be bloody miserable. But I'll tell you one thing. I refuse to pretend to be happy so you can be happy about how happy I am, okay?

SADIE. I don't think you like that jumper I bought you. If you don't like it, just give it back to me and I'll wear it for working in, pet.

BARBS. Mum, I love the jumper.

SADIE. You don't, I can tell.

BARBS. I do. I do.

SADIE. Nor have you said if you enjoyed your strippergram.

BARBS. So it was you!

SADIE. Ach, you ought to lighten up. Be a wee bit broad-minded. I am. Mina and I might go the Guild Outing to the Chippendales.

Black.

Music bridge: Clare Grogan's 'Happy Birthday to You, Happy Birthday'.

Scene Three

Later the same night. Tinfoil catering packages and mess across the coffee table among the birthday cards. BRENDAN BOYLE, BARBS*'s best friend (gorgeous – but gay of course) and* BARBS *have just demolished a Chinese meal and their first bottle of champagne. He is in mid-mock harangue of* BARBS, *who he's really got squirming.*

BRENDAN. ... *So* she's only the wee shampoo lassie and sweeper-upper, right? Sixteen and seldom been shagged –

BARBS. Don't!

BRENDAN. – Nice enough wee lassie –

BARBS. I know...

BRENDAN. – Nice wee lassie wee Kimberly! Poor wee Kimberly, the Sowell, whit does she know? Nothing.

So she's well into it. Giving it that. And we haven't the heart, huv we, to go Heard It Heard It? We're like dead polite. We're like all agog. As if. She's like: The shampoo girl's just rinsed off the conditioner at the backwash when she sees the guy's hauns gaun like that, right? Under his robe. Hits him a clatter roon the back of the heid with the shampoo spray, lays him oot cold, and here it turns oot –

You swan in and go: He was only polishing his glasses!

BARBS. Och stop it.

BRENDAN. You go: Kimberly. Kindly, before you come out with all this keech from your day-release classes, before you bore your colleagues with jejeune reruns of ancient urban myths concerning Panda cars, cats with internal injuries keeling over and snuffing it after eating innocent dinner-party leftovers, or women dying of heart attacks when they see the dog devouring the turkey giblets their son has stuffed down their drunken husband's flies – *kindly* check with us, Kimberly, you goes, whether we've heard this one before, eh? You will probably find the answer is: Many Times. Many, many times. Right?

You go: I – for one – have got an eight-thirty. Has nobody *else* around here got work to go to? And off you go. El Boss Barbara 'Claus' Barbie wi your face like fizz.

We're like that.

Wee Kimberly's like… Ooyah! Pure scarlet.

I'm like: I wonder who shat in her handbag?

BARBS. I am a monster…

BRENDAN. I mean, Barbs, give us a break, if you don't even give us a clue how are we supposed to mind it's your birthday? We would've done something, obviously –

BARBS. A complete monster.

BRENDAN. Sure are, Barbo. But then so were all the women I adore. Bette Davis. Joan Crawford…

BRENDAN *and* BARBS. …Marilyn Monroe. Princess Diana. Judy Garland…

BARBS. And you, Brendan, you are totally a complete nelly cliché.

BRENDAN. Totally. But then you see, growing up a Glesga Boy in No Mean City – yeah, among all the easy-affrontit mammies and all the daddies that were pure frozen-arsed hardmen wi jaws made oot o girders, well, I found out very early that the world and its wife were quite happy and totally tane oan wi the local token Wee-Bit-of-a-Mary-Anne-God-Love-Him. Even Father Hugh and Father Thomas used to pure crease themsels at my antics when I took centre stage cross-dressed at the Legion of Mary Conversazzione.

Anyway some of us might be clichés, but we are seldom short of a shag.

BARBS. Ooyah. Unike certain other folk, you mean? Okay, Brendan, you bastard, ye, don't rub it in.

Sometimes I doubt I'll ever have sex again.

BRENDAN. Eh?

BARBS. I mean it. I mean there is bound to be a last time isn't there? I mean, there is bound to be a last time, in your life, but you would tend to hope that, unlike the first time, you wouldny know it while it was happening because you'd think Christ this better be good.

BRENDAN. You're mad.

BARBS. How?

BRENDAN. Look at you. Sexy as fuck.

BARBS. Yeah… Says you. What would *you* know?

BRENDAN. I know. Drop-dead fucking gorgeous.

BARBS. Old.

BRENDAN. Bollox.

BARBS. I am. Ancient. Thirty-nine. This is my fortieth year, Brendan…

BRENDAN. You don't look it, but.

BARBS. I feel it. After a day like the day and a night like the night. My mother. My mother would put years on you…

Anyway it was very very kind of you to make an Auld Wummin very happy and schlep up here wi that bottle of champagne and carry-out chinky. Who cares if I never see another willy as long as there is Szechuan king prawns?

She skewers a last one out of the tinfoil with her chopstick and devours.

BRENDAN. Ooyah!

BARBS. Crunch. Crunch.

BRENDAN. No wonder men forget you. Correction no wonder men have bad dreams about you, no wonder they hit the grunn running and don't stop till they've got the protection of ten doted wee blonde dolly birds between them and big bad brainy women with sharp tongues and sharp teeth like you.

BARBS. Oh, speaking of doted wee blonde dolly birds, that wee model Stefan is shacking up with is up the duff apparently.

BRENDAN. Christ, is there nae end to that prick's fecundity?

BARBS. Apparently not. Over the moon according to Tiff.

BRENDAN. Has he forgot he's got five already plus an ex-wife that's drinking herself to death in Drymen?

BARBS. That was Tash's point exactly but Tiff says dee-lighted. Like a cat with two tails.

BRENDAN. Dog!

BARBS. Now I wouldn't say that she is a gorgeous-looking lassie!

They both laugh.

BRENDAN. You should ditch Stefan and open up a new wan wi me. He doesny know where it's at these days. The cutting edge, that's moi.

BARBS. Last prawn?

BRENDAN. – You should but!

No takers in either direction. She skewers the prawn, devours.

BARBS. They were quite delicious. Thank you.

BRENDAN. You're very welcome. Many happy returns.

He raises his glass to her.

BARBS. But was it entirely kindly meant, I wonder, to bring us a bottle of Youth Dew and a copy of Germaine Greer's book on the menopause?

BRENDAN. Gie's a brekk, time I'd finished that full-head highlights and you'd finally let us oot of work the night, ya bliddy slave-driver ye, there was bugger all open except Waterstone's and the Nine O' Clock Chemists on the corner, and it was either that or a box of foosty Quality Street oot the Asian grocer's for which I did not think you'd thank me.

BARBS. But I do thank you, Brendan. You're a darling.

BRENDAN. I was gonny get you that *Men Are From Mars Women Are From Venus* but I thought to myself –

BARBS *and* BRENDAN. – Read it!

They nod simultaneously.

BARBS. I've also read that *Women Who Love Too Much*, *The Cinderella Syndrome*, *The Rules*, *The Little Book of Calm*, *Promises Lovers Make When It's Getting Late*, *Why Women Need Chocolate* and *Feel the Fear And Do It Anyway.*

I was going to write one of my own: *Women Who Fancy Men So That Is Them Fucked Forget It…* Yup. I've read them all, plus *Rosemary Connelly's Hip And Thigh Diet*, but this is still me, since yesterday…

BRENDAN. Fuck you got on anyway?

BARBS. Don't start me.

BRENDAN. Great taste your mother!

BARBS. Fabulous. But listen, it really was nice of you…

BRENDAN. Ach…

BARBS. No honestly…

BRENDAN. I was dead dead sorry I'd forgot. You never forget mines.

BARBS. I thought I wanted it just to go by me, unmarked and unremarked on, then when that big bouquet arrived at work – and it would be today – for flaming Tash…

BRENDAN. Tiff –

BARBS. Tiff or Tash, whoever… Anyway, I was disappointed I have to admit it, but, see, when yon bloody birthday strippergram arrived, Christ I could've seen *him* far enough.

BRENDAN. I thought he was quite cute.

BARBS. I know you did. Capone-o-gram! Capone-O-Gram. My bloody mother. That *Full Monty*'s got a lot to answer for I'll tell you… 'Parently he's a boy Binnie, brought up a Plymouth Brethren but got elbowed out the fold when he set up as a strippergram. Originally under the Enterprise allowance scheme according to my bloody mother. Who got suckered into clubbing together with Mina next door on his 'This Month Special Offer Two for the Price of One'. Uh-huh.

Mina sent her Auld Mammy a birthday Tarzanogram up at the Eastern Star Whist Drive. Brought the house down. Poor guy was lucky to get out alive.

BRENDAN. Well, he does have a tasty torso. As we all saw. I was like ooyah! Get that waashed and brung round to my Winnebago.

BARBS. Don't! I was in the middle of Carol Smillie's lowlights, I could have Saint Valentine's Day *Massacred* the bugger… Talk about a right rid neck…

BRENDAN. Ach lighten up.

BARBS. Don't you start.

BARBS. Plus – what a day – there would have to be yon 'Mother of the Bride' that I was in the same class as in primary school. As she would keep flaming reminding me.

BRENDAN. You're joking! She was ancient.

BARBS. Same age as me.

BRENDAN. Nah! Her that got the Bergen Beige Blonde foils and the graduated bob? That Big Fat Wan? Wi the face like a burst tomatta? Her that was the spitting image of Rab C. Nesbitt? I had to bite my tongue no to say to her: See you and Rab C? Youse could be *sisters*.

BARBS. Well, her and me could be twins. 'Cept I'm six month older than her.

BRENDAN. Get tae!

BARBS. Brendan, do I look as old as her?

BRENDAN. I'm no even gonny answer that.

A beat or two.

BARBS. I lied to my mother.

BRENDAN. Oh-wah! What about, Barbsie?

BARBS. I do. I do know what I want to do next. I want to have a baby.

BRENDAN. You asking?

BARBS. You dancing?

BRENDAN *has caught up. Is silenced. Looks away.* BARBS *wanders, picks up her wedding photograph. Puts it down.*

What's the matter with me? I should be divorced. This should be put away in a drawer.

BRENDAN *comes over, takes it off her, looks at it, looks at her, puts it back down on the table.*

BRENDAN. Nice. It's a nice photy, Barbs. Of both y you… Apart fae the His'n'Her matching feather haircuts. Fucksake…

But BARBS *is unreachable. To herself –*

BARBS. When I was nineteen I married Davie. Nineteen. Christ, I couldnae even walk right in high heels…

BRENDAN. I like Davie.

BARBS. I like Davie. Liking him isny the problem. I married him to get away from my mammy. Plus I fancied myself entering my twenties as a grown-up married lady…

When I was twenty-nine I left Davie. Well, I fancied myself entering my thirties as a swinging single career woman unencumbered by an ageing hippy that couldn't seem to grasp that this was the nineteen-freaking-eighties.

And now I'm thirty-nine…

BRENDAN *looks away from her. Nodding.*

I do. I want to have a baby.

Silence. They are not looking at each other. BRENDAN *nods again.*

I mean my biological clock –

BRENDAN. I ken, Germaine…

BARBS. I never used to. Do you remember that advert in the pictures? For hot dogs? 'An hour from now you'll wish you'd had one.' I used to think, that'll be me, one day I'll wake up old and grey and childless and I'll wish I'd had one, but –

BRENDAN. You… wereny hungry?

BARBS. Nope. But see now? All of a sudden… I'm ravenous!

I want a baby. But who with, that is the question?

BRENDAN. How about that guy from the Citizens Theatre?

BARBS. Brendan, he was more interested in cheap haircuts than sex.

BRENDAN. Well, there's Handsome we met in the lift yon time. He was all over you.

BARBS. Howard? He's flitted –

BRENDAN. – That's a sin, cos –

BARBS. – And, please. I really would have to have been helluva desperate to have shagged Howard.

BRENDAN. I'd shag him.

BARBS. You'd shag anything.

BRENDAN. Please. That is very hurtful. I'm gonna turn over a new leaf and find myself a deep and meaningful.

BARBS. Hah.

BRENDAN. You wait and see. Anyway you were talking about a sperminator. Shouldn't be difficult. What's the problem? You could just ask somebody –

BARBS. Brendan, I *am* asking.

BRENDAN. Oh.

BARBS. Listen, Brendan, do not assume – necessarily – that I want – necessarily – to have the baby the old-fashioned way where the father is present at the conception.

BRENDAN. Oh, you mod-ren girls…!

BARBS. I mean all I absolutely need is a well-timed syringeful of spunk that I can keep warm in a jar up my jumper until I get the chance to skoosh it up. (*Beat.*) Cool!

BRENDAN. What?

BARBS. I don't want to keep it *warm* up my jumper, sorry, I want to keep it cool, don't I? Cold. In my knickers presumably. (*Beat.*) Brendan, it is basically just like being a blood donor.

BRENDAN. Barbs, it is not 'just like being a blood donor'.

BARBS. I'd buy you the magazine!

BRENDAN. Hah!

BARBS. Just… don't reject it out of hand.

BRENDAN. 'Overheard at a party!' (*Beat.*) Sorry.

BARBS. No, Brendan, I'm sorry…

BRENDAN. No, don't be sorry… I'll… think about it. I will think about it, but I don't think I'll think about it very seriously. (*Beat.*) Sorry…

BARBS. That is quite okay.

BRENDAN. Sure?

BARBS. Yup.

Anyway, dear heart, excuse me, but I have to go to bed now. because I am bushed. Pished and bushed.

BRENDAN. Oh, that's okay. Because I've got a date.

BARBS. So late? A date? *Who* with?

BRENDAN. Oh God. You'll never guess!

BARBS. Fuck, I don't know. Richard Gere. My Davie. *Tell* me.

BRENDAN. Guess!

BARBS. I can't. (*Beat.*) Oh yes I can. I'm getting pinstripe suit… I'm getting fedora… black-and-white-two-tone correspondent shoes… I'm getting a bulging posing pouch… (*Laughing.*) My fucking mother's strippergram. For me! For me you bugger! Bren-dan, Brendan, Brendan!… What's his name?

BRENDAN. Cammy…

BARBS. As in – *knicker?*

BRENDAN. Naw as in *Cameron*. Cameron Binnie. A *Prodd*estant I hud presumed, but you know me, I'm no fussy, I've tried all creeds and colours, the hale gammy…

BARBS. How did this come about?

BRENDAN. Well, you know how you hunted him?

BARBS. I sure did. Carol fucking Smillie laughing up her sleeve at me!

BRENDAN. Well, he came back. While you were out for lunch. Looking for his kipper tie. Plus in the kerfuffle he'd lost wan of the knobs aff his tommy gun. We got chatt'n. This and that. Blah blah. And blabbity… So, eh, it's an ill wind.

BARBS. Aye, that blaws nae cunt fuck all good.

She is laughing and shooing him out the door.

En-joy.

BRENDAN. Sleep tight.

BRENDAN *turns to go. Whirls back in to close to* BARBS.

Well, what do I know, it isny my biological clock, but, haw, Barbs, are you not panicking far too early? I mean, my Auntie Sybill had a wean at fifty-four, didny even know she was expecting, thought it was a bad plate of wulks on the *Maid of the Loch*, but it wisny.

BARBS. And was the baby all right?

BRENDAN. Christ no! Fact he was a congenital every-syndrome-in-the-medical-dictionary, wee Freddie…

BRENDAN *perks up.*

But he might not have been!

BARBS *is laughing.*

Fade to black.

Music bridge: Dr Hook's 'Who's Gonna Iron My Shirts? Who's Gonna Kiss Me Where It Hurts? (If Not You)'.

Scene Four

In BARBS*'s empty place it is intimately lit, an ice bucket has appeared on the table with a bottle of champagne sticking out of it. The telephone rings, answer machine kicks in.*

BARBS, *a Japanese kimono falling open over her seduction undies, sticks her head round the door to listen to who it is, then immediately she re-exits towards the bathroom without picking up when it's only her mother.*

SADIE*'s voice speaks out. Awkward, uncomfortable. Too loud.*

SADIE'S VOICE. Hello. Hello, this is Mrs Sadie Kirkwood leaving a message for Barbara Marshall…

Hello? Hello? Hello are you there? I hate this thing…
Eh, Barbara? Emm I was wondering… Mina's wee club is looking for speakers. They've a good speaker for next week, it's the home economics teacher up the high school doing food hygiene in the light of E. Coli, and the week after they thought they'd got old Mr Simpson that used to run the Co doing his slides of his safari up the Zambesi, but, here, he's been taken in for tests, so I volunteered you in as an emergency. Nothing complicated. Mibbe a makeover or a make-up demonstration. Anything. Celebrity gossip… The sort of thing you can do standing on your head, Barbara. Let me know if you canny manage it, okay?

During this last BARBS *has re-entered still in her kimono with her whole face covered in a white or pale-greenish face mask and has been advancing towards the machine, glaring murderously at it.*

A daft pause then an abrupt and weirdly formal –

Thank you!

It clicks off –

BARBS. Nae tother a baw! Christ, Mother, if you don't take the fucking shortbread biscuit…

BARBS *goes out to the kitchen, brings cutlery for two, napkins, lights candles, quite unconsciously singing away to herself (no conscious agenda, it's only the CD she's just been playing, that's all) the old Scott Walker classic, 'Make It Easy On Yourself… ' without ever quite completing the 'cos breakin' up is so hard to do' line. The ground-floor buzzer rings.*

Christ…

BARBS *looks at her watch in horror. Goes and presses intercom.*

Hello?

DAVIE (*over intercom*). It's me…

BARBS. Jesus, Davie, you're early.

The inside doorbell shrills, and, fastening the sash of the kimono round her and climbing on to some high silly mules, she opens the door to DAVIE MARSHALL, *forty-one, in a smart and stylish suit and holding a couple of old plastic carrier bags.*

Yonks early by the way!

DAVIE. That's nice, doll! No that much, we says seven, right.

BARBS. Half seven. It's ten to! Plus you're always *late*. I can depend on it…

DAVIE. Well, I've turned over a new leaf, doll, how are you? You're looking *pale*…

He finds this funny. BARBS *looks in the mirror, remembers her face mask. But is buggered if she's going to take it off early because he's here. It's only* DAVIE.

BARBS. Anyway, a drink. Now you're here. How are *you*? Davie, I wouldn't have recognised you. You look great.

BARBS *moves towards the wine in the ice bucket.*

DAVIE. Open this!

He hands her a parcel, hastily and shambolically wrapped in newspaper and a third-hand polythene poke.

She pulls out a junk-shop treasure of a framed blow-up of the classic kids' shoe ad of the fifties. Back view, a wee boy and girl walk off into the sunset…

BARBS. The Start-rite kids!

DAVIE. Don't smile, then. Your face'll crack!

BARBS. Thank you, Davie, you're a darling so you are… What's it in aid of?

DAVIE. Nothing. I just thought it was you. Go wi thon Bisto Kids thing – have you still got that up in the kitchen?

BARBS. Nuh.

DAVIE. Naw? Oh… Plus I brung you up some classic vinyl.

She removes an LP in a beat-up cover.

BARBS. The Lovin' Spoonful…?

DAVIE. You loved thame.

BARBS. Oh so I did…

DAVIE. Aye. You were into sixties retro by the seventies. Before your time so you were! Put it on.

BARBS. After.

DAVIE. Well, long time no see, eh? When did I last see you? Been ages, doll. I've phoned you several times. You're never ever in…

BARBS. I wouldn't say that.

DAVIE. I've left you messages several times, but did you phone me back…? Nuh…

BARBS. Anyway, when did you get the haircut?

DAVIE. Ach, it was time. I thought to myself I don't want to look like wan of they sad bastards. The auld baldy wans wi the scraggy wee ponytails…

BARBS. You look great, you really do. *Plus* the suit…

She picks out the bottle of champagne from the ice bucket, but just as she goes to untwist the wire –

DAVIE. Eh, doll, don't open that for me. You any mineral water or anything? Appletise? I mean obviously if you want it –

BARBS. You not drinking?

DAVIE. I'm not, no…

BARBS. Wow. Anything you should tell me?

DAVIE. No really. Nuh.

She shrugs and puts the bottle unopened back into the bucket. As she exits kitchen-ward –

BARBS. Mineral water it is. It'll do me good a night on the wagon an all.

DAVIE. Anyway, my big sister was telling me she was round, you done her hair for her?

BARBS *reappears with an almost empty plastic bottle of Highland Spring and pours it into the two wine glasses.*

BARBS. You've seen her?

DAVIE. I have yes…

BARBS. This is flat… Ach, it's likely too flat, Davie, I'm sorry…

DAVIE. How did you think she was?

BARBS. Did she, eh, tell you? –

DAVIE. Aye, she did, yeah… What did you think?

BARBS*'s face says she was gobsmacked. She shakes her head.*

BARBS. I mean, how could she have kept that a secret for all these years…? I mean it was a secret? You never ever mentioned anything about it…

DAVIE. I knew nothing. Nothing at all. Although looking back… I was only, what? Fourteen year aul at the time but I mind Alice was 'working away from home', that was the story.

See when you saw her? What did you think?

BARBS. What did you think yourself… ?

DAVIE. I think that cunt's at it!

BARBS. The boy? But she was really –

DAVIE. Some boy. He's a grown man. Just swanning back into her life after – whit – twenty-five year because he's 'curious about his roots'? Never mind what kind of a havoc – do you know she's *told* Tommy by the way, and introduced him to him. *And* the girls…

BARBS. Surely Tommy knew?

DAVIE. Oh, course he *knew*. Haw, how do you think Noelene and Andrea felt all of a sudden having this half-brother they'd never even heard of?

BARBS. Did you ask them?

DAVIE. No.

BARBS. Did you ask Alice?

DAVIE. She said they were delighted.

BARBS. Well then…

DAVIE. Did she tell you whose wean it was?

BARBS. She did, yes...

Very forcefully –

DAVIE. The worst badyin in the whole scheme, Hannegan. Why on earth would she –

BARBS. But, Davie, he was very handsome. Very clever and all. It takes brains to be a villain, and he was very charming with it. Could be... when he wanted to...

DAVIE. Well, he came to a very sticky end anyway.

BARBS. I wonder how Alice's boy felt to hear all that?

DAVIE. Well, I hope he was satisfied.

BARBS. Have you met him yet?

DAVIE. No. No and I don't want to.

BARBS. Davie, Alice is absolutely over the moon!

He remains unconvinced.

DAVIE. Anyway, I wanted to tell you my big news. When last was I in touch with you? –

BARBS. My birthday.

DAVIE. So it was, so it was, doll. Hey, did you like your record?

BARBS. What? That request? God that DJ! Yuch. All that slush about 'it was twenty years ago today that Barbara and Davie walked down the aisle, she was only a teenager at the time and that boy wasn't a whole lot older, but that boy and that girl they couldn't have loved each other more'...

DAVIE. I thought you'd like it. It was anonymous, the 'Mystic Memories' slot – only you and me knew what it was about, Barbra...

BARBS. Christ.

DAVIE. I thought you'd be pleased.

BARBS. 'There's been a lot of water under the bridge, *he's* had other relationships' – yeah, not fucking half, starting from a year after the wedding when you were never off the road with those ginks in that band –

DAVIE. We nearly made it. (*Pause.*) We came that close to getting the record deal.

BARBS. – '*She's* had other relationships.' – Yeah, but not till after we split up!

DAVIE. That's what split us up. That 'affair' you had. Coming to me and telling me you were 'having an affair'... I never had an affair. The girls in the van after the gigs were not an affair...

BARBS. 'But he wanted me to tell Barbara: happy birthday and to remember that in all his life there'll only ever be one you.'

I was choked, Davie. It got to me, I must admit. Tell you, I was stood there in my kitchen, my thirty-ninth birthday, bawling my eyes out. I was looking down into the depths of my fruitbowl, where there lurked in the bottom the classic and oh-so-fucking-poignant still life of one leprous banana flanked with two shrivelled blue-furred balls that mibbe had once been... what... plums?... peaches?... some fucking Sweet Thing That Had Been Left To Rot...

Then on came the song you had requested for me: 'Here's Dr Hook and "If Not You"...'

DAVIE. Beautiful song, Barbs, you always loved it, doll. It was a toss-up between that and 'Hey, You Look Wonderful Tonight'...

He does the Eric Clapton number, air guitar and all, laughing at himself, and swings her round the floor. She counters with the words of the Dr Hook hit –

BARBS (*singing*). 'Who is going to water my plants?
Who is gonna *patch my pants*?'

DAVIE *keeps dancing her and laughing as he joins in.*

DAVIE (*singing*). 'And who is gonna give me the chance
To feel brand new... '

BARBS (*singing*). 'Who is going to *iron my shirts*?
Who's going to kiss where it hurts?
And who needs a man when he flirts – '

DAVIE (*singing*). ' – The way I do?'

BARBS (*singing*). 'Oo–oo if not you–oo... Oo if not you.'

(*Speaking.*) Well, I lifted out that poxetten brown banana, seized my biggest *Sabatier* and I sliced the fucker into three, just for badness, oh, it was long past the edible stage, and I tipped it into the waste-disposal unit and timmed the pair of plums in after and I whirred it all up and sent it all scooshing to oblivion shouting out at the radio: 'Well, I'll tell you, pal, it fucking won't be me!'

And now, Davie, you're going to tell me you've Met Someone…

DAVIE. I have. And I'm going to be a daddy!

BARBS. Oh. Oh. Congratulations.

DAVIE. I knew you'd be pleased for me!

BARBS. Course I am, Davie. Who is the lucky girl?

DAVIE. Her name is Colette…

BARBS. And she is twenty-three!

DAVIE. Twenty-two actually. I met her at the Arcade. She was at the Caledonian University, know, doing an interior-design degree and she came in looking to see what I had in Deco, because there's been a revival again, Bakelite's back. Well, I helped her with her degree show…

BARBS. You never wanted kids.

DAVIE. Neither did you.

BARBS. She better be nice.

DAVIE. Colette? Oh she's great. We're going to open a shop, get a wee business going, specialise in retro and good handmade one-offs. Colette's got a great eye…

BARBS. Oh, and you're going to be all right with the bank loan? Because I don't like to piss on your parade, Davie, but, I tell you, the banks at the moment are basically being bastards.

DAVIE. Oh, Colette's dad has got a right few bob, you know, and her grandmother left her a trust fund that she inherited, there, when she was twenty-one.

BARBS. Well… Congratulations, Davie, my darling, what can I say?

DAVIE. Say you're happy for us.

BARBS. I'm happy for you, Davie. Maybe it'll who knows happen for me someday, haha…

DAVIE. Course it will. *If* it's what you want. You've always – and I don't mean anything, nothing bar admiration, Barbs, by this – been totally brilliant at Getting What You Want.

BARBS. Oh good…

DAVIE. Because that lawyer guy –

Involuntarily –

BARBS. – Gordon?

DAVIE. Yes, that Gordon twat, him, couple of year back… you did not want *him*, he didn't deserve you.

BARBS. No? No, I did not want him. At least not while his wife was dying of cancer and he had that boy and girl to bring through it all, no, I did not want that on my conscience thank you very much, I was glad when we agreed we wouldn't see each other any more, fine, but I must admit it did hurt when he married the Macmillan nurse…

DAVIE. The guy was a tube.

BARBS. The guy was a tube. Who broke my heart. But never mind, time is a great healer et cetera et cetera. At the ratio, I find, of *minimum* two years' agony and suffering for one of true love and happiness, but I've done my time, I'm over Gordon.

I no longer love him…

Anyway I don't think, these days, it is a man I want.

DAVIE. No! Hey, you don't mean –

BARBS. No I don't mean! No. Actually what I was planning was to wine you and dine you and seduce you and persuade you we should try again.

DAVIE. You're kidding.

BARBS. Yeah, I'm kidding.

BARBS *takes her first swig of the water. Gets up abruptly.*

Jesus, Davie, this is flat as piss. I'm going to throw it out.

BARBS *disappears swiftly offstage kitchen-side with the plastic bottle and both glasses.* DAVIE *sits back, swivels his neck, gets up, begins to wander round trying – in vain – to see the right place to hang the Start-rite kids. He admits it to himself, calling out to offstage* BARBS –

DAVIE. This is wrong.

He shakes his head. Takes it off the other side – bedroom-ward, bathroom-ward.

BARBS (*offstage*). What…?

DAVIE *backs back on without the Start-rite poster. He looks as if at a distance to where he's propped it. Decides it's probably not right there either.*

DAVIE. I says, I don't think it's gonny fit in, doll.

BARBS. Overheard at a party!

DAVIE. Acht!

DAVIE *is not very keen on camp* BRENDAN-*style remarks. He gives up on the poster too, leaving it there offstage. He goes and looks in towards her in the kitchen, smells the cooking, looks back towards the cutlery set out on the table by the unopened bottle in its bucket. The penny finally dropping.*

Barbs, haw, what you doing?

BARBS *re-enters, barefaced, shiny and pink.*

BARBS. Nothing. It was just time I washed off that mask, that's all.

DAVIE. I didny eh realise you'd be cooking…

BARBS. Marks & Spencers did.

DAVIE. Only… what I was hoping… well, I wanted to take you out… you know… a wee bite… and meet Colette.

BARBS. Bring her up!

DAVIE. Don't be daft, no, I was going to take you – she's dying to meet you.

BARBS. And me her. Go get her.

DAVIE. Well, I said I'd meet her down… you know that Bar Bargo? Half-sevenish…

BARBS. Well, go go go.

And, eh, give me half an hour, eh? To put my face and the rest of my clothes on. While I work out some creative way of splitting two chicken breasts stuffed with mushroom in wine sauce into three!

DAVIE. C'mere…

He gives her a hug. She pushes him away.

BARBS. Go on!

DAVIE *goes. Looking behind him… she's managing to smile. Till he gets out the door at least. Then she's alone with her feelings.*

BARBS *goes to the CD player, puts on Scott Walker's 'No Regrets' then briskly goes to the table, picks up the champagne, ice bucket and cutlery, dumps it unceremoniously through in the kitchen. She picks up the wedding photograph, glances at it once and takes it off bedroom/bathroom-wards, comes back immediately with her make-up bag. All the while singing along with Scott W. On 'No tears goodbye, I don't want you back, we'd only cry again', she sits down on the sofa, picks up her make-up bag and begins to paint a bright-red mouth on her face.*

Black.

Music continues as bridge:

Scene Five

Lights come up on BARBS*'s empty loft apartment.*

Darkness. Night. Door opens and BARBS *enters talking. With* GRANT STEEL, *an extremely attractive young man in his early to mid-twenties, in tow. They are both nervous but both fancy themselves good at hiding it.*

She switches on lights. He looks around, appraising, taking it all in for, clearly, the very first time.

BARBS. – about eighteen months ago. Well, the flat I had, out west – it was a nice flat but I had outgrown it, basically, and I knew the architect that was developing this building… and the idea of a *loft*, designing it by myself for myself, lots of space…

GRANT. Great! Wow! A bed platform I've always loved these.

She motions him towards the chair.

BARBS. Oh, that's just the guest sleep-space. Drinks…? I'll get you a drink. Grant. Sit down. Relax. What would you like?

He sits down considering the single chair then going for the sofa.

GRANT. What have you got?

BARBS *goes to the rather well-stocked drinks trolley and begins to rummage.*

BARBS. Everything. All the usual stuff. I mean, there's vodka, G and T, brandy, correction there's just *about* a cognac left in here. There is a very nice, well, I don't myself, but my husband says this is a very good malt?

GRANT. You're, eh, married then?

BARBS. Separated. Amicably. He's my best friend. One of my best friends.

GRANT. Do you have maybe a beer?

BARBS. Sure… I think I've got a couple in the fridge.

She goes to the kitchen to fetch it. He gets up and wanders around, even climbs a step or two of the loft-bed steps.

GRANT. Wicked place this…!

BARBS *re-enters with a beer by the neck, goes towards him.*

BARBS. Thank you… Glass?

GRANT. Bottle.

Seizing all of same, he takes it and pulls her towards him with the other arm and kisses her full on the mouth. She stands back amazed.

BARBS. I'm sorry… I think you've got the wrong idea…

GRANT. Listen, I should go.

BARBS. No. No. Sit down. Grant. Please…

GRANT. I'm sorry… I just… well, when you asked me up here for a drink –

BARBS. I said for a drink, not 'for coffee'!

GRANT. I apologise. I was way out of line there. Wires crossed.

BARBS. Please. Have a drink. Grant. Relax… I'm going to.

Silence. They both drink. An awkward silence. He tries to backtrack.

GRANT. Fantastic space! It must be great to be downtown like this, near all the clubs… Merchant City, eh?

BARBS. Merchant City! As my auld mammy calls it, the Back o Goldbergs.

He looks puzzled.

BARBS, *more rattled than she'd like to let on, starts rabbiting.*

Sorry, course you don't know what I'm talking about, you didn't grow up in Glasgow plus you're too young anyway, but Goldbergs, just round the block there, Goldbergs was this big warehouse where you had to get a line for it, you know, you paid things up? Provident cheques, I believe. My mother was a widow so she paid up everything. My brother and I used to get brought into the town twice a year, given a shot up and down the escalator in Lewis's, and taken into Goldbergs – July sales and January – to get kitted out wi school clothes a size too big for us that we'd grow in to.

Once they were worn out.

Goldbergs! See Goldbergs, see glamorous! They had this pool, a pond, you know, like sunk in the ground sales floor with *goldfish* –

GRANT. Samuel Goldwyn's name was Goldfish!

BARBS. Eh…?

GRANT. Samuel Goldfish. Originally. Maybe Goldberg's real name was Goldfish, so –

You know, 'Include me out'…? 'Let's have some new clichés'…?

BARBS. Right! 'In two words – '

Their eyes meet.

BARBS *and* GRANT. 'Im-Possible!'

They smile. Then have to look away from each other. He clears his throat. Silence again.

BARBS. Have you been up here long?

Puzzled, he almost goes to look at his watch.

GRANT. Oh, you mean up in *Glasgow*? Ages. No, not long actually, I suppose. Not that long. Relatively.

I only came up to go to college. A post-graduate thing. Film and TV. But that was a bummer so I left. And I stayed.

BARBS. Right…

Silence. He swigs his beer.

Listen, Grant, when I met you in that bar last week…

GRANT. That wasn't your husband you were with then, was it?

BARBS. No, that was my friend Brendan. And that was his boyfriend Cammy…

GRANT. I thought so.

BARBS. Well, it must've looked like I was picking you up or something, I do realise that.

GRANT. And you definitely weren't.

I mean, you don't actually, do you, want me to do any modelling for those pictures for the salon?

BARBS. No – well, at least, I *do*. I think it would be really great if you did our photo session. I mean, I think you'd be great, perfect in fact, well, if you fancied it…? And it would be a bit of pin money –

GRANT. – which would be fine by me. I'm saving like mad at the moment. To go travelling. Which is why I'm working nights in that bar anyway.

BARBS. Well, great.

But, you're right. It was… a pretext so that I could get – Grant, when I asked you if you would meet me briefly, tonight, for a quick drink, there was something else I wanted to talk to you about. In private. And, och, I suppose it was daft of me to think I could just meet you quietly across the road for a quick cappuccino –

GRANT. That bloody woman was all over you like a rash, wasn't she? Who was she? Really seemed to think you'd changed her life –

BARBS. – Yup, where actually all I had done was cut off five inches of bad perm and tired highlights and pluck her eyebrows. On TV though, so I suppose you can't blame her for being all obsessed with her five minutes of fame.

GRANT. Sorry?

BARBS. It's just this silly *Morningtime* television thing, it's quite camp actually, that they've decided to make out of Glasgow. Seeing as we're your regional style capital of Europe.

GRANT. Are you?

BARBS. Are we buggery, it's all a lot of bollox but am I complaining? Except when, like tonight, I'm trying to have a private conversation… So, I invited you up here. There was something I wanted to ask you…

GRANT. Ask away…

BARBS. No. Forget it. Just let's have a quiet drink… (*Beat.*)

So you're off round the world then as soon as you get the money together.

GRANT *nods.*

GRANT. Soon as poss…

BARBS. Great! I mean, travel. Fantastic. Wish I'd done that at your age. Another beer?

GRANT. I won't thanks.

BARBS *gives herself another slug of vodka.*

BARBS. Music…?

GRANT *shakes his head slowly, looks at her very directly.*

Silence.

GRANT. And there is, unfortunately, no chance you are after my body?

BARBS. No.

GRANT. Number-one fantasy bites the dust. Oh well. Cheers.

He takes a long and draining swig of his beer. Looks at her.

Shoot.

BARBS. I know your mother.

GRANT. You know my…? Oh, you mean you know *Alice*.

BARBS. Yes.

GRANT. And?

BARBS. And she was telling me you wanted to… cool the relationship.

GRANT. And this has exactly what to do with you?

BARBS. It is none of my business, no. But Alice is my friend. She and I, we go way back.

GRANT. And?

BARBS. She is heartbroken. Heart broken. Devastated.

GRANT. And who are you? I mean who exactly the fuck are you? To try to tell me –

He gets up and picks up his jacket, heads for the door. BARBS *gets between him and it.*

BARBS. She is my sister. In-law. I married her brother. But that's irrelevant. Look, she doesn't know anything about me talking to you like this. She would go apeshit. Don't you dare tell her I invited you up here!

GRANT. You are a bit of an interfering old cow, aren't you?

BARBS. Yes, I am. Yes.

Look, Grant, I knew nothing about your existence till a couple of months ago. She just… all these years. Said nothing.

But, if you had heard how happy she was that you'd tracked her down… She was ecstatic.

Then last week she turns up at the aerobics in bits.

Well, couple of nights later, I'm in that club with Brendan and Cammy and I spy you behind the bar –

GRANT. How did you know who I was?

BARBS. I saw you together. You and Alice. It must've been your first meeting.

GRANT. You what?

BARBS. Saw you. Having lunch.

GRANT. What the fuck was going on? You mean she brought you along to give me the once over from behind the pillars or what?

BARBS. No, no nothing like –

GRANT. This makes me feel… spied on, actually. Look, I am out of here –

BARBS. No. Don't go, please. Not yet. I mean, think about it from her point of view… Alice. She gets pregnant. At the age of seventeen. These were very different days then, Grant, you probably wouldn't believe how different…

GRANT. Had she never heard of the pill?

BARBS. Oh, yes, I expect she had! The swinging sixties, all that stuff, they were past and gone already, I expect she'd read the *Honey* magazine with all the rest of us.

Anyway, she had you, had you adopted and you've had a nice life, haven't you?

GRANT. So-so.

BARBS. Legally it is up to the adopted child to get in touch isn't it?

So it was up to you.

Alice said your eighteenth birthday went past, the nineteenth, twentieth…

GRANT. I am nearly twenty-six.

BARBS. So what made you do it now?

GRANT. I don't know… I… wanted to know. (*Beat.*) Did you know my father?

BARBS. I did, actually… Though I never knew Alice went out with him.

GRANT. They tell me he was a right evil bastard.

BARBS. Well, I don't know that I'd say evil…

GRANT. Stabbed to death in a prison brawl in Barlinnie in 1981. That is quite a thing to find out about your biological parent.

BARBS. I expect it is…

GRANT. What was he like?

BARBS. Physically… he looked a lot like you, Hannegan. He was very handsome. Famously so, round our scheme.

GRANT. Did you go out with him?

A beat –

BARBS. No.

Alice and he were never an item either. Not openly. Not really. She says when he found out she was pregnant he just did not want to know…

GRANT. Bastard, eh?

BARBS. And now, you turn up, the spitting image of him, and then you say you don't want to see her any more.

GRANT. Listen, Barbara… I've got a mum and dad.

I always knew I had been adopted. 'We chose you because we loved you.' All that.

I didn't say anything to them about looking for my natural parents. I don't know why. I didn't know if I'd get anywhere anyway…

Finding Alice, well, it was curiosity. A curiosity satisfied.

And I *liked* her. You couldn't not. I mean, I think my own mother would like her actually…

But when I told my mum about tracking down Alice… Well, I felt disloyal, that's what I felt…

BARBS. And you feel no need to continue the contact?

GRANT. I'd like to… keep in touch.

BARBS. You mean in a Christmas-card sort of a way?

GRANT. Yeah. Why not. Yeah.

Take all this… extended-family stuff. I can't handle it. Well, Alice has a husband. Fair enough. Great. And daughters. They are my half-sisters. By blood anyway. But what I felt about them… well, they're lovely girls, yeah, but I didn't feel as if I could feel what I felt I was expected to feel.

Which made me feel really shitty.

It was… too much…

What got to me was this business of Noelene's eighteenth birthday party. *I* don't want to go. Noelene certainly doesn't want me to go…

So I thought… as I am leaving anyway, soon – I told you I am planning on going to Australia, New Zealand, Japan –

BARBS. But why cut off like that? Break things… I mean, if you are leaving anyway, can't you just let it cool down naturally?

Grant, Alice doesn't want anything of you.

GRANT. No? She wants me to be her son. You see the big problem is: to Alice I'm her son. But to me she's not my mother.

BARBS. I will give you some money for your travel fund if you just don't do this to Alice.

He looks long and hard at her as if she is dirt, turns and leaves. The door shuts with a slam behind him.

BARBS *sits on the sofa deeply troubled. Silence. No music.*

Fade to black.

End of Act One.

ACT TWO

Scene One

BRENDAN, *alone in* BARBS*'s living room, is looking at an old 'Anniversary of Death of Diana' issue of* HELLO!, *or something similar. Facing the audience is a big enough picture of the princess to register loud and clear. He turns a page and sighs.*

BRENDAN. Totally tragic… And jist when she'd finally got her hair lukkin haulfwey decent as well…

BARBS *comes from the kitchen, hands him a glass of red wine.*

BARBS. So what did you think of her?

BRENDAN. – Who? Davie's Colette? She seemed nice enough, aye!

BARBS *sweeps back into the kitchen.*

I thought to myself, well, Teenie-fae-Troon, you're no feart, putting yourself into my hands, swanning in here to Razor City without an appointment. I thought, see if Barbs had any *agenda*, or see if she was afflicted with a vindictive nature, she'd give you Tash and a month of bad-herr days…

All I done actually, boss, was to do a deep conditioning and just take the very ends off because she's growing out a Rachel…

Bonny-lookin lassie… Pleasant to talk to… A bit kinna… Kilmal*colm*.

The question is: what does she see in Davie?

I mean, yous vanilla breeders, eh? Whit like urr ye? A closed book tae me…

Smells great. Spicy, eh? Cammy will be pleased. More Tastier Snax Later… Marinade me…

Want any help?

BARBS *calls from kitchen.*

BARBS. Nope!

BRENDAN. Okay, I'll put oan some music. If I can find anything. Your taste is in your arse, no your ears!

He begins to look through a pile of old vinyl, holding up a vintage Sinatra, a Nat King Cole, not fancying any of it. He continues calling out to her offstage –

Anyway what I really wanted to tell you – and I have talked it over with Cammy, because, obviously, he's my partner, right? It affects him if I decide to take on a parenting role...

Well, I've not said anything up till now, well, obviously I've thought a lot about it ever since your birthday, ever since that night you asked us –

And yes... well, when it came down to it... Ach, Barbsie, I don't want you to think I was one of those Big-Void-In-My-Life Queens with the strong maternal instinct girning on about their secret sadness. Because I don't honestly think I was.

BARBS *enters, her eyes like saucers. Stands there.*

But I thought to myself: yes I would like to have a baby.

Correction, I'd like to have Barbs's baby. If – and only if – I can have a continuing... presence... in that baby's life. A connection. Commitment. Of some sort.

So Cammy's attitude was: it's up to me.

Well I know I've been a while getting back to you on this one, but obviously I had to have an AIDS test – oh, I can see it on your face, you never thought of that, did you, Barbs, you never thought it through, you just came out with it and asked me, the question expecting the answer No... I had to have the Test. And Cammy had to have the Test.

It is a thought to do it. Because obviously the best way to live your life is to assume you're not but everybody else could be, so practise safe sex anyway. And I have been practising. I'm even getting quite good at it... But anyway me 'n' Cammy, we decided: this is the Start of Our Relationship, it's *serious* we want this to work out, we'll both go and Get Tested.

Well obviously it takes a wee while. For the results. And to be sure...

But it was fine. We are both free from HIV.

So do you know what this is? Correct. Useful Utensil Number Sixty-Nine. A. Turkey. Baster. (Naw, I'd never seen wan either I'd *wondered* what like it was.) This mother is meant to put that magic elixir, that 10cc, that lovin' spoonful up therr wherr the sun don't shine…

Listen, Barbs Marshall, hey, don't you dare kid on that night you were only kidding on because you wereny, I know you wereny. Say yes. 'Yes I would like us to try for a baby.' Say it!

BARBS *opens her mouth and shuts it again. She rushes into his arms. They embrace.*

Black.

Music bridge. Billy Swan's 'I Can Help'.

Scene Two

One single exciting, eye-catching and beautiful designer Christmas decoration, perhaps fairy-lit, on the table tells the audience it's coming on Christmas.

BARBS *is lying on the floor with her legs up.* BRENDAN *sits on the couch, painting her toenails with nail varnish.*

BRENDAN. How long do you have to keep your feet up?

BARBS. Lot longer than it'll take that to dry anyway.

BRENDAN. Wonder if it'll work this time?

BARBS. Time will tell…

BRENDAN. How do you feel?

BARBS. Pregnant.

BRENDAN. Do you?

BARBS. No. Not yet. Did you wash out the middleman?

BRENDAN. Sappled it through in warm soapy watter, dried it aff, and put it by in your bathroom cabinet for the next shot.

BARBS. Brendan, this might take a wee while to work. I mean your auld Auntie Barbara isny as young as she used to be.

BRENDAN. By the way, this nail varnish is gonny take three coats an' all…

BARBS. At this point in time, Brendan, if we have done it right, there are more than two hundred million motile sperm currently swimming up my fanny towards The One And Only out of my dwindling supply of my somewhat elderly eggs which has hopefully ripened, travelled along the clagged-up old fallopian plumbing and got itself into position for the moon-shot. I mean two hundred million. Constantly replenishing themselves. To one. Out of a finite number that were there since before the day I was born female.

Two hundred million. To one. That's not equal. How can we say men and women are the same or ever could be?

I mean, Brendan, *you*, you bastard, are – and this is you till you're ninety – just sitting there manufacturing more sperm to replace the two hundred million you just flang away.

BRENDAN. Huv you been reading books again? Actually I didny find it aw that easy to manage my Wee Fling to tell you the truth…

BARBS. How come?

BRENDAN. That was the question…! Och, I'm shy, Hairy Melon, I'm shy…

BARBS. Canny get aff in a lassie's bedroom, is that the trouble?

BRENDAN. Nor in thon designer bathroom of yours neither without giving myself a severe talking-to. And normally I've only got to smell the *paper* of Farm Boys in Gingham and that's me. Faster than shite aff a shovel. Tellin' you, Barbsie, if it's all the same with you – *if* we've got to try again next month – I'll produce it at home and bring it round like we did last month, okay?

BARBS. 'S up to yourself… Enlist the help of Cammy for all I care. Just as long as you hotfoot it round here with the product…

BRENDAN. When will you know?

BARBS. I'll keep you posted. (*Beat.*) Away down and get us both some Häagen-Dazs, go an', it's *ER* night. The deli downstairs is still open, you'll just catch it. Take my keys, they're on the table, I'm no about to get up and open the door to you, am I?

BRENDAN. Don't say I'm not – extremely – good to you.

The phone rings. And rings.

BARBS. Shit, the machine's not on. Give us it over.

BRENDAN. Belgian Chocolate?

She lifts the receiver.

BARBS. Hello? Hello, stranger! (*To* BRENDAN.) Cookie Dough!

BRENDAN *leaves waving keys.*

No, I was talking to somebody else… It's okay he's just going. Well, well, wee bro, how's things?

She listens swivelling her ankles and surveying her bonny red toenails.

Me? Oh fine and dandy, right now. Totally… laid back.

Well, of course we're busy, yeah, right through Christmas up till the New Year. All go.

Ninety what? I don't want to hear it. Here it's the dreich, dark, days of Glesca in December, remember?

Mm-hm. Mm-hm. Oh Ma is fine. She is the same as ever. She's indestructible. Indefensible most of the time, but och aye, just the same. She's taken up aromatherapy, her and Mina. Up the community centre. Had to shell out a fortune for her basic kit so here's hoping she sticks in at it.

Last Thursday, yup same as ever. Shake-'n'-vac'd the shagpile then advanced on my pressure points with neroli oil and lavender. Set my teeth on edge and all my nerve ends a-jangle but then that's likely just me…

The downstairs buzzer goes. She covers the receiver.

Come in, Brendan, you daft bastard you've got the keys! (*Back to Billy and the phone call.*) Sorry. Christmas? Ma's. I did ask her here, but no joy. It is the duty of every singleton, divorcée and sadfuck to pack their fluffy pyjamas and allow themselves to be sucked back into the bosom of the parental home for a three-day torporfest.

Listens. A smile begins to spread across her face.

You're on! She would come, she would, if I came too. Why not? Next Christmas. Yes! Australia! Christmas Day on a beach for once in my life. This time next year…

She looks down at her hands cupping her flat belly. Crosses fingers.

Who knows…? We'll *all* come… I'll just book the tickets and surprise her. Yeah… We'll do it. Let Ma spend some perfect time with all her grandchildren…

The door opens and SADIE *enters with her key and a shopping bag and a plastic bag too.*

BARBS *is of course unable to see who has come in –*

Hi, Brendan!

SADIE. What you daen, Barbara, I rang the buzzer but nae answer…

BARBS. Mum! I'm just on the phone to our Billy. Do you want a wee word…?

SADIE. No thanks. I spoke to him last night. Tell him no to waste money on the phone.

BARBS. Billy, I'll phone you back later, Bills, all right? Time is it there anyway? Okay.

She hangs up.

SADIE. What the hell are you daen lying on your back like that. Have you slipped a disc?

BARBS. No.

SADIE. Well, get up, you dizzy article, the back of your jumper will get aw oose.

BARBS *gets up.*

BARBS. Ma, what are you doing here?

From out of the plastic bag, SADIE *sets a light up novelty talking Christmas tree on the table. Shoving* BARBS*'s decor aside.*

SADIE. Look what they were selling in Argyle Street, I was in doing ma late-night Christmas shopping. Cheery intit? I thought to myself oor Barbs does a lot of enter*tain*ing…

The tree winks and blinks and says 'Merry Christmas, ho ho ho'.

BARBS *looks at it, amazed.* SADIE *with delighted triumph.*

Well, I wisny going to humph it all the way home on the bus and humph it all the way back in here on Thursday. I thought to myself I'll pop up.

BARBS. And you're very welcome. My pal Brendan – you remember Brendan?

SADIE. Aye, him that's right yon wey? Nice enough laddie…

BARBS. He's great! Well, he'll be back up in a minute. He's away for ice cream. The three of us could have a bowl of ice cream and watch the telly together. *ER*'s on later. You know, with Him You Like? Away through and get three bowls and some spoons…

SADIE *exits kitchen-ward,* BARBS *following her.*

BRENDAN *enters with his key and two tubs of Häagen-Dazs. Shouting loudly as he comes in.*

BRENDAN. Pralines and Cream and Belgian Chocolate. Quickie-quick because that George Clooney is *such* a shag!

BARBS *shoots out of the kitchen pantomiming frantically for him to shut up.*

What the fuck are you doing on your pins, missus, because you'll be *spilling*!

Behind him SADIE *re-enters with bowls and spoons.* BRENDAN*'s attention is fixated on the talking Christmas tree.*

Knock ma pan in wanking out hard-won spunk for you to just let scale down your silken thighs and go to w– what the *fuck* is that?

BARBS. It's a present. From my mum here.

SADIE. Hello, Brendan.

BRENDAN. Mrs Kirkwood! Sadie…!

BARBS. Mum, siddown…

SADIE. I think I'll maybe better get up the road…

BARBS. Not at all, Mother, sit down, please.

SADIE. I'll see you Thursday, pet, same as usual…

BARBS. Mother, Brendan and I have Just Been Making Babies.

SADIE *looks from one to the other astonished. Appalled.*

BRENDAN. Yes, well, time for a quick-sharp exit…

BRENDAN *goes and gets his jacket from the peg.*

BARBS. Hopefully. We hope to get me pregnant. Don't we, Brendan?

BRENDAN. Barbs, I think you and your ma need a wee –

BARBS. Sit down, Brendan. Sit down, Mother.

SADIE. You're only doing this to upset me!

BARBS *laughs.*

BARBS. Ha! No – and I do go to great lengths for you, Mother, granted – but strangely enough I'm doing this to make me happy.

SADIE. What about the child? And anyway what do you think children have to do with happiness?

BARBS. Ach, here we go!

SADIE. All you had to do was ask me!

BARBS. Ah yes. And I know what you'd've said. 'I was a widow by the time I was thirty' –

SADIE. I was. And you and Billy had my heart roasted.

BARBS. Mother, you don't mean that.

SADIE. By God and I do. Disgusting! That's what it is. He's a bloody homosexual! You can't –

BRENDAN. It isny hereditary, Mrs Kirkwood. Obviously. Work it out. I mean, think about it.

Sadie, eh, we didn't actually –

BARBS. That is none of her business!

SADIE. With a test tube! That's hellish! It's perverted! Plus AIDS. Think of that.

BARBS. Ah, Brendan, we are talking to the biggest bigot in the west here. You are in the presence of the woman who went in the huff, went *in the huff* with our dog Trooper when she caught him humping Blackie, Mrs Bain's big butch labrador up Hinshelwood Quadrant. In the huff. With a dug!

SADIE. No harm to you, Brendan, but to me it's not and never will be natural.

BRENDAN. Listen, I'm away, Barbara. You and your ma have some talking to do. In private.

BARBS. Don't you dare go anywhere!

BRENDAN. Barbs, darlin', you want me phone me later. Night, Mrs Kirkwood, nice Christmas and, eh, All the Best When It Comes...

BRENDAN *exits, depositing* BARB*'s keys on the table.*

SADIE. You just don't know what to be at!

BARBS. On the contrary I have never actually been so one hundred per cent clear about what I want.

SADIE. Stupid. You think you are so bloody smart but you do not have a clue. Dream world, that's what you live in. Selfish. Selfish to the core. Think it is a joke to bring up a child on your own?

BARBS. No. No I don't. You did it. You did it well. For two of us. We turned out all right, me and our Billy.

SADIE *makes a noise of disgust and scorn.*

Say it. Say we turned out okay. Say it!

SADIE. I don't know you. Either of the bloody two of you.

BARBS. You did it. You did it all by yourself!

SADIE. And what choice did I have? Do you think I'd have chosen that for my life?

And you want to *deliberately*... Ach!

Well, I will tell you one thing, I won't be up here babysitting, bailing you out, the same as I've done with everything else.

Once the novelty wears off and you want your life back and your freedom back don't think I'll be here watching it and loving it and helping you out because I won't.

BARBS. Mum, I am nearly forty. Mum, my life is not your life. Mammy, please don't go in the huff.

SADIE *does. She goes, takes her present and leaves.* BARBS *is alone, distraught.*

The bell goes.

Thank Christ!

She throws open the door. To GRANT.

Oh!

GRANT. I've just been out with Alice. Having a drink.

BARBS. Oh.

GRANT. We talked and stuff. I just thought you'd want to know. I mean I was pissed off at the time. But I thought, later, you know… About what you said. I mean, you're right, she's not nothing to me. I thought I should tell you. The outside door was open. Sorry, I should have buzzed. Have I come at a bad time?

BARBS. Bad time, good time, who knows… Come on in anyway.

Black.

Music bridge: The Loving Spoonful's 'Darling Be Home Soon'.

Scene Three

It is Valentine's Day almost two months later.

On the table are a single red rose in a tall vase and a large card which is just a big red heart on silver.

Lights come up on BARBS *and* GRANT, *post-shower, she's in a huge white fluffy robe, he's in Calvin Klein underpants. She's on the sofa, he's on the floor, she's towelling his wet hair, he's reading to himself the sleeve notes on the album cover. It's that present* DAVIE *gave her months ago. The Lovin' Spoonful LP.*

The song ends and it clicks off.

GRANT. Hey listen to this! I love it!... 'The car radio suddenly burst into "Do You Believe in Magic" which is how I met The Lovin' Spoonful... First they were only a name and that great song so immediately touching, so perfect in its presence... Despite the song they had trouble believing in the magic of rock and roll When The Rock And Roll Was Them.'

Brilliant! Where do you get this stuff?

BARBS *swipes away the album cover.*

BARBS. Never mind. It's old!

GRANT. Can I have it?

BARBS. I'll make you a tape.

GRANT. Just a loan of?

BARBS. I'll tape it for you. With all the other golden oldies you're so keen on. You better hurry up, you're late for your work already.

GRANT. Maybe I won't go. It is Valentine's after all. Surely all the good-time people will be staying home tonight like what we did. Like what we do all the time, Barbarella.

BARBS. Don't start that again!

GRANT. Well, is there something wrong with wanting to go out with you? In Public. My flatmates don't believe you're real. C'mon, let your hair down, Rapunzel. Why can't we go to the movies – ?

BARBS. What's wrong with staying home with the Classic Video Collection.

GRANT. Nothing. You know I love the Classic Video Collection. *Schweet*heart.

BARBS. Well then. Away and work!

GRANT. Can I come up after I finish? I'll promise not to wake you.

BARBS. Hah!

GRANT. Well, there's a first time for everything...

BARBS. Hey! I wasn't complaining...

GRANT. I should think not.

BARBS. Not even a toty wee bit. Do you want a sandwich before you go?

GRANT. Here's yet another way I'm good for you! Before you met me your fridge was full of make-up. Now there's Real Food, bacon and bagels and everything –

BARBS. Well, you are a growing boy.

GRANT. – and yogurt with wheatgerm...

BARBS. – and I need all my strength to keep up with you, don't I?

They kiss.

GRANT. C'mere!

He takes her over to the bottom of the steps up to the loft bed.

Well, you know we've made love just about everywhere in this apartment? We've had the snogs on the sofa, the knee-tremblers in the shower and the table-enders in the kitchen, not to speak of all the lay-lady-lays across your big brass bed...

BARBS. So?

GRANT. One place we've never done it is up in the loft bed here. And I've always wanted to.

BARBS. So?

GRANT. We're going to. I'm going to put on this hippy music, and we'll smoke a joint and we'll make long slow summer of love hippy love...

BARBS. Hey, what age do you think I am? Oh God, Grant, I don't think I've smoked a joint since the Tories got into power...

GRANT *puts on the music. The sound of The Lovin' Spoonful fills the room again. This time it is 'Full Measure'.* GRANT *goes over to the couch and takes a packet of Rizlas and a tin out of his jeans pocket, singing and jiving away.*

One sec. Bathroom. One sec.

BARBS *disappears bathroom-wards and* GRANT *still dancing climbs up into the loft-bed space. He takes out a rolled joint, lights it, inhales. Looks down over the edge.* BARBS *reappears.* GRANT *throws those white underpants at her. She ducks then picks them up –*

GRANT. Hey, Marshall, get your gorgeous ass up here.

– And BARBS *clowns around flashing at him and dancing and singing along to the music.*

Suddenly the inside doorbell goes and the letter box is raised and rattled.

ALICE*'s eyes peek through. Very loudly –*

ALICE. Haw! Haw, Barbara, open the door will you? It's me. Alice.

BARBS. Christ!

BARBS *runs back to the wall by the door, flattens herself against it, panicking.* GRANT *leans over the loft signalling at her to ignore it. She crawls under the letter box on the door, trying ludicrously to keep out of sight and puts the music up louder. Crawls back, waving up at* GRANT *to stay there. It's a ridiculous routine only stopped by* ALICE *shouting through again.*

ALICE. I know you're there, open up?

BARBS *waves at* GRANT *to keep out of sight and, giving up, opens the door.* ALICE *comes in, invited or not.*

Christ, that music's deafening!

BARBS. Sorry…

BARBS *swiches off the music.*

ALICE. Are you… on your own?

BARBS. Yeah! Sometimes I'm in myself I just like to play old records really loud…!

ALICE. Aye well, that's three weeks in a row you've missed the aerobics. (*Beat.*) Have you been smoking dope?

BARBS. I've been really busy. (Dope, please, no since I split up wi Davie!) Awfy busy! Work stuff. Well, not tonight, obviously. Shaving my legs. How did you get in here?

ALICE. You opened the door…

BARBS. Naw I mean into the building. Is the entrance lock buggered again?

ALICE. Not as far as I know. Somebody came out just as I arrived and I asked them to hold open the door for me. I didny want to buzz up and have you no answer.

BARBS. Why wouldn't I answer?

BARBS *suddenly realises she's holding the underpants and looks at them with horror before stuffing them into her pocket.* ALICE *does not register this though.*

ALICE. I asked Brendan, he says the same. You never go out with him and Whatsisname any more. He's worried about you.

BARBS. Is he stuff!

ALICE. Have you gone agoraphobic? Or what? Hey, check the –

BARBS. I'm fine!

ALICE. – Valentine! And a single red rose! Do tell!

BARBS. Nothing *to* tell. Stefan gave every girl at work one. Probably cynically meant but you know me, I'll refuse nothing but blows. And a rose is a rose is a rose. And the Valentine –

BARBS *opens and shuts the card to reveal that it says* 'all my love' *and is signed* '?'

– Doesny say! Traditional eh no? No, it was actually the wan wi a bit of taste from the fan-mail sack at the programme this morning. I couldny resist bringing it back to cheer myself up. Sad eh?

ALICE. Some poor sucker went to the bother of making this imagine! For a total stranger?

BARBS. Telly's weird.

ALICE. Even Buns of Steel was asking for you.

BARBS. What did she say?

ALICE. Said she'd thought she was a good judge of character after all these years as an aerobics instructor and she hadn't taken you for a backslider. Told me to remind you to make sure you kept up the pelvic thrusts.

BARBS. Jesus...

ALICE. Anyway I haveny seen you since Noelene's eighteenth. What did you think of it? I thought it was quite a nice night.

BARBS. A smashing night, Alice. And Noelene looked gorgeous.

ALICE. Thanks to the swanky haircut.

BARBS. Brendan's very good.

ALICE. She's a lucky lucky girl. I says to her I hope your Auntie Barbara knows you appreciate her. Anyway, did you get to meet Grant? What did you think?

BARBS. He seemed… a nice boy.

ALICE. I hope so. I want him to be happy, Barbara.

BARBS *tries to get* ALICE *to the door and out.*

BARBS. I know… Anyway, Alice, dear heart, why don't I take you out for lunch –

ALICE. What I really wanted to ask you was: did you phone your mother yet?

BARBS. I don't want to talk about it!

Alice, she went in the huff with me, she should be the one – Ach, I will. I will do, okay? Alice, why can't she treat me like a human being and no like 'her daughter'.

ALICE. Because you *are* her daughter. But phone her, eh? Because I saw her on Sunday there when I was in The Place visiting my ma.

BARBS. Eh?

ALICE. No! No! She was in visiting. With her pal Mina visiting an old lady they had been in the church club with or something.

BARBS. How was she?

ALICE. Oh, fine, fine. She's very sparky your ma. Wonderful appearance too when she's done up.

BARBS. She's not old, Alice.

ALICE. Neither she is. Unlike mines.

BARBS. How is she?

ALICE. Dear oh dear oh dear.

Ach, you have to laugh sometimes. It can be quite funny. Some of what she comes out with, you know. Doesn't know me! At least your mother has all her marbles.

BARBS. Hah!

ALICE. She does. You're lucky! Your ma can be very funny! *Intentionally* funny! She told me a joke. In The Place on Sunday there, that wan of the orderlies tellt her: What's sixty feet long and smells of pish? A conga line in an old folk's home!

BARBS. Christ!

ALICE. She has a sense of humour, Barbs, sometimes I think you just don't appreciate it.

BARBS. Obviously not overburdened with empathy for the poor old terminally bewildered…

ALICE. Ach, Barbs, she's no old yet! Plus you do have to laugh. (*Beat.*) Look, I know she really offended you saying what she said about Brendan – and ach, I know you are probably waiting for a result before –

BARBS. I said I really really don't want to talk about it!

With the hot bit of the roach catching the back of his throat, GRANT *coughs unwittingly.* BARBS *coughs, trying to cover it up.* ALICE *finally catches on. She pantomimes 'is somebody up there?'* BARBS *– eventually – nods.* ALICE *pantomimes 'Who?'* BARBS *pantomimes back 'Brendan'.* ALICE *repeat pantomimes 'Brendan?' and, realising what he must be there for, pantomimes wanking. Loudly –*

ALICE. Jeez oh, Barbs, is that the time? Jings, I'll better away. Tommy says he'd pick me up the back of nine… Anyway, Barbs, I'll phone you, we'll have our lunch and a good blether, eh? (I'm *so* sorry!)

And she's away. The letter box rises again.

Oh, and Phone Your Mother.

BARBS *just stands there wating for* GRANT *to come down. She takes the underpants out of her pocket and tosses them up to the silence of the loft bed.*

Pulling on the pants he descends the staircase, then, unsmiling and unspeaking, he goes to the bedroom, fetches his clothes brings them back and puts them on.

BARBS. Don't say anything!

GRANT. I'm saying nothing!

BARBS. I will tell her! Honestly, I will. When the time is right…

GRANT. I almost came down. Bollock naked as I was I nearly came down. But it's not for me to tell her, is it? I want you to tell her. I want us to tell her *together*… How did you think I felt stuck up there like Jesus Christ being denied thrice? Stefan gave you my rose. The Valentine was from a fucking fan. I am a nice boy.

Hey! Who the fuck did she think I was anyway?

BARBS. Nobody!

GRANT. Nobody?

BARBS. Just… somebody.

GRANT. Why did you let her in?

BARBS. She knew I was here!

GRANT. I tell you, Barbara, I aint gonna put up with this shit for ever.

BARBS. I know… Will I see you later? I'll sleep up there and you can come and surprise me.

GRANT. Surprise you I fuck off home to my own bed for once.

BARBS. You wouldny…

GRANT. Naw, I wouldny.' (*Kisses her once then smiles.*)
I suppose.

He goes. She leans against the door shaking her head. Aargh. After a moment the (outside) buzzer goes. She jumps, then puts record off, goes to the intercom.

BARBS. Hello?

BRENDAN. It's me!

BARBS. Brendan?

BRENDAN. Have you forgot what day it is?

BARBS. No! (*Beat.*) I had! Come in, darlin'. Come on up! Perfect!

Music starts: Frank Sinatra singing 'My Funny Valentine'. The doorbell goes. BARBS *opens it.* BRENDAN *sticks out his arm, a little brown-bagged parcel in his hand. After 'Sweet comic Valentine – '*

BRENDAN. Pro-duct!

Black.

Music bridge continues.

Scene Four

Lights up on BARBS*'s living room.*

DAVIE *stands with an empty whisky glass, looking down into it.*

Standing apart from him, holding a full glass, absently, not drinking it, is BRENDAN. *Both men have black ties, sober dark clothes, funeral-smart.*

ALICE *is there too, wearing her good dark coat, open, over dark dress and stockings. Everyone edgy, isolated from each other.*

BRENDAN. Barbs okay, Alice?

ALICE. I think so. She'll be out in a wee minute, Brendan. I think she wanted, you know, to get changed…

BRENDAN *nods, looks towards the bedroom.*

DAVIE *goes and pours himself another large whisky.*

Davie, don't you be drinking too much!

DAVIE *glowers at her, advances to* BRENDAN *with the bottle.*

DAVIE. Brendan! See's your glass…

BRENDAN *puts his hand over his glass, shakes his head as* GRANT, *in white shirt, dark jacket and black tie, comes out of the kitchen with a huge bunch of funeral lilies in an impressive glass vase. He puts them down on the table.*

ALICE. Beautiful, son…

She indicates the door.

On you go too, Grant, if you want. The girls are just away. Andrea's exhausted. She's upset. She's never been to a funeral before. I says, I'll say bye for you to your Auntie Barbs, she'll be awful glad you came, 'preciate it… Run, you'll catch them. You can go up the road with the girls.

GRANT. No it's all right, Alice, I'll stay a little while.

DAVIE *glowers at him. He doesn't see it, but* ALICE *does. She glowers back in a warning way.*

ALICE. Thanks, son… (*Reads the card which was with the flowers.*) 'With deepest sympathy from Tiffany, Natasha, Stefan and all at Razor City.' Our Barbara, well, she has a lot of good friends there is no doubt about it. But there is nothing – nothing on Earth – which can ever make up for losing your mother…

BRENDAN. One helluva shock.

ALICE. I know, I know, it's very hard to take in.

DAVIE. *Sadie*… unbelievable… She was some Sadie…

ALICE. That minister did very well with his speech didn't he?

DAVIE *glowers at her again. She takes his point.*

I can't believe I just came out with that!

GRANT *exits again towards the bedroom.* DAVIE *glowers after him.*

DAVIE. Fuck's *he* daen' here?

ALICE. Leave him alone, Davie, he just came to support me. It was very good of him.

Ach, it's just terrible. Out of the blue like that. Hellish. Never a day's illness in her life.

BRENDAN. No warning at all, eh?

ALICE. None. No, her old neighbour said the pair of them had been up the community centre the night before and she was the same as ever.

BRENDAN. That's sore. I just hope Barbs'll be okay… She'd never made up with Sadie, had she?

DAVIE. What the fuck did they fight about anyway? Sadie and Barbs, there was always these wee spats and that, but, basically, the two of them were *like that*. I never heard of such a thing as them no speaking for three months.

BRENDAN. I know she'd bought her something for Mother's Day. She said she was going to go round with a bunch of flowers –

ALICE. I know, son, she told me...

When I was up there at the house with Barbs... you know, day it happened...? And I was looking in cupboards to see if we could find anything... Like a will or anything. And thae cupboards were chock-a-block jampacked wi things Barbs gave her. Still in their wrapping paper the most of them. Untouched. (*Beat.*) Perfume. Silk scarves...

BRENDAN. Tragic eh...?

DAVIE. Where's Billy?

ALICE. Where's Billy Kirkwood? Barbs said he's away with that couple of friends of his.

DAVIE. That bugger's never around when he's needed...

ALICE. Och, Davie, wheesht don't you be causing trouble on a day like the day.

DAVIE. Well, bastard fucks off to Australia leaving Barbs to carry the whole can with Sadie.

ALICE. Now, now, that's not what Barbs thinks. Plus he was great at keeping in touch. He had her out there visiting.

DAVIE. Aye, comes home for the funeral once we've got everything arranged and starts putting in his tuppenceworth. The minute the sit-down tea's done he just buggers off –

ALICE. Davie, Barbs was pleased he was getting the chance to see his friends. It was nice of them to come. Nice-looking couple.

BRENDAN. Them in the Saab?

ALICE. As well if Billy gets a wee drink and a chance to relax wi his pals because it'll have been a right sorrowful homecoming for him. That long flight with a heartache at the end of it.

BRENDAN. I think I'll go through and put the kettle on. Barbs'll mibbe just prefer a wee cup of tea.

BRENDAN *exits kitchen-ward with his whisky glass.*

ALICE. Och, the endless cups of tea, eh? That's what I remember about the time, endless time it seemed, between my dad going, eh, and the funeral. All the neighbours, mind, Davie? Coming in with cakes and baking… A sour mouth and dry sponge cake and gallons of hot sweet tea.

It was awful good you helped Barbs with all the arrangements and everything.

DAVIE. Who else was gonny dae it? I'm still her husband after all.

ALICE. Davie, can I ask you something? Do you and Barbs ever still…

DAVIE. What? Get thegether? Like…? Naw. No recently, anyway. Whiles, when we were first split, or yon time she was really upset ower yon lawyer eejit we used to… Thing is, Alice, Barbara stopped fancying me, it's as simple as that.

ALICE. Then you wereny lying up there on that bed up there smoking a joint on Valentine's Day?

DAVIE. Me? Not guilty, naw. How?

ALICE *shrugs. Says nothing.*

Christ! What's that bliddy Brendan hinging aboot here for? Does it never occur to emdy Barbra'll be exhausted after a day like the day? Certain times are for family. Know what I mean?

ALICE. Davie, he's her best pal. A big help to her. In many ways that you know nothing about. Can you no just wheesht about things you know nothing about?

DAVIE. Some folk cling on to Barbara – I've told her this – looking for all they can get.

And where's that big gink, Grant? He doesny even know Barbs!

ALICE. He's met her. He met her at Noelene's eighteenth. He's doing no harm, Davie.

DAVIE. I says to Colette to no bother coming. She sent a card.

ALICE. He makes me happy, Davie, to see that he turned out all right.

DAVIE. He's curious about you, you're curious about him, fine… But then can he no just bugger off?

ALICE. Do you think my da knew?

I often think, Ma and I, who were we fooling? And for what?

DAVIE. Different days, Alice.

ALICE. Did you not guess, Davie?

DAVIE. I was only about fourteen-year-aul. I was just a daft boy.

ALICE. I was just a daft girl.

DAVIE. Could you no have kept it? If you wanted? I mean my da was strict. But he would've come round. Like everybody else does.

ALICE. I didn't want a baby. I wanted a life.

DAVIE. You could've got an abortion.

ALICE. I went as far as the wummin's close. Cat's pish and cabbage. Then I phoned that number. Hah! There was this advert. 'Pregnant? And don't want to be?' I thought it was an abortion advisory service… Pro-lifers. They put the fear of death into me!

Ach, I just did what girls in my situation have always done, which is pretend it wasn't happening to me until it was too late and I had to tell my mammy. Oh, she gets me away to the Church of Scotland home in the Highlands, all that, keeps it a big secret from you, a big secret from my da. Which I doubt. But in those days…

Anyway. Nothing Was Ever Said.

I've been thinking a lot about them. The last few days. My ma and my da…

DAVIE. I know what you mean. What wi Sadie… Makes you look back. On the past, like, know? Ach, I really, literally, can't take it in. You feel that helpless. For Barbara.

ALICE. There's Our Ma… in yon place. Like that. And then there's Sadie…

DAVIE. Aye. She was one helluva gal, old Sadie. Like mother, like daughter.

ALICE. Could Colette no have come today? No, maybe you're right enough that wouldny have been right…?

DAVIE. I didny think so.

ALICE. They get on though, her and Barbs?

DAVIE. Oh, aye, well enough… though I think Colette is that wee bit jealous of Barbs, know what I mean?

ALICE. Yeah…

DAVIE. Alice, Colette had a termination.

ALICE. Oh no, Davie, and you were that excited.

ALICE *goes towards her brother. Touches his arm.*

Was there… something wrong? With the baby?

DAVIE. No, no. (*Beat.*) No, Colette decided to listen to her mother and father and all their stuff about her having her whole life in front of her. They booked her into a private clinic. Six weeks ago. It was getting near the cut-off point, know?

I was not consulted. I got presented with a fait accompli… We've not split up, nor nothing. No, as Colette says, her and me, we've got all the time in the world.

BRENDAN *re-enters with a set tea tray, puts it down.*

BRENDAN. I put out this cake. Likely nobody hungry, but ocht…

BARBS *enters with the awful Scene One jersey her mother gave her over her sober black skirt and funeral shoes.*

BARBS. Anybody want a drink?

Beautiful flowers…

The minister did well.

ALICE. I was just saying that. Very moving.

GRANT *re-enters and goes up to* BARBS *tries to put his arm around her.*

GRANT. Barbs, don't just walk away from me.

BARBS. Grant, sit down and have a drink, please.

DAVIE. Don't you be upsetting my Barbs on a day like today. What exactly are you on, pal?

ALICE. Davie, shut up!

GRANT. Barbara, I want you to tell them who I am.

BARBS. This is Alice's son, Grant Steel. Grant, I think you know everyone with the possible exception of Brendan Boyle.

BRENDAN. I know him. He is the model for the spring photoshoot.

GRANT. I am in love with Barbara Marshall. She is my lover. Tell them, Barbs.

BARBS. I have been having a relationship with this… young man.

Alice –

ALICE. Don't touch me!

GRANT. I want you to tell them. Tell them you're in love with me.

BARBS. Grant, please. My mother is dead and I don't know how I am going to live without her.

GRANT. Let me comfort you.

You know I am in love with you and you know how sick I am of being your dirty secret for some reason.

Gets nothing, so has to appeal to ALICE *for help.*

I was here, Alice, on Valentine's Day but –

ALICE. You?

GRANT. I wanted to tell you –

Back to BARBS.

Why not? I told you, Barbs. I want to go out with you. Oh, staying in with you is all very lovely. This Christmas, yeah, it was the best Christmas of my life. For you too, Barbs, you know it was. Say it! Say it.

Silence. She won't. He keeps trying. Won't give up.

But I want to go *out* with you. I want you to come to my seedy flat and meet my – actually it's not seedy, I am going to pack in all this apologising for myself.

I am a grown-up man of twenty-six and I am in love with you, Barbara.

Is there something strange in that? Am I missing something?

I want to go to the movies with you, eat dinner in public. And I'm never – never – going to be in the position again, Barbs, where I am at Noelene's eighteenth birthday party and you are at Noelene's eighteenth birthday party but I am not even allowed to dance with you. Never again.

Why are you ashamed of me?

Today – today of all days, I want you to tell all them you are in love with me.

BRENDAN. Have you been shagging somebody else while we were trying to have a baby?

GRANT. While you what?

BARBS. I want you all to go away and leave me alone.

GRANT. No.

BARBS. You will do anyway. Soon. Oh yes you will, Grant, you're going away, remember? Australia, Japan –

GRANT. That was before I met you.

BARBS. Grant, you are a young man. With places to go. I am pushing forty.

GRANT. Thirteen years, Barbs. Look at you! What difference does it make.

BARBS. All the difference in the world.

BRENDAN. All that while we were trying for a baby you were having it off with him? Christ, that makes me feel sick.

DAVIE. You never wanted a baby…

BARBS. Neither did you.

GRANT. You were trying to have a baby with that poof while you were so totally paranoid about me being careful?

BARBS. Yes I was. And more than you know. I used my cap as well. Condoms and cap. Belt and braces. Because the last thing I wanted was to trap you, Grant. You have to go…

BRENDAN. Well, as it turns out we were wasting our time, Barbara.

I went and got a sperm count. Because it sort of bothered me we'd been trying for a few months and no joy. I know, I know, we said we'd give it the six months, then we'd go for tests together, see if all was well. Because there was things could be done, *assisted* things you'd been reading about in all yon books… Well, there was nothing could have been done for you and me, Barbs, because – oh, and this came as big a shock to me as it would to the next man, believe me – I have just about the lowest sperm count they have ever registered. Less than a million per millilitre and zero motility. No chance, Barbs. We'd never – never in a million years – have been parents.

BARBS. I am pregnant.

A silence. BARBS *begins to laugh weirdly. Stops again.*

I thought to myself, no, I'll only be late because of… Everything. This week of all weeks, eh? I thought don't get all excited. But I just did a pregnancy test. And it was positive. The stick changed colour.

BRENDAN, GRANT *and* DAVIE. Whose baby is it?

BARBS. It is mine!

BRENDAN. Well, I am out of here. Barbs, bye, that is you and me finished.

BRENDAN *walks out the door.*

BARBS. I want you all to go.

GRANT. I'm going nowhere.

DAVIE. Barbs, just you say the word, doll, and I'll stiffen this bastard.

BARBS. Leave me alone, Davie.

DAVIE. I'll stay with you, doll. Long as you need me.

BARBS. Leave me!

He does finally. Walks out the door. Leaving BARBS, ALICE *and* GRANT.

ALICE. You just couldn't see me happy, could you, without you having to take him away from me?

GRANT. I won't ever leave till you tell me to my face you don't want me.

BARBS. I want my mother!

She breaks down at last. Eventually –

ALICE. Grant, there's tea made. Pour the three of us, c'mon, a wee cup of tea…

He doesn't. Folds his arms. Eventually ALICE *is forced to go to the tea tray and pour it herself.*

Aye well, I suppose I'll better be mother…

She starts to laugh. Not a particularly merry laugh, but she does find it – literally – absolutely – hysterical.

I do not believe I said that! (*Beat.*) *Grand*mother I suppose I should say…

ALICE *looks up to see* GRANT *and* BARBS *in each other's arms. He's rocking her, stroking her back, soothing her, holding her.*

To herself –

Ach well, as they say, you'd think I'd no home to go to, eh?… Ah'll better away…

ALICE *goes to the door.*

BARBS. Alice, please don't go. I need you.

BARBS *disentangles herself from* GRANT*'s arms.*

Grant. Darling. It's not yours.

GRANT. But he said –

She pushes him gently away from her with one hand.

BARBS. I am absolutely sure, my darling, this baby isn't yours.

Black.

Music bridge: Annie Lennox: 'No More I Love You's'.

Scene Five

BARBS *alone, zonked out on the sofa. Asleep. She wears a loose almost Greek-looking nightgown and is barefooted. The picture of the classic dreaming girl…*

The ghost of SADIE *appears. As a young mother in 1961 or 1962,* SADIE *has a puffball or a pencil skirt, stilettos, big hair and she wheels one of those sixties coach-built prams. She crosses the stage simply and exits. Singing 'I love you a bushel and a peck'.*

BARBS *wakes up and joins in '…A bushel and a peck and a hug around the neck.' She does not look at* SADIE *but seems to quite simply feel her presence as she passes by.* SADIE *disappears as lights change.*

Standing on the floor is a large plastic bronze-coloured bottle. A little larger than a sweetie jar. On the table is a beautiful empty shallow dish. BARBS *opens the jar and solemnly, experimentally, pours some of these, her mother's, ashes into the dish. There is a sifting of fine grey ash, but a few carbon-y coke-like black burnt bone lumps too. She goes to touch, curious.*

As she does, the downstairs buzzer goes.

BARBS *jumps. Then, slipping her feet into giant silly novelty furry slippers, she goes and answers at the intercom.*

BARBS. Hello? Who is it?

BRENDAN (*on intercom*). It's me…

BARBS. Brendan? It's late, Brendan. But, yeah. Yeah come on up.

She presses the button then goes back to the table, puts the plastic crematorium jar down behind it. The inside bell goes. She opens the door.

BRENDAN *comes in.*

BRENDAN. Hello, Barbs.

BARBS. Hello, stranger.

BRENDAN. I met Tiff – first time I've even seen anybody – I bumped into her on Waverley Station and she told me you were moving!

BARBS. – Need a garden. This place is on the market. Offers over a hundred and ninety-five would you believe –

BRENDAN. Oh, well, I'll speak to my broker right away! (*Beat.*) I've missed you, Barbara. Very very long time no see, eh?

BARBS. A whole year. You missed my birthday. Bastard. You missed my big Four-O.

BRENDAN. How was that?

BARBS. Very quiet. I was nearly five months pregnant at the time, so…

BRENDAN. How is she?

BARBS. Perfect. It's hard work. She's beautiful.

BRENDAN. Like her mammy, eh? I, emm, brung her up a wee lamb.

He produces a soft-toy lamb. Small and very sweet.

Grace, eh?

BARBS. That's right. That's lovely, Brendan. She'll love it. She's sleeping, but she's due to wake up soon.

BRENDAN. Grace. Imagine.

BARBS. Grace Sarah Kirkwood. After my mum.

BRENDAN. Was that her name? Sadie?

BARBS. She was Sarah Grace Kirkwood…

I couldn't call her Marshall. The baby. I mean, I am stuck with Davie's name for the duration I suppose, but I couldn't give it to Grace, could I? So she has my family name. The one I grew up with. My father's name…

BRENDAN. Him that you don't remember?

BARBS. Yeah… Davie and I got divorced, by the way.

BRENDAN. How was that?

BARBS. Fine. He came up with a bottle of champagne and two of milk stout and made Black Velvet which he said was good for my breastfeeding.

BRENDAN. How's his… relationship?

BARBS. Oh… (*Makes a so-so gesture with her hand.*) Things will never be right until when and if the lovely Colette tells her rich father to fuck off. But, that's between her and Davie…

BRENDAN. I broke up with Cammy.

BARBS. Oh, Brendan…

She hugs him. They hold a moment.

BRENDAN. A couple of months back. But, och, you know what they say about gay relationships being measured in dog years… In that case Cammy and I made it well past the seven-year-itch stage.

BARBS. Och, Brendan, I'm sorry. Was it hellish?

BRENDAN. Pretty bad. But, och, I'm back amongst the walking wounded…

BARBS. How is the job?

BRENDAN. That *is* hellish. Plus the commute to Edinburgh is doing my head in. I was thinking of flitting through, but then I thought do I want to live in a gay scene dominated by QC's and candidates for the new Scottish Parliament…?

BARBS. Wanting to come back to Razor City?

BRENDAN. In a minute. But what would Stefan say?

BARBS. Please. Maternity may have turned my brain to mince, but in Razor City I do still have an equal say. Plus Stefan would be the first to admit we have never found, nor ever will find, a cutter to match you.

You can come back if you'll come with me tomorrow.

BRENDAN. What's tomorrow?

BARBS. Tomorrow is the anniversary of my mother's funeral.

BRENDAN. I remembered, yes. (*Beat.*) It's Mother's Day tomorrow.

BARBS. Yeah, well, I'm a mother, amn't I? So I can do what I want.

What I was going to do tomorrow, well, the weather's been nice, so I thought I'd like to take Grace, she loves it in her backpack, we are going to take my mother's ashes up to the top of this hill – my mother was always talking about this place, my father used to take us there. I don't remember it but I remember my mother talking about it, Mum, Dad, me, Our Billy, well, he was only a baby, maybe wasn't even born yet. We'd go for picnics and there was a waterfall called the Grey Mare's Tail. It's south, down the main road, near Moffat, I found it on the map, not far…

I want you to come with us. I want us to take Sadie's ashes and let them go. Over the waterfall. Then I want us to have a picnic. Family only. You, me and Grace.

BRENDAN. What can I say?

BARBS. Say yes. Say it!

BRENDAN. Yes.

BARBS. Perfect.

BRENDAN. Speaking of perfect, how's whatsisface? My… rival for your affections?

BARBS. Grant? Very good I think. Last I heard was a postcard from Ayers Rock at Christmas. Alice and I got the exact same one.

BRENDAN. Do you miss him?

BARBS. No. (*Beat.*) Definitely not as much as Alice does.

BRENDAN. Did you love him?

BARBS. Oh yes. I did do.

BRENDAN. I solved the mystery.

BARBS. What mystery?

BRENDAN. The… paternity. Didn't it worry you?

BARBS. No.

BRENDAN. Christ, that's honest.

BARBS. Brendan, I have, for the last year, had more to bother me than that. Pregnancy. Do you know how you are meant to blossom? Glow? Forget it. I felt like shit the whole time. Physically. Inside myself I never regretted it for a minute.

Giving birth. Agony. I can't tell you. Ask Alice! Alice was my birth partner. She stayed with me. Held my hand. Through absolute bloody agony. Till my nails gouged into her hand, made her bleed. Kept on hanging on.

And Grace… Changed everything.

(*Beat.*) Sometimes I even feel as if I can understand my own mother.

BRENDAN (*amazed*). Can you?

BARBS. No. But I miss her.

BRENDAN. The baby is Cammy's. In the matter of her… biological paternity.

BARBS. What?

BRENDAN. He switched jars.

BARBS. He what?

BRENDAN. Remember how we used to – then I'd bring it round? He was jealous. He –

BARBS. – Produced his own and switched the jars! That is brilliant. When Ma sent me that strippergram she didn't know it but she was certainly sending me quite a present. Thank you, Sadie…

BRENDAN. Can I go through and see her?

BARBS. Course you can… bring her through, she's due a feed anyway.

BRENDAN *takes the lamb and goes off.*

BRENDAN (*offstage*). Hello. Hello, darling… (*Beat. Then loudly.*) She's gorgeous, Barbsie! Beautiful.

He comes on with a baby of four months wrapped in his arms.

Hello! Hello, it's your Auntie Brenda, your fairy godmother…

BARBS *goes to him. They make a beautiful tender family tableau.*

Do you know who she is the spitting image of? Across the eyes?

BARBS. Don't!

BRENDAN. Your mother…

They laugh together in sheer joy. It coming streaming out from them, expanding, lifting.

Music: Lou Reed's 'Perfect Day' in the multi-voiced and soaring BBC version.

The End.

GOOD THINGS

For Marion Marshall – and The Girls

Good Things was first performed by Borderline Theatre Company, in association with the Byre Theatre, St Andrews and Perth Theatre, at the Tron Theatre, Glasgow on Thursday 16 September 2004.

The production then toured to Eastgate Theatre and Arts Centre, Peebles; Barrfields Theatre, Largs; Howden Park Centre, Livingston; Lochside Theatre, Castle Douglas; Falkirk Town Hall; MacRobert Theatre, Stirling; Gaiety Theatre, Ayr; Arts Guild Theatre, Greenock; Carnegie Hall, Dunfermline; Eden Court Theatre, Inverness; Cumbernauld Theatre; Brunton Theatre, Musselburgh; The Palace, Kilmarnock; Byre Theatre, St Andrews and Perth Theatre.

The cast was as follows:

ACTRESS ONE (SUSAN)	Annette Staines
ACTOR ONE (DAVID)	Vincent Friell
ACTRESS TWO (MARJORIE, DORIS, et al)	Molly Innes
ACTOR TWO (FRAZER, TONY, et al)	Kenneth Bryans
Director	Maureen Beattie
Designer	Finlay McLay
Lighting Designer	Simon Wilkinson

Thanks to Eddie Jackson at Borderline for the imaginative and exceptionally extensive series of workshops on this script and to all the different actors and directors who contributed at various times.

Liz Lochhead

Characters

SUSAN LOVE, *forty-nine* *played by* ACTRESS ONE
DAVID, *fifty-one* *played by* ACTOR ONE

SCOTCH DORIS, *sixty-ish*
CHERYL, *forty-ish*
MARJORIE, *forty-five-ish*
WELL-DRESSED WOMAN
NATALIE, *thirty-two*
SHARP YOUNG POLICEWOMAN
HELENA, *twenty-two*
all played by ACTRESS TWO

FRAZER, *forty-ish*
ARCHIE, *eighty-four*
TONY, *fifty-ish*
SCRUFFY LITTLE MAN, *sixty*
FLOWER DELIVERY MAN
INSENSITIVE POLICEMAN
all played by ACTOR TWO

'Scotch Doris' is Scottish, obviously, and has a lot of strongly idiomatic dialogue, but – this is entirely optional – Susan could well be too, albeit with only a Scots accent on her perfectly standard English vocabulary and syntax.

The town, or big city suburb, could be anywhere, but the scene is the little charity shop on the corner – very much Frazer's designer-palace – on three different days in one year.

There should be as miraculous and swift a transformation as possible between Act One, 6 January, and Act Two, Valentine's Day.

Act Three should have a very different Christmas tree and decorations from Act One.

Possibly on one of the three days (perhaps Act One?), it is pouring with rain outside, and people come in from the outside wet. A cold dry bright winter's day for Act Two would therefore contrast beautifully.

ACT ONE

TWELFTH NIGHT

Music: 'Time is On My Side' (Rolling Stones), loud.

6 January. A little charity shop on the corner. The rather spectacular Christmas decorations are more than half down but a last section on one side is very much still to do. There's the A-frame of an open step-ladder and under it a full box spilling gorgeously coloured tinsel.

Stage right, on the back wall, there is a doorway to backshop with a door, currently closed, clearly marked 'Private'.

Stage left, on the back wall, behind a single full-length front curtain, currently closed, there are two slightly angled, adjoining, tiny changing-room spaces, each with a curtain stopping well short of the floor, which shows the legs and feet, though covers the heads, if and when the long front curtain is open.

The shop's front door entrance/exit from street is stage left.

FRAZER, *a dapper man in early middle age and* SUSAN, *attractive, warm, likeable, youthful-looking for her late forties, stand near each other, poised.* FRAZER *is looking at his watch, waiting for the second hand to reach the twelve. He points at* SUSAN: *Go!* SUSAN *takes a deep breath, then –*

SUSAN. Okay, what I'll say, I'll say: Susan. Friendship. Friendship and fun really. Nothing too serious! Susan Love –

(But you know, Frazer, I'm seriously thinking of reverting to my maiden name, only I've not used it for so long – obviously it's not me, though what is? I mean, there could be pluses, well, in the self-esteem department? I suppose.)

My counsellor suggested it, that the time would come I might feel that taking back my own name would be appropriate – not that I go in much for therapy or counselling or stuff – but he was helpful. Definitely.

I thought, avail yourself of everything, Susan, everything that's going – and it was part of a package at work, my friend Mel that's just moved to Macclesfield with her husband, she recommended it, she said, 'Susan, see a counsellor, I would, it's free, there's no shame, did wonders for me with that second miscarriage before little Benny was born when I just couldn't see light at the end of the tunnel, he's very good, he helps you get in touch with your feelings.'

I said, 'Mel, I've got no problem feeling my feelings, I wish I could stop feeling them, I'm awash with the bloody things.' She said, 'I know but he helps you accept your grief and move through it, realise you're not always going to feel like this and, well, put it in perspective sort of thing. You know… grieve and move on?'

I said, 'I don't know if *grief's* what I'd call it exactly' but – he helped! Oh, it was only the six free sessions, no way would I or could I ever get into that sort of self-indulgence and expense long-term.

And I'm fine. D'you know, eighteen months on, some days I feel quite excited. Exhilarated. A clean slate. Hence ditch the Love, though why should I change the person I've been for the last twenty-four years because my husband ups sticks? And it's my daughter's name, so I'm probably stuck with Love for the duration.

FRAZER (*tapping watch, c'mon!*). Sus-ann!

SUSAN. Right what? God… My interests? Macrame, origami and aqua-nooky!

Well… Music. All sorts. Stones, Sinatra, Springsteen, Sibelius. Ella, anybody good! Except folk. Folk or jazz. Can't stand jazz, too jangly. Nor can I abide dance or house or rap. None of the stuff that our Stephi drives me up the wall with. Easy listening? I find that hard to take.

Love going to the pictures! Just about anything. Old black-and-whites on the telly on a Sunday afternoon –

FRAZER. Time's up.

SUSAN. Really? That's what I'm afraid of. Game over.

FRAZER. Why?

SUSAN. Past it. That's me! Most probably. Face it, Frazer, I'm forty-eight, forty-nine in February.

FRAZER. Yes, but you don't need to tell them that!

SUSAN. Why not? It's the truth. This year I'll be hitting my fiftieth year.

FRAZER. Is fifty not supposed to be the new thirty?

SUSAN. – The full half-century. How the hell did that happen?

DORIS, *a regular, sixty-ish, known as 'Scotch Doris', sticks her head round one side of the changing-room area's front curtain.*

DORIS. You don't look it, darlin'. Do you have this in a size bigger?

FRAZER. Perhaps 'modom' would prefer it in the aubergine? This is a *charity* shop, Doris! All one-offs, obviously. Duh!

DORIS *sweeps the front curtain wide open and emerges. She looks a fright in whatever (much too tight).*

Stage-right cubicle's short curtain is shut, no legs showing in there, it's clearly empty. DORIS*'s stage-left cubicle has its short curtain wide open. She has a colourful half of the shop's stock in there to try on.*

DORIS. Mibbe I could let the darts out?

FRAZER *rolls his eyes.*

Mibbe I could put in a gusset up the back in a contrast fabric or make an insert out of an elastic placket and wear it under a cardigan?

FRAZER. Doris –

DORIS. Anybody haufweys handy with a Singer could save themselves a pure fortune in here.

FRAZER. Doris, did you try the navy?

DORIS. Don't know that I fancy it.

FRAZER. Try it. For me!

DORIS *sighs and indulges him, disappears back into the inner-curtained cubicle.* SUSAN *pulls across the full-length outer curtain for (her own) privacy's sake.*

SUSAN. When did *she* come in?

FRAZER *shrugs.*

Did you know she was in there?

FRAZER. I forgot.

He scuttles back up the stepladder to demolish more decorations.

SUSAN. Honestly! I'm back there sorting out the post-Christmas-unwanted-present mountain into some sort of order for Her Majesty Marjorie to price when she deigns to come in, I come back through here, you don't even bother to tell me there's someone in the changing room and we are Not Alone.

Could've been anybody! But, oh, you've got to get me – Ooh!

Laughing, she throws a cushion from the soft-furnishings pile. He chucks it back.

FRAZER. – Practising your sales pitch for the speed dating. Tonight! Which was hopeless to be perfectly frank and honest.

SUSAN. Really?

Listen, not a *word* to Marjorie about this! I don't want her to start trying to fix me up with one of Douglas's golfing cronies again. Spare me. Please!

Was I really so rubbish? What should I say?

FRAZER. Well, skip the past for a start! Forget it. Just… answer those questions I asked you in the first place: 'Who are you? And what do you want to get out of this?' Sell yourself, Susan. You're a lovely lady.

SUSAN. No point in telling any lies. This is it. Here I am. What you see is what you get.

God! Sell myself? I don't think I could give myself away.

Snogging? Couldn't! What do you do with your face? Do you pucker up or open up?

FRAZER, *up the top of the ladder, holds out a sprig of mistletoe above her and puckers up, eyes shut. She snatches it, bins it, laughing.*

Hey! Hey, you know how my old dad's in his second childhood? I think I've hit my second adolescence. It's exactly the same as the first time. I can't conceive of anyone of the opposite sex treating me as a sexual being.

Or what the hell I'd do if they did.

FRAZER *takes down the last tinsel.*

FRAZER. There's more to life, Susan! (There better be, says me!)

He comes down the ladder.

Hey! Remember how you were saying you fancy trying that salsa dancing? There's a class advertised up the sports centre. Beginners. Let's give it a shot, mmm?

SUSAN. Why not! You never know, I might meet my ideal man – don't they tell you to try evening classes? (Mind you, I'm not stupid, all you ever meet are other women looking for their ideal man...)

But let's give the salsa a whirl! The worst that could happen is we learn to dance.

He gives her a whirl and backwards dip, copied from the telly.

FRAZER. Absolutely! I might not be your ideal partner, missus, but I'm keen!

SUSAN (*laughing*). And it was our new year resolution that we'd try something new...

SUSAN *sits at the counter, fishes a book out from her handbag, opens it, starts reading, so now talks automatically, distractedly.*

FRAZER. So it was. Ooh, hope this is a good year for us, eh? Here's hoping we each get our heart's desire.

Nice if we could both move on and get out of here, eh, the pair of us?

SUSAN. Any chance of anything?

FRAZER. Well, there's a movie I heard about, supposed to be definitely going to go in the spring, fingers crossed, director I did the frocks for, for his first costume epic at the Beeb in '87 for two and six on an education and documentary budget, so you'd think I'd be in with a chance there. I e-mailed my CV but quite honestly the so-called 'producers' these days are about twelve-and-a-half years old, the lot of them.

SUSAN (*automatic*). I suppose it's Who You Know…

FRAZER. And of course with what I went through with my mother, I've let myself fall out of the loop somewhat. Oh, no regrets! (*Kisses fairy and dumps her.*) Well, there's the Christmas-tree fairy back in her box for another year, aren't you, pet?

Well, Frazer son, what theme are you going to use for the window dressing this month, eh? Should I skip straight to Valentine's? WH Smith has already!

What you reading?

Grabs it, she grabs it back, reads.

SUSAN. *Doctor Zhivago*. I'm getting into it. Course, nothing could touch the film. Remember Julie Christie and Omar Sharif and at the end they just kept passing each other and missing – Oh, it was so romantic. Not a dry eye in the two and nines. Certainly not mine!

FRAZER. I'm not a big reader.

SUSAN. Stephi bought me it for my Christmas last Christmas and I only got round to finally starting it this Christmas because the TV was so utterly appalling.

FRAZER. Wasn't it just? Have you no work to do?

SUSAN. No. Give me a break, I'm at a good bit. Put the kettle on, go on.

He blows a kiss and indulges her, then goes backshop. SUSAN *reads. From cubicle comes some harrumphing and groaning.* SUSAN *registers it, ignores it. It gets louder.*

DORIS (*off*). Haw! Am I supposed tae tie masel in knots like Houdini in here? Is there naebody can gie me a wee haun wi these press-fasteners?

SUSAN. Certainly, Doris, certainly. Your servant, I'm sure.

SUSAN *fashions herself a bookmark, places it, sighs, shuts book, goes behind the front curtain.*

A very scruffy little MAN *enters, stands, surveys the empty shop imperiously, then nods to himself.*

MAN. Right…

SUSAN *comes out of cubicle.*

SUSAN. Ah! Sir, can I – ?

MAN. Old things, eh?

SUSAN. Many with a lot of good wear in them! For instance this overcoat would –

MAN. No, no, I'm not *buying*.

DORIS (*off*). Well, you can beat it well!

The scruffy MAN *looks amazed.*

MAN (*to* SUSAN). Are you throwing your voice?

DORIS *sticks her head out from the long front curtain.*

DORIS. Because you'll be getting bugger all buckshee by the way! All the money's in a good cause!

MAN. Who asked you for your tuppenceworth?

He exits.

SUSAN. Now, Doris, you've no call to go insulting our customers!

DORIS. Him! He was mingin'. He was honkin'. From here!

Your trouble is you've got too much time for timewasters. You shouldnae give them the time of day!

SUSAN. You never said a truer word. So, Doris, how was your Christmas?

DORIS. Very quiet.

SUSAN (*commiserating*). Well…

DORIS. I've got high hopes for this New Year, but!

SUSAN. Ever the optimist, eh?

DORIS. Like yoursel'!

SUSAN (*doubting it*). Am I?

DORIS. Oh aye! See, the good thing about getting to our age, you get to the 'Know Thyself' stage. Or you should, anyway.

Optimist rather than pessimist, extrovert no introvert, ectomorph, no, mesamorph, that's me!

DORIS *disappears behind the curtain.*

Laughing, SUSAN *makes for her book. Picks it up again and reads.*

Enter an attractive likeable man of SUSAN*'s age or a little older, with a couple of bin bags. This is* DAVID. *He has to come right up to her before she registers his presence.*

DAVID. Emm..

SUSAN. Sorry, I was… a bit engrossed! Just we've been very quiet this morning so far. Think everyone is at home hoovering up pine needles and going on detoxes. This some stuff for us?

DAVID. If it would be any use at all to you.

SUSAN. That's very kind –

Enter CHERYL, *an energetic and determinedly good-looking forty-ish woman. Ignoring* SUSAN *utterly, she pulls* DAVID *aside.*

CHERYL. There you are, darling! I just popped down for some soya milk.

DAVID. I've got milk.

CHERYL. Yes but, darling, I don't do dairy. I wondered where you'd got to.

DAVID. Brought over a couple of bags…

CHERYL. Well, I'm all for the big clear-out as you know. It's time. But, darling – (*Whispers.*) where did you get to? Came out the shower and you'd gone!

Okay, let's have ourselves some brunch, babes, then would it not be nice to do something with our day?

DAVID. Sure. Sure, yes, but –

CHERYL. Because what was that new year resolution about gathering our rosebuds?

And, rather embarassed, he exits with her. SUSAN *picks up her book again, determinedly reads.*

FRAZER *appears from backshop, wanders, catches sight of something out of the window out front.*

FRAZER. There she is! Here she comes…

SUSAN *gives up, shuts her book and leaves it on the counter, gets up and joins him, looking out.*

SUSAN. No rest for the wicked! Oh, don't park the Beamer there, Marjorie, or else you'll get a ticket and we'll never hear the end of it.

FRAZER. Oh my. She's talking to that horrible woman that owns Scandalrags next door.

SUSAN. So she is!

FRAZER *scurries to put the stepladders away backshop, then quickly reappears.*

(*Shouts.*) Doris, have you ever maxed out the plastic and bought yourself a dressy little frock out of Scandalrags?

DORIS (*off*). Oot o whit?

SUSAN. The posh dress shop next door!

DORIS (*off*). I wouldn't give stuff out of there houseroom!

SUSAN. Oh I would… I would! (*To* FRAZER.) Apparently, Natalie shops in Scandalrags, according to our Stephi.

FRAZER. She would.

SUSAN. Oh, don't get me started!

FRAZER. Oh look… Oh no! Marjorie's getting stuff out of the boot, uh-oh, I see Tupperware…

SUSAN. Marjorie, please don't bring us in your post-Christmas glut! Remember last year, Frazer? We were up to here with your surplus panettone. We were pâtéd out. Let's tell her she can stick her stinky old stilton!

Oh, I know I shouldn't take the piss out of Marjorie, she means well, I love her dearly. She's got a good heart, Frazer. A helluva good heart.

It's just you really have to be feeling stout-hearted yourself to be up to it.

Enter MARJORIE, *a middle-class matron in her mid-forties, through the shop door.*

MARJORIE. Morning, Frazer!

FRAZER. Morning, Marjorie! Happy New Year!

He helps her with her Tupperware, taking it from her.

MARJORIE. You too!

FRAZER. Want a cuppa? Kettle's on.

FRAZER *exits backshop.*

MARJORIE. Morning, Susan, Happy New Year! My, it's marvellous to be out of that madhouse! Douglas and the boys are adorable, particularly when their chums are in and out like that – it's a hoot, but it's hard work!

Have you ever felt you can just get too much socialising?

SUSAN. Morning, Marjorie.

MARJORIE. Oh, I'm sorry, Susan, that was tactless of me. How was your Christmas? Did Stephi spend it with you... or was she with her dad and er...?

SUSAN. Natalie. No, Marjorie – Tony and the famous Natalie, they spent Christmas in the sun somewhere. Stephi told me where but I can't remember, I wasn't interested, could it have been the Caribbean? Anyway, Stephi – very much on sufferance as she made bloody clear – was with me. And her old granddad, of course, who frankly didn't know if it was New Year or New York but what's new? Anyway, overall it was a fairly continent Christmas so we have to be grateful for small mercies.

MARJORIE. I'm full of admiration, so I am, Susan. I think you're marvellous. Out of the blue, your husband just up and offs with the younger woman, leaving you with the stroppy adolescent, during the following year you sell your house and move in with your old dad because he's no longer coping, you get made redundant – any single one, far less all these things together, are supposed to be Big Stressful Life Events, some of *the most* stressful – but you, you just take it all in your stride, you're not bitter, you're always exactly the same, you've got a smile for everybody –

SUSAN. Marjorie, have you seen all the super stuff that's come in?

MARJORIE. – I think you're marvellous, I really do!

SUSAN. I really think you should take a peek –

MARJORIE (*mildly irritated*). Oh, I will do. I've just got in the door!

SUSAN. – because there are some really good things!

MARJORIE. Well, excellent! (*Confides.*) Joanne from Head Office is coming in later to check my pricing policy. They are trying to standardise across the branches. As far as is feasible.

Enter TONY *through the shop door, a conspicuously youthfully well-dressed, fiftyish man (just the type who has a young girlfriend).*

TONY. Susan.

SUSAN. For God's sake, what do you mean coming here, disturbing me at my work?

TONY. I was passing – you won't so much as talk to me on the phone if I've not made an appointment.

I want you to get Stephi to see sense.

MARJORIE. Do you need any help, Susan?

SUSAN. No thanks, Marjorie, I'm fine. Could you, eh, give us a bit of privacy?

MARJORIE. Oh certainly, Susan, sorry I spoke. You're sure you're okay?

MARJORIE *reluctantly goes through to backshop.*

SUSAN. Nice tan, Tony.

TONY. Thank you, Susan.

SUSAN. Listen, what the hell do you mean by –

MARJORIE *pokes her head out from backshop.*

MARJORIE. Because if That One gives you any bother, Susan –

SUSAN. Marjorie, I'm fine! Stephi to see sense about what?

TONY. You know very well what.

SUSAN. Enlighten me.

TONY. Don't try and pretend you never put her up to it.

SUSAN. Up to what?

TONY. Because it's just like you to pressurise her into refusing to come to the wedding.

SUSAN. Whose wedding?

TONY. She'll not even talk to me on the phone.

SUSAN. Whose wedding?

TONY. Don't you try and make out Stephi didn't tell you Natalie asked her to be her bridesmaid?

SUSAN. No. No, she never did.

TONY. It'll have been your attitude that made her scared to bring it up.

SUSAN. No, Tony, not so. But I think you could have told me. Yourself.

TONY. You've made it very clear you don't want to discuss anything with me except the welfare of our daughter.

SUSAN. That's true. And I don't. If Stephi doesn't want to be a bridesmaid at your wedding, you'll just have to take no for an answer.

TONY. That's nice! Well, tell Stephi from me that it goes two ways. She'll learn that if she don't play ball with me, I won't be playing ball with her either, okay?

Exit TONY.

SUSAN (*after him*). Oh, you and your balls, you stupid, stupid – Clear off! You're good at that.

SUSAN *sits down, weeping in anger.* MARJORIE, *coat off now, stands in entrance from backshop looking down, shaking her head. She approaches and touches* SUSAN*'s arm, full of sympathy.*

MARJORIE. Susan…

SUSAN. Leave it, Marjorie, please!

MARJORIE. Poor you, Susan, what a –

SUSAN. Don't!

MARJORIE. Unbelievable! I heard every word…

SUSAN. I was afraid you would.

MARJORIE. You're better off without him, pet.

SUSAN *breathes deep, pulls herself together as best she can.*

SUSAN. That would seem to be the general consensus.

MARJORIE*'s eyes widen as she catches sight of something through the front window.*

MARJORIE. – I don't believe it! (*Making for the door.*) Oh, they're absolute 'B's – excuse my French.

Hello, excuse me, that's mine!

Exit MARJORIE *out of the front door. From off, as she goes:*

And I tried to get a ticket but the blinking machine's not working!

SUSAN *wipes eyes, breathes deep.*

SUSAN. Well, Marjorie, if there's anyone could get the better of a parking warden, it's you.

Oooh! That's right, Marjorie, you just tell them! Don't take it lying down! Do your stuff!

Immediately, the same little scruffy MAN *enters again through front door with a heavy binbag. He drags it up to desk and dumps it.*

MAN. So, you take stuff?

SUSAN. Depends. What sort of stuff?

Nothing electrical –

MAN. There might be a couple of electric things in there.

SUSAN. We're not allowed. For safety reasons.

MAN. S'all right, they're not working.

Enter a meek, nicely-dressed WOMAN.

SUSAN (*to* MAN). But –

The WOMAN *begins rifling through clothes and immediately finds both a dress and a raincoat.*

MAN. Just you chuck them out, my dear, if they're no use to you. Clothes! Old clothes. Plenty more. Lots more stuff. I'm clearing out. Moving house.

WOMAN. Excuse me, can I try these on?

SUSAN (*to* MAN). Yes, but you see actually – (*To* WOMAN.) Certainly, no problem. Just –

SUSAN *pulls back the right side of the long outer curtain and shows the* WOMAN *into the clearly empty cubicle next to the one where we saw* DORIS. *Now the* WOMAN*'s feet in her smart shoes and the bottom of her legs are still clearly visible as she draws the short inner curtain over.*

MAN (*exiting*). I'll bring you the other stuff in soon, okay?

A harrumphing noise from DORIS *in her (currently curtained-over) side.*

SUSAN (*of the binbag*). Ooh! (*Beat.*) You all right in there, Doris?

SUSAN *pulls back the outer curtain in the stage-left changing room so we can see* DORIS*'s legs and boots, struggling in a pair of red-and-white spotted cotton trousers. We can now see two pairs of legs* (DORIS*'s and the* WOMAN*'s) and two pairs of moving elbows behind the closed inner curtains.*

DORIS (*off*). I'll just have to unfankle my feet oot this perr of pedalpushers. I should of perhaps took ma buits aff first.

SUSAN. Take your time, take your time, Doris, nobody's rushing you –

WOMAN (*off*). Excuse me, can you possibly give me a hand with this zip?

SUSAN. Certainly.

SUSAN *goes in to help the* WOMAN. *She closes the full-length outer curtain as she steps inside. For a nanosecond there's an empty stage.*

FRAZER*'s head pops out of the backroom entrance.*

FRAZER. Tea's up! Where is everybody?

Puzzled, FRAZER *goes backshop again.*

SUSAN *comes out and goes towards the* MAN*'s bag trepidatiously and gingerly looks inside. She recoils.*

SUSAN. Oh well, saved you hiring a skip!

FRAZER *enters from the backroom with his outdoor coat on.*

FRAZER. Oh, there you are. Where's Marjorie?

SUSAN. Traffic wardens.

FRAZER. Right. (Do they know who they're messing with?)

Listen, my Number One New Year Resolution, Susie Q, is No More Marvel, we deserve better –

FRAZER *heads for the front door crossing with* MARJORIE *entering as he exits.*

So I'm just away for a pint of proper milk, ladies!

Tea's made, Marjorie! Through there!

Oooh... Perhaps a Belgian biscuit out of Rockingham's and break New Year Resolution Number Two?

Exit FRAZER.

MARJORIE (*after him*). Thanks, Frazer, you're a sweetheart! So he is, eh, Susan?

SUSAN. Yes, Frazer's lovely!

MARJORIE. Does he have a friend?

SUSAN. Stacks and stacks of them.

MARJORIE. No, I mean –

SUSAN. I know exactly what you mean and I don't know. No one live-in anyway, nobody he talks about particularly.

MARJORIE. There's an awfully nice chap in Douglas's office, nice type, as they say a confirmed bachelor, I wonder –

SUSAN. Marjorie, leave the boy alone! Frazer's perfectly happy how he is!

MARJORIE. If you say so.

SUSAN. I do!

MARJORIE *looks out of the window.*

MARJORIE. Blooming parking attendants! There they go, harassing some other innocent motorist. Ugly uniform, isn't it? Ugly job. I was just in time out there. They'd not actually started writing out the ticket.

MARJORIE *spots the bag of rubbish.*

What's this?

SUSAN. Don't ask, Marjorie, just go and get your tea, you've had a stressful experience.

MARJORIE. I'll give these so-and-sos a stressful experience all right! Blinking Little Hitlers!

MARJORIE *exits backshop.*

SUSAN. Oh I know Marjorie, I know…

SUSAN *looks down at the disgusting bag, dispirited. She looks in again, then ties the top of it back up firmly, shaking her head. The meek, well-dressed* WOMAN *comes out, and twirls in front of the mirror in her coat, preening herself almost apologetically.*

(*Of bag.*) Completely and utterly dis-bloody-gusting!

WOMAN. Sorry?

SUSAN. – Absolutely stinking!

WOMAN. Pardon?

SUSAN (*leaving bag*). No! Sorry… I…

WOMAN. I was just saying, what do you think of it? Really?

Scruffy MAN *comes in dragging another bag.*

SUSAN (*to* WOMAN). Very nice!

MAN. Oh, it's no bother! Phwaugh! I'm done in. This is even heavier than the last one…

SUSAN *whirls to stop him, bumping into and tripping over the first bag.*

SUSAN. Sir! At the moment we really are overstocked, so –

WOMAN. But you know, I don't know if it's really me…

The WOMAN *goes back into the changing room.* SUSAN *gets up. The* MAN *leaves his second bag and exits.*

MAN (*calling*). I've more. Plenty more where that came from! I'll be back!

SUSAN. Sir! Sir! We can't –

SUSAN *runs towards the second bag but he's gone. She speaks through the inner curtain to well-dressed* WOMAN.

What about the dress then? Was that any use?

The WOMAN*'s arm comes through the inner curtain, handing the dress over.* SUSAN *takes it.*

WOMAN. No… no… I'm not sure…

As SUSAN *walks by the second bag, she's hit by a whiff.*

SUSAN. Oh, what a smell!

WOMAN (*off*). Sorry?

SUSAN. No. No. Sorry, not you!

SUSAN *hangs up the dress, goes back and bends to the second bag.*

The WOMAN *comes out of the changing room holding the coat on a hanger, all her attention on it, not looking at* SUSAN, *shaking her head at the sight of herself.*

WOMAN. No. No, d'you know, I don't really think so…

SUSAN (*shouting at bag*). We're not a bloody rag-and-bone shop, you know!

WOMAN. No, no! I just mean I don't –

SUSAN. Oh, not you! Sorry, is it no use?

The worm turns.

WOMAN (*very brusquely*). No! No, it is not!

The WOMAN *thrusts the coat on its hanger at* SUSAN *and exits through front door in high dudgeon.*

SUSAN. That's nice!

(*Of the coat.*) Here, that *is* nice! This is a good thing. It really is fantastic quality. Astonishing what some folk chuck out, it really is! And weatherproof! Wonder if our Stephi would wear that? It's very smart. So I don't suppose she'd be seen dead in it.

MARJORIE *shouts out from backshop.*

MARJORIE (*off*). Are you not having any tea then, Susan?

SUSAN. Oh yes indeedy. In a mo, Marjorie.

SUSAN *puts the coat back on the rail, shouts.*

(*Shouts.*) How you doing in there, Doris?

DORIS (*off*). Ach, I don't think this is my lucky day!

SUSAN. Yours neither, eh?

Marjorie! Marjorie, we've got a Code Three here. Situation Red Alert! Toxic Waste.

There's a couple of bags here. Well, obviously we'll have to go through them…

Enter MARJORIE *from backshop.*

MARJORIE. Who brought them in?

SUSAN. A scruffy little sod.

MARJORIE. Well, Susan, you should've known not to accept them. You just say – politely but firmly – thanks very much! Thanks but no thanks!

SUSAN. Well, we will have to go through them now, because, as Frazer says, you never know the minute. (The clothes, no, but there could be valuable bric-a-brac. Has happened!) But I'll tell you one thing, it's not a task for anybody without their Marigolds, Marjorie.

MARJORIE *sees something out of the window.*

MARJORIE. Is that him? There's a man coming across the road with a big bag…

SUSAN. Sorry, Marjorie, you deal with it! I'm going to wash my hands and get a cuppa.

SUSAN *drags the two heavy, smelly bags behind her towards backshop.*

MARJORIE. – Because I'll give him short shrift!

MARJORIE *bends down behind the counter.*

DAVID, *an attractive man of about fifty, enters to the sight of* SUSAN *disappearing as she hums a few bars from the theme tune to* Steptoe & Son.

DAVID. Em…!

But the swing doors shut on him: 'Private'.

Ah!

As he looks round, MARJORIE *pops up behind the counter, her hands up with rubber gloves on, and an insane smile on her face.*

MARJORIE. Can I help you?

FRAZER *enters with a pint of milk and box of cookies, to see –*

DAVID. Well, I just…

MARJORIE. No, thank you!

MARJORIE *picks up* DAVID*'s bag and runs with it to the door where she dumps it unceremoniously outside. She comes back and glares.*

FRAZER, *amazed, dumps the milk and cookies beside* SUSAN*'s book on the desk, goes out, picks the bag back up, and brings it in again.*

FRAZER. Can I give you a hand, Marjorie?

DAVID. I have some things and I wondered if you –

MARJORIE (*beady*). Are they good things?

DAVID. Yes. Yes, I think so. If –

FRAZER. You *sure* I can't give you a hand, Marjorie?

MARJORIE. No, it's okay, Frazer, thank you!

FRAZER *opens the bag, pulls out from the top an elegant classic and simple dress which he holds up against himself with a flourish.*

Oh, that –

MARJORIE *and* FRAZER (*in unison*). – is beautiful!

DAVID. It's just… Well, there's a couple of these dresses and coats and ladies jackets and so on. Good quality, so I thought –

MARJORIE. Oh excellent! (*Sympathetic.*) Have you had a bereavement?

FRAZER *grabs* MARJORIE *and drags her away.*

FRAZER. For God's sake, Marjorie! Obviously the man's had a bereavement. Either that or he's a bloody transvestite!

He goes to DAVID, *touches his arm.*

Did you lose your mother? Oh, I know how you feel. I lost mine more than two years ago and I'm still not right, am I, Marjorie?

DAVID. My wife actually. She died. Almost a year ago. I thought it was time to –

MARJORIE. Oh absolutely!

DAVID. And it's a waste.

MARJORIE. Oh absolutely.

DAVID. Somebody should be getting the good –

MARJORIE. Oh absolutely.

FRAZER. Marjorie! Why don't you go through and join Susan in that cup of tea that must be getting freezing cold by now!

FRAZER *thrusts the pint of milk and the box of biscuits at her. She takes them, and exits with the dress over her arm to backroom, her embarassment dawning on her.*

She's got a heart of gold! She really has.

DAVID. Seemed quite a character.

FRAZER. She is. She's a good woman. Really. Can I help you with anything else?

DAVID. No thanks.

He goes to leave but FRAZER *puts his hand on his arm, detaining him.*

FRAZER. The charity will make a lot from your kind donation – we do charge proper economic prices, you know. They don't go for fifty pence! Never! And you know what a good cause…

Not to speak of the pleasure it'll be for me to have some really classy stuff to work with. Unless that is – are you local? You're not, are you? Say you're not!

DAVID. Couldn't be more so, I'm just across the road!

FRAZER. Well, then no way, Mr…

DAVID. David.

FRAZER (*shaking his hand*). Frazer! How'd you do, David! Well, you see, there is generally a policy of swapping, so that the goods you brought will be sold in another branch and some of their best stock will come to us. It's a courtesy thing, you know, so you won't be distressed by seeing your wife's things –

DAVID. No. No, that wouldn't bother me at all. Christine's done with them now.

I mean, we sorted through everything, gave it all away just after she died, but I must have missed that cupboard in the spare bedroom – I was looking for my badminton racquet and there they all were! You know, I don't think she'd ever worn half of them. There was this pair of shoes, look, here, I found them still in the box! Think she must've bought these for our son's wedding then ended up in something comfier so she could dance the night away. And she sure did!

He pulls out a shoebox, and leaves it on the counter.

FRAZER. Well, we're always very grateful for good stock.

DAVID. She had a lot of style, my wife, she loved clothes but... She was a really practical person, you know? She hated waste, she was very green, a great recycler – I was always in her bad books for putting glass in the plastic bin or plastic in with glass!

She always made me laugh! Oh – !

He gestures his embarrassment at 'going on like this', and turns to go.

FRAZER (*decisively*). David. David, don't go away. There's a number I want to give you. It's in my address book through the back. Bear with me –

DAVID (*indicating door, he's in a hurry*). Frazer, I'm –

FRAZER. Please!

DAVID. Okay.

FRAZER *exits to backroom.*

DAVID *idly picks up* SUSAN*'s* Doctor Zhivago, *looks at it, whistles 'Lara's Theme' from the film, smiles, and decides to buy it.*

He crouches down to rifle through a small heap of books on the downstage side of the counter as SUSAN *enters from the backroom. They are both hidden from each other's sight.* SUSAN *is carrying the good dress that* DAVID *brought to the shop. It's on a hanger and prominently priced by* MARJORIE. *She gives a little twirl as she passes the mirror, holding it up to herself.*

SUSAN. No, Susan, sweetheart, definitely not for you!

She hangs it up and is exiting again, just as DAVID, *hearing her and about to ask her something stands up. But she's gone. He puts another book on top of* Doctor Zhivago, *obscuring it.*

FRAZER *enters, holding out a piece of paper with a number on it.*

DAVID. Didn't know you did books.

FRAZER. Books, vinyl – oh, those down there, they've still to be sorted and shelved.

DAVID. This *Halliwell's Film Guide* is a lot more recent than mine!

FRAZER. David. David don't take this the wrong way but there's this Bereavement Group –

DAVID. Thanks. No, really, thank you, I know you mean it kindly but –

FRAZER. It helped me a lot. Still does.

DAVID. But yes, as Christine was fond of saying, it wouldn't do if we were all the same.

FRAZER. See, it's a process –

DAVID. It's a fact. A fact I have to be getting on with.

I'm sorry, but if there is one thing that gives me the heebie-jeebies it's all this counselling crap and therapy-speak. Just not my cup of tea! At all.

See, I don't think there is anything wrong with me. If there is then I think that it's only right there's something wrong this stage of the game.

I miss her. What's wrong with that?

FRAZER. Will you take the number?

DAVID (*a beat, evenly*). Sure, if you tell me how much these books are.

FRAZER. Oh, I'll need to go and get Marjorie. She's the manageress, she does all the pricing.

DAVID. Frazer, don't disturb her, don't! I'll be back. I'll get them then. I'll need to do a clear-out, I've plenty of books I'll never read again that I can bring over.

FRAZER. It's no bother. One second!

FRAZER *exits backshop*. DAVID *looks at his watch*. MARJORIE *enters*.

MARJORIE. Fifty pence! No! No, altogether!

She grabs the books, and shoves them in a bag for him.

DAVID. Take the quid. At least. I insist.

MARJORIE. Not at all –

DAVID. But there's a last year's *Halliwell's* and an as-new *Doctor Zhiva–*

MARJORIE. For goodness' sake, the amount of good things you brought in for us!

DAVID. And there's more! I'll bring them!

Exit DAVID. *Just the moment he is gone,* SUSAN *appears with more things, and hangs them up.*

MARJORIE. Charming man!

SUSAN (*automatically*). Really? Was he married?

Re-enter FRAZER. MARJORIE *picks up the shoebox.*

MARJORIE. What on earth is this? Oh my! Look at the make! They are an arm and a leg! You always see them with the Jimmy Choo's and the Manolo Thingy's in *Elle* and *Vogue* –

SUSAN *takes the box from* MARJORIE *and she is the one to open it and, breathlessly, to take the beautiful shoes out of their tissue in the box.* MARJORIE *takes them.*

Oh! Oh those are just gorgeous. They wouldn't even look at me with my high instep but they are just lovely!

Never been worn, look. Not a mark on the sole!

She puts them on the counter and, shaking her head at such profligacy, she exits backshop.

SUSAN. They're my size, but they look far too narrow.

FRAZER. Oh, try them on!

She does.

Oh my God. Do they fit?

She nods.

SUSAN. Like a glove.

SUSAN *dances and twirls about the place, smiling.*

FRAZER. Oh, Cinders, you shall go to the ball! Some day your prince will come! That is a gorgeous shoe! Not what you would call a wearing-shoe but very chic!

Hey, Susan, buy them and wear them tonight for… you know! Hey, if you don't get a feller in lovely shoes like that with a pair of perfect pins like you've got, then I don't know what's wrong with men.

Re-enter MARJORIE.

MARJORIE. Off! You can't buy them! You know that! It's against the rules –

Shocked, SUSAN *takes them off.*

FRAZER. Marjorie, don't be so bloody stupid. Price them at your highest, I'll put in an extra fiver on top – we are not trying to cheat our charity, we're just trying to give Susan a treat.

MARJORIE. You know the rules and why they exist. For goodness' sake! With Joanne from Head Office due any moment!

MARJORIE *closes the box and, taking the shoes, she exits.*

SUSAN *can't speak. She is near tears. Walking away, almost comically upset, she waves her hands in front of her, as if to say 'Don't you say anything, especially anything nice to me.'*

FRAZER. She'll relent, Susan! Why does she have to be like that?

Winding herself up further, SUSAN *shakes her head, tears about to spill, dumb-showing: 'Just keep away from me, Frazer, you're making it worse…'*

They were so elegant! So *you*! You could've gone anywhere in those shoes. They would have given you confidence. Class. For a classy lady.

SUSAN *could weep. Doesn't of course. Shuts her eyes, has to suffer it.* FRAZER *has a rebellious thought which thrills him.*

I'm going to put the wrong size on them or hide one till the six weeks are up and I'm allowed to buy you them. I will!

Enter DORIS *from the changing room.*

DORIS. Naw. No nothing! Tried oan the hale shoap but there was nothing suitable. Know thae days you lukk at yourself and you say I'm nicer in what I came in wi? Thanks.

She dumps a mess of clothes on counter, but, perversely, she returns a huge wedding hat to its proper place on a head in the window. She wheels round to reveal that the fitted coat she is wearing, and which looks, relatively, all right from the front, has two flaring contrast panel inserts in the back. She exits, but right at the door she wheels back in.

(*To* SUSAN.) Haw, whit is speed dating when it's at hame? Hope it's no whit I think it is!

Blackout.

End of Act One.

ACT TWO

FUNNY VALENTINE

Music: Jazzy instrumental of 'Love for Sale' (*Cole Porter*).

14 February, and the shop's been transformed to a place spectacularly decorated in red hearts for Valentine's Day.

As music fades, lights up on SUSAN *and* FRAZER. SUSAN, *with dusters, Pledge and Windolene, is cleaning off and on throughout this exchange.*

FRAZER *is at the counter, sorting through a box of period textiles, embroidered cushion covers, etc.*

SUSAN. I mean, what is the point?

FRAZER (*shrugs*). Search me, Susan.

SUSAN. Lying about your height? To somebody you're going to meet?

FRAZER *finds a lovely, fifties-style, red-and-white-checked, frilly pinny and pops it on* SUSAN, *tying the strings behind her back to camp up her housework, and try to make her laugh. She lets him, but she's not to be deflected or distracted.*

Lies. That's what you get, basically. Okay, I've only done it three times and I've yet to get past the 'meet for a coffee' stage but what I'd say is it's often rubbish. Most people e-mail tripe about themselves, they really do.

They're all 'I run my own business' or 'financial services' or 'IT'. (*Sceptically.*) I'm sure!

(*Beat.*) I've seen some terrible toupees.

FRAZER. Is there any other sort?

SUSAN. Probably not. Last night's was a corker.

FRAZER. Last night's toupee?

SUSAN (*spelling it out*). No, last night's Internet Cupid's Connection.

FRAZER. What?

SUSAN. You heard me!

FRAZER. Look at what happened with that speed-dating carry-on.

SUSAN. That was then, this is now.

FRAZER. – And not content with that, now you've got to… go *online* and look for a 'cyber sweetheart'.

SUSAN. Frazer, get modern. Everybody does computer dating these days.

FRAZER. – Posting your intimate details on the web for all and sundry.

SUSAN. Anybody would think you didn't want me to find True Love and Happiness!

FRAZER. Darling, of course I do. It's just –

SUSAN. I know!

But it's not dangerous. You don't put down any details that could identify you, no addresses or anything, just first names, in fact your *nom de plume* –

FRAZER (*hands in the air*). Up to yourself!

SUSAN. Anyway, I was telling you about last night's Geek of the Week. Supposed to be forty-seven – uh-huh, and the rest! Former social worker suffering from burn-out, now a 'consultant'. 'Darkly handsome' – well, is that not for me to say, not him?

You'd think so.

He was… Swarthy, that's what I'd say. Sallow. Terrible blackheads, totally bald, broader than he was long but I thought to myself, 'Susan, you've got to stop judging by appearances – because I'm ashamed to say I do – the man's p'rhaps an interesting man, give him a chance', so I thought, 'Okay, I'll meet him again, perhaps I'll go for a drink with him,' and he says to me he hopes I'm not offended but he won't ask to see me again because 'the spark is just there or it isn't' and he thinks it's better to be honest about these things, I'm a very nice lady but no spark.

FRAZER. I couldn't. I just couldn't. Imagine getting the thumbs-down from somebody you don't even fancy.

SUSAN. No. No, it didn't bother me to be quite honest. Rejection. When Tony left, yes. But a stranger? That I've never met before and I'll never meet again? (He said, 'Good luck with your quest!' Imagine! I nearly died!)

But I'm going to stick at all this carry-on and persevere because how else am I going to meet anyone? At my age?

FRAZER. Is that what you do? When you whatsit on the internet? Step it up from 'go for a coffee' to 'go for a drink'?

SUSAN. I think so. I'm hardly the expert but I think that's how it works. Meet in, say, Starbucks in somewhere impersonal, say, middle of town on late opening night, so if it doesn't work out – (Why should it work out? You do this stuff you take the long-term view, Frazer) – when it doesn't work out you can cut your losses and do a good freezer shop in Marks' and be back home before soap-time on the telly.

FRAZER. And if it works out?

SUSAN. If!

Well… I suppose next time you could meet for a drink? And if that worked out, following week you could arrange to go for a drink and a bite to eat. Perhaps swap phone numbers –

FRAZER. Oh my God, you better promise me you'll take good care of yourself! Because –

SUSAN. I'm hardly somebody some suave Casanova Conman's going to marry and murder for her money, am I?

FRAZER. You can't be too careful.

(Actually p'rhaps you can, I think that's been me all my life.)

But, oh, is it not kind of, I don't know – unnatural? Forced?

SUSAN. Like rhubarb?

FRAZER. No. Yes. I mean, you'll meet someone, Susan –

SUSAN. How? Where?

FRAZER. I honestly think you want to meet someone, you're meant to meet someone, you'll meet someone.

(Where does that leave me?)

SUSAN. There's no stigma nowadays. I'd even try that speed dating again.

FRAZER. Look where that got you!

SUSAN. He's got the message!

FRAZER. Eventually! Is that not a syndrome, that?

SUSAN. What?

FRAZER. De Somebody or Other's Syndrome. Being deluded that somebody's in love with you. I saw a programme about it on the telly: woman thought King George the Something was madly in love with her and sending her secret messages depending on how many curtains were drawn and how many not drawn on the front of Buckingham Palace.

SUSAN. He was harmless.

FRAZER. King George?

SUSAN. No, the guy that pestered me for a date, stupid!

The organiser of the speed dating told him she refused to forward any more correspondence to me and that was that.

FRAZER. – and there was a pair of identical twins both mad about some poor lorry driver whose life they made an absolute misery.

SUSAN. He was just a little bit persistent, that was all.

FRAZER. And the rest were all losers and weirdos as well; admit it.

SUSAN. Frazer, you want something, you've got to go for it. Take Positive Steps.

I'd do it again. And the internet. I'm even going to do an old-fashioned ad in that lonely hearts' column in the local rag. I'm not even particularly hopeful but I'll try.

FRAZER. GSOH?

SUSAN. What?

FRAZER. Good Sense of Humour.

SUSAN. Of course I have. I'll need it no doubt.

FRAZER. WLTM. You've got a good day for it, eh?

SUSAN. What? My birthday?

FRAZER. No, Valentine's! (*Dawns.*) Gosh –

SUSAN. – Forget it!

FRAZER. Oh, it is your birthday. I forgot! Some pal I am.

Valentine's Day! I knew that! You'd think I could've remembered –

SUSAN. It was perfect for Tony. He could kill two birds with one stone and forget Valentine's Day and my birthday in a one-er.

Ooh! My advert! Because I'm going to do one. Help me write it. Go on!

(*As she cleans.*) These mirrors! Who let in that mum with the sticky toddler?

SUSAN*'s housekeeping has taken her to the changing rooms.*

FRAZER. She wanted to try on a blouse.

SUSAN. And did she take it?

FRAZER. No…

SUSAN. Give me up the Windolene.

SUSAN *is inside the changing rooms now, behind the curtain. Pops back out again:*

– And the air freshener while you're at it!

She pops back in. During the following, SUSAN *keeps sticking her head out to chip in, then back inside again.* FRAZER *begins writing on a bit of paper.*

FRAZER. Attractive lady –

SUSAN. That means plain as a plate of chips but with a nice-enough nature.

FRAZER. Beautiful lady –

SUSAN. Hey! Steady on. Trade Descriptions Act.

FRAZER. Lovely lady. That's more like it? Strike a balance. Lovely lady (you are though)! Late forties –

SUSAN *and* FRAZER (*in unison*). Forty-something!

SUSAN *pops head back inside and now stays in.*

FRAZER. Young-looking, young-acting forty-something WLTM.

MARJORIE *appears from backshop. Caught by what* FRAZER, *apparently alone, is saying and doing, she stands at the door, quietly listening.*

Would like to meet… Man. Mature. Genuine. Caring. GSOH. Faithful. No, loyal. (Loyal's lovely.) Sensitive. A man… In touch with his feminine side. Own hair and teeth. OHAT.

For…

Fun. Companionship. Maybe more. Long winter afternoons curled up watching old black-and-whites on the telly.

MARJORIE *comes right out and touches his shoulder.*

MARJORIE. – Oh, Frazer, that's lovely!

FRAZER. What?

MARJORIE. I think it's so lovely that you've decided to… to 'come out of the closet', is that what they say? At your age. And look for love. And why not?

I'm not shocked, Frazer.

I think you'll find it's a changed climate generally.

People are broad-minded. These days. But I still think you're very brave.

(*Confiding.*) If you don't mind me saying so, I'm not actually totally one hundred per cent surprised.

FRAZER. Marjorie, it's not –

MARJORIE. Well, it won't be! Tea's up through the back, pet. Come through, yeah? And we can 'talk'.

If you want to…

MARJORIE *exits backshop.* SUSAN *comes out in hysterics of laughter.*

FRAZER. I know who should've come out the closet!

SUSAN. Oh Frazer, darling, I couldn't. I really, really don't want Marjorie's sympathy. Or her help. Christ, no.

FRAZER. But she thinks –

SUSAN. Let her. For me. Go on.

FRAZER. Ooh… *You!* What would I not do for you!

Smiling, SUSAN *picks up the ad copy, reads and sighs.*

FRAZER *covers up his (perhaps) over-fondness for* SUSAN *by camping it up, making light of his worry.*

Hey, Suze!

See once you've hooked your dream lover, what about our salsa nights, eh? Will you still chum me on a Tuesday?

SUSAN. Damn tootin'! (*Beat.*) Oh, I'll never meet anyone anyway.

FRAZER. Why not? Susan, you've got so much to offer.

SUSAN. Oh, I know that. My self-esteem hasn't slipped that low. I do have a lot to offer and of course I'm not about to offer it to just anyone.

'member that Stones' song? 'Ti-i-i-ime is on my side, yes it is…'?

'*Not'* – as Stephi would say.

Bloke my age with his own hair and teeth – no, strike the condition. Too stringent.

Bloke my age with a pulse, he can start over dead easy, find himself some fresh young bit and begin again.

Was reading an article in the *GQ* there. At the dentist. And it was perfectly brazen about it, it had a little formula about Every Man's Ideal Age for a Girlfriend or Partner and it went like this: Half Your Age Plus Seven. So… it works. It does.

Try it out. Okay… Marjorie's big son Steven, what age is he? Sixteen. Half his age that's eight, plus seven that's fifteen, I'm sure that'd do him very nicely, thank you.

And take Tony. Take my husband. Please…

(And she certainly did.)

Well, Tony's fifty, half that is twenty-five plus seven that's thirty-two. I believe the Dreaded Natalie is a youngish thirty-something…? No doubt with tits out to here, I wouldn't know. I'm yet to clap eyes on the bitch, anyway, anyway…

Now, I'm forty-nine, do the sum backwards. So take away seven, that's forty-two, double it. I'm the ideal age of girlfriend for a man of eighty-four. Which is Dad's age.

And I'm living with my Old Dad so there's got to be an irony there somewhere.

Enter DORIS *in the same coat and tea-cosy hat as before.*

DORIS. Did yous get a Valentine? Neither did Ah.

They acknowledge her: an exhausted wave from SUSAN, *a flamboyant ironic bow from* FRAZER. DORIS *begins to browse.*

SUSAN. Do you know, I don't really blame men, Frazer.

FRAZER. Oh, I do!

SUSAN. If I'm in the street and I see some attractive man, invariably I think about it, he'll be… oh, late thirties maximum, and certainly not about to be interested in me!

My 'Oh, He's Nice!' meter is stuck way back in the era I used to be using it last!

I don't think I fancy men over forty, frankly.

FRAZER. Some of us are okay, surely?

DORIS *has found something, and shows it to* SUSAN.

DORIS. Here, that's nice. What would you say that shade was?

SUSAN. Lovatt?

DORIS. Aye, so do I, but what would you cry it? Sortae sage? Kinna dark odeneel, intit? Between that and a sortae pale greenish donkey.

The phone rings and SUSAN *answers it.* DORIS *gathers a garment or two, eavesdropping.*

SUSAN. Speaking. (*Listens.*) Oh. (*Listens.*) Oh dear. (*Listens.*) Without his trous…? (*Listens.*) Oh dear. (*Listens.*) Oh dear. Yes, I can see that. (*Listens.*) No, he's never done that before. (*Listens.*) No, I'll come over the road. I'll come home, it's no bother, be right there.

She hangs up.

The home help. Little bit of a domestic emergency. With Dad. I'll have to pop home, I'm sure I'll be right back –

SUSAN *exits backshop.*

DORIS. Can I try them?

FRAZER. You know where to go, Doris.

DORIS *disappears into the changing room as* SUSAN *rushes out from backshop with her coat flung on. Grabbing her bag,* SUSAN *exits by the front door, bumping hard into* DAVID *who is carrying a big cardboard box before him. He drops the box.*

DAVID. Sorry! (*Meaning: 'Manners! Can't you apologise too?'*)

FRAZER. Hello! Back again! David, isn't it?

DAVID *dumps the box on the counter. A couple of sad suits still in hangers are sticking out. He grabs a bag off the top and grabs a handful of ties from inside it, spilling them onto the counter –*

DAVID. Ties! Who needs them?

– in a not-very-brightly-coloured silken heap of mainly striped and rather conservative numbers.

I mean, what a stupid appendage! One little strip of cloth to express ourselves.

And women have all this! Rainbows! Herbaceous borders –

He indicates the rows of dresses. MARJORIE *enters, and stands in the doorway, listening, concerned.*

FRAZER. Oh, I know! I often envy women their clothes, don't you?

DAVID. Well… I wouldn't say that, but –

MARJORIE. Frazer –

FRAZER. You are looking so fine. There is something different about you since the last time you were in here –

DAVID. Big clear-out! Psychologically good for you, don't they say? None of the young guys at work would be seen dead with a tie on. And these suits! What an old sad-sack I've been going to work, it's unnecessary.

FRAZER. Do you remember David, Marjorie? Isn't he looking great?

MARJORIE. Frazer –

DAVID. Dumping the whole damn lot of them, 'cept kept the bow tie for my dinner jacket and the black one for funerals.

FRAZER. And we hope, David, it'll be a long long while before either you or me's got another one of them.

MARJORIE. Oh, absolutely –

FRAZER. Looking fine! You really are.

DAVID. Thanks a lot! Emm… You're looking fit yourself…

MARJORIE. Frazer –

DAVID. I sort of took myself in hand, I thought Christine'd have been the first to remind me that life's for the living –

FRAZER. Oh, so it is, you should try new things! Speaking of… Tell me… Did you ring That Number…?

MARJORIE. Frazer –

FRAZER. Remember? That number I suggested –

MARJORIE. Frazer! There's a beautiful little cashmere cardie come in but it unfortunately needs debobbling, it's in urgent need of your services. Through the back.

FRAZER. Marjorie, I'm just having a little chat with –

MARJORIE. Yes, I do know David –

FRAZER. Can't it wait?

MARJORIE. You're our ultimate defuzzer, Frazer, as well you know!

FRAZER. Marjorie –

MARJORIE. Can I just have a little moment here, please, Frazer!

What can he say? FRAZER *exits backshop.* MARJORIE *makes a beeline for* DAVID *and touches his arm.*

(*Very confidentially.*) I hope he's not coming on too strong, David.

DAVID. No, not at all, Marjorie. I can call you Marjorie, can I? You don't mind me calling you by your first name? Because I don't think we've actually been formally introduced.

If she's being (*nicely and subtly*) *rebuked it's wasted on her.*

MARJORIE (*grandly*). Feel free, David, of course. It's just that I was concerned that he… Bit much? Eh?

DAVID. He's only got my interests at heart, Marjorie.

MARJORIE. Well, if you –

DAVID. He means well.

MARJORIE. That's very –

DAVID. Of course, I'm not that way inclined myself.

MARJORIE. I didn't think so.

DAVID. I'm not, and he knows that. I said, 'Not my cup of tea, no, sorry!'

But it's not as if he's the type to ram it down your throat, is he?

MARJORIE. I hope not.

DAVID. I was absolutely straight with him, and that was no problem. I think he preferred it.

But see, Marjorie, I look at it this way: it's very kind of him, I mean, from his point of view if something does something for you, well, obviously you can't help being… what? That little bit messianic about it? Can you? It's only natural.

MARJORIE. I'm glad you look at it that way.

DAVID. I do.

MARJORIE. Because I was worried in case…

DAVID. I can see that, but no need on my behalf, I can assure you.

MARJORIE. Because you see it's very very recent…

DAVID. Really? Oh, I thought it was a little while…

MARJORIE. Well, as far as him acknowledging it. Openly.

DAVID. So it was hard for him to accept it?

MARJORIE. Oh yes, oh, I think so, and of course denial…

DAVID. Touch of the Anthony Perkins's, eh?

MARJORIE. I don't follow…

DAVID *makes stabbing motions and imitates the* Psycho *soundtrack as her bafflement increases.*

DAVID. Ee! Ee! Ee! Ee! Bates Motel – Sorry, Marjorie, that was a sick joke and the last thing I'd ever want to do is make a fool of Frazer's feelings. (*Coughs.*) Sorry… Sorry?

No, no, I understand, that makes things a lot clearer. He was in denial. I see. I see… That'll be why the telephone thing'll have been somewhat of a lifeline for him?

MARJORIE. You're very tolerant.

DAVID. Of course!

MARJORIE. I'm glad to say!

DAVID. Well, the way I see it is everybody deals with these things in very different ways. Some folk like to get together in big touchy-feely groups, others – like me – are just more inclined to grin and bear it, just sort of stick it out in private.

MARJORIE *gives him a look –*

MARJORIE. Right…

DAVID. Or maybe, God help us, accidentally end up leading other folk up the garden path sort of a thing – because if you end up getting too close to somebody who's maybe not the right person to get close to, not right for you at all, and it's not the right time for you to be getting close to anybody in the first place far less the wrong person, well when you extricate yourself from the situation you should never have got into – because you've got to, because it's kinder in the long run, kinder all round obviously – well somebody can end up being hurt.

Sorry. See what I mean? Never mind it's not… sorry…

MARJORIE *is baffled. Exits backshop, sharpish. As* DAVID *makes for the door,* SUSAN*'s father* ARCHIE*, an old man of eighty-four, somewhat bewildered, enters and grabs him by the sleeve.*

ARCHIE.… Where's our Susan? Somebody said to me I'll find our Susan in here.

DAVID. Sorry, I'm not –

ARCHIE.… What are all these clothes doing in Fullerton the Ironmongers'? Where's Jack Fullerton?

DAVID. Mr Dickinson, it's you, isn't it?

ARCHIE.… Yes, Archibald Dickinson, that's me, do I know your face? You're familiar… but to tell you the truth, I've been diagnosed with a little bit of memory loss.

DAVID. I know you. You're Mr Dickinson the plumber. You put in a bathroom for us but you'll not remember that, why should you?

ARCHIE.…I do a lot of bathrooms. How's your wife?

DAVID. I'm afraid my wife died.

ARCHIE.…Oh, I'm sorry to hear that.

DAVID. Made a lovely job of our bathroom, you did!

ARCHIE.…Do you know, I think I came out the house there for a pound and a half of mince for the wife but I can't find Gardeners the Butchers'.

DAVID. Ah well…

ARCHIE.…Because our Susan's supposed to be coming up tonight with her Spanish boyfriend so of course she's wanting to make them Spaghetti Bolognese…

DAVID. Aaah… Frazer! Frazer! Marjorie!

Enter MARJORIE *from backshop.*

MARJORIE. He's away out the back at the bins, David, it's collection day. (*Shouting as if to a deaf person.*) Mr Dickinson, what are you doing here, I thought Susan was away home looking for you?

ARCHIE (*shouting back*). What is she looking for me for, because I'm normally at my work?

MARJORIE (*confidentially to* DAVID, *shaking head*). Confused.

Well, just you sit there for a minute, Mr Dickinson. I'm sure she'll be back in just a little minute.

ARCHIE.…No, I can't stop because I'm to get something or other for the wife. Wonder what it was…

MARJORIE (*confidentially to* DAVID, *shaking head*). Dead. Years ago!

Mr Dickinson, why don't you go through the back with David here and sit and have yourself a little cup of tea?

ARCHIE.…Because I'm getting forgetful, you know. To tell the truth, I've been diagnosed with a little bit of memory loss.

MARJORIE (*confidentially to* DAVID, *shaking head*). Tragic!

That's a good idea, come on through here with David…

ARCHIE (*to* DAVID). Who are you? Any relation of Jack Fullerton?

How's your wife? Is she keeping okay?

DAVID *manoeuvres* ARCHIE *backshop as* MARJORIE *looks out of the window.*

MARJORIE. Och Susan! Susan, where are you, for goodness' sake… No sign… I wonder if she's got her mobile?

MARJORIE *dials the phone.*

Susan, there you are! Where are you? Your dad's here! (*Listens.*) Mmm. Mmm. No, he's fine. Well, a little bit confused for sure, but he's fine, we've got him having a little cuppa through the back with Frazer and David. (*Listens.*) You know David! You do!

Oh, never mind, your dad's just dandy! Okay, okay, see you in a little minute. Susan, don't rush, he's perfectly all right.

DAVID *returns from backshop.*

DAVID. I'm just off. Frazer seems to be having a job finding the Empire Biscuits he's promised Mr Dickinson.

MARJORIE *rolls her eyes at the incompetence she puts up with.*

MARJORIE. I can't tempt you?

MARJORIE *exits backshop. Grinning,* DAVID *nods his goodbye, but he is beaten to his exit by a muffled* DELIVERY MAN *who enters with big bunch of red roses and a heart card, blocking him.*

DELIVERY MAN. I'll need a signature, please.

DAVID. Can't help you, pal, sorry, I don't work here.

DAVID *tries again for the door, but the* DELIVERY MAN *stops him.*

DELIVERY MAN. Flowers for Love, it's a same-day delivery. Just sign for them.

DAVID. Frazer! Marjorie!

MARJORIE *comes back out.*

MARJORIE. Oh my! These are beautiful!

Wait there just one little second, David, please, could you? (*Signs chit and reads card.*) Seems our Susan must have a secret admirer! Well, well, there's a turn-up for the books.

The DELIVERY MAN *exits.*

David, I meant to ask you, you couldn't do me a favour and bring that box of yours – (it was awfully good of you) – through the back for me, only, poor old Frazer's disc's playing up again and the consultant was adamant I'm not supposed to do any heavy lifting for a full year after my little op.

DAVID. Of course.

Ushered by MARJORIE, DAVID *begins to lift the box and bring it through the back. Leaving the plastic bag with the spilling bundle of ties on the counter.*

MARJORIE. Course it was keyhole and quite frankly, a couple of weeks later there was damn all wrong with me.

What on earth have you been bringing us? Books! They're so blinking heavy, aren't they –

DAVID. Books, CDs, videos, two fondue sets…

MARJORIE. Oh absolutely!

They exit backshop just as SUSAN *comes in through the front door and, on her way towards the back, does a double take, arrested by the sight of the roses.*

SUSAN. Oh my! Somebody loves somebody.

She looks at the card. And backs off as if it's radioactive.

Is somebody taking the piss? Frazer! Frazer!

FRAZER *sticks his head out from backshop.*

FRAZER. Hi there, Susan, the old fella's fine. Wants to put a new washer on our tap. That'll be him for hours, eh? Happy as Larry…

SUSAN *is still examining the roses, amazed. Behind* SUSAN, DAVID *comes out from backshop, dusting his hands.*

Hearing his footsteps, SUSAN, *thinking it's* FRAZER, *turns and hugs him.*

SUSAN. Did you send these? Frazer, you're –

DAVID. Not guilty, no. Flowers for Love, that's what the man said!

SUSAN. Oh! Sorry, sorry, I thought you were… Excuse me!

SUSAN, *covered in confusion, flees backshop, dropping the bouquet.* FRAZER *enters from backshop crossing with her.* DAVID *picks up the roses from the floor.*

DAVID. These don't seem to have had the desired effect...

FRAZER. You sent roses...?

DAVID. No. Why'd I send anybody roses? I just meant, somebody –

FRAZER *is reading the card.*

FRAZER. Sent roses to Susan? 'All My Love from You Know Who...'? You'd think she'd be pleased...

DAVID. My point entirely.

FRAZER. Anyway, David, as I was trying to ask you earlier before I got so rudely interrupted – (Marjorie, honest to God, what is she on?) – how are you? In yourself.

DAVID. I'm fine. Most of the time. I'm sleeping better. I seem to accept now that Christine's gone. I still miss her. Always will, no question about that, but... Things've changed. The house feels different now. Don't laugh – perhaps you'll know what I'm talking about? – but for months and months I'd go into a room and I'd feel she'd just left. Not her perfume exactly – and there was nothing spooky about this feeling, quite the reverse, it was a comfort if anything. Her presence, you know? Often as if she was in the house but in another room. I mean, I knew it was just in my imagination but it felt quite real to me and... Recently it's changed. She's gone.

FRAZER. Oh, I know what you mean, sometimes when I go in that door I'm just expecting my old mum to be sat there in that kitchen!

DAVID. No, what I'm saying, I *don't* –

FRAZER. No, I know exactly what you mean!

DAVID. The worse thing I can do to Christine's memory is try and turn her into some kind of saint. Cos she sure wasn't. Neither of us were! We made a lot of mistakes, had a lot of ups and downs like anybody else, two or three bad patches where I tell you it was touch and go if we made it as a couple... but we had the boys, and we got through it. Somehow. (*Smiles.*) And the last four or five years, before she was diagnosed, yes, and after it too – well, that is often the way of it, is it not?

FRAZER. I don't think I'll ever get over my mother!

DAVID. No, no, I can see that. (*Beat.*) Have you redecorated?

FRAZER. Eh? I'm changing things around. Got rid of the television. Phoned up the Salvation Army and they came up and took it off my hands. I don't miss it, not one bit. I've been reading a lot and listening to music, I used to be a big jazz buff, you know, but some of those LPs I've not listened to for years.

I've tried taking myself out to the movies, but –

Anyway, life moves on. New beginnings. I can't help but feel that something is about to happen. Well… for instance –

Through the door comes a youngish thirty-something woman, festooned with expensive carriers from Scandalrags boutique. This (though we are yet to know it) is NATALIE.

NATALIE. Excuse me, can I try that shoe in the window?

FRAZER. Surely.

FRAZER *remembers the provenance of the shoe and wishes to protect* DAVID.

Is that you off, David?

NATALIE. It's the one on the heart-shaped cushion, I'm sure it's a –

FRAZER. Yes, it is! I know just the shoe you're talking about, only –

NATALIE. Can I try it?

FRAZER. Surely.

FRAZER *reluctantly goes to window, brings it back to her.*

NATALIE. I think it says… Am I right, is it a thirty-seven? Oh, right foot, is it?

FRAZER. It is, but…

NATALIE. That's my size normally. It's brand new! Oh gosh, oh gosh, that is just perfect, isn't it? What do you think?

She tries the shoe on and stretches out her leg like Anne Bancroft in The Graduate, *skirt above knee, right at* DAVID *who, of course, recognises the shoe. He is affected by a sudden pang of grief.*

DAVID. Oh! Oh, very nice, I'm sure. Excuse me.

DAVID *exits.*

NATALIE. What's the matter with your other assistant? Did I offend him?

FRAZER. No. No. He doesn't work here, no, just a little… emotional moment there, I suspect.

For emotional reasons.

NATALIE *is puzzled, but much more interested in swivelling her ankle and admiring her own shapely leg in the lovely shoe.*

NATALIE. Right… Can I try the other foot?

FRAZER. The left?

NATALIE. Yeah, right.

FRAZER. No, that's the thing, I'm sorry. We've only got the one.

NATALIE. The what?

FRAZER. The one.

NATALIE. The one?

FRAZER. Uh-huh.

NATALIE. Of the pair?

FRAZER. Uh-huh. I assume. If they were a pair.

NATALIE. Really? Surely –

FRAZER. Well, we've mislaid it, obviously. Or else it came in like that.

NATALIE. The one shoe?

FRAZER. Or it was stolen.

NATALIE. One shoe? Somebody…?

FRAZER. Well, the other's here, so…

SUSAN *enters, waving her book.*

SUSAN. I don't believe it. My *Doctor Zhivago* that I lost! (I take it all back, Marjorie! I was sure she'd sold it because she so very vehemently denied it.)

SUSAN *sees* NATALIE *wearing 'her' shoe.*

Oh, sorry! Oh! Somebody's found a bargain!

SUSAN *and* FRAZER *are quite complicit throughout the following. It's not the first time they've pulled this stunt.* SUSAN *is slightly shocked at herself, which makes her enjoy it even more; she's quite near the giggles throughout.*

NATALIE. Well, I thought so, only –

SUSAN. *Don't* tell me it's still not turned up, Frazer?

FRAZER. Neither hide nor hair of it unfortunately.

SUSAN. Really?

FRAZER. And do you know, I'm beginning to think it never will.

NATALIE. You're joking! Oh well, I should have known I wasn't the get-a-great-bargain-in-a-charity-shop type! Girl in my office kits herself out constantly from top to toe in secondhand shops and looks a million dollars.

SUSAN. I know, some people just seem to have an eye, don't they? And the knack.

NATALIE. – She got a Nicole Farhi in the Marie Curie!

SUSAN. Oh, it wouldn't be me!

NATALIE. – She *says*. Yeah, right! Because of course it's nothing but a reverse sort of one-upmanship, if you ask me.

You know: 'I got that exact Versace jacket in Oxfam.'

'Paid full price for your Prada bag, did you? You're a mug, cos I got mine in TK Maxx for a fiver.'

(*Beat.*) Basically, you want to kill the cow.

FRAZER. Is the one no good to you?

NATALIE. Eh?

FRAZER. Because it'd just be the half price, obviously…

NATALIE. Pardon?

SUSAN. Frazer!

FRAZER. What? Well, somebody's going to want it…

With a theatrical sigh he replaces the shoe in the window, then goes to the counter and picks up the roses.

NATALIE. Look, if you would just take a look –

FRAZER. I'll take these through –

NATALIE. Please! Okay?

FRAZER. – and I'll put them in water because if you ask me, somebody round here is very ungrateful indeed!

SUSAN. Frazer, I'm –

But he's off through the back. To herself, though NATALIE *overhears:*

Shouldn't have, he really shouldn't…

NATALIE. Little crush on you, has he? You can't tell can you, like my hairdresser, you'd totally swear he was camp as Chloë but, no, as you were, he's happily married with three kids!

SUSAN. My someone's been splashing out today already! Scandalrags, eh, lucky you, I always look in their window and wish.

NATALIE. You should go in!

SUSAN. They're beyond my budget and that's for sure!

NATALIE. No, you get to your age, you need a bit of class in the clothes department. Look at this…

She drags out a simple but classy top from one carrier bag, and holds it up.

See, this would suit you. Because you've got a lovely figure.

SUSAN. Me!

NATALIE. Oh, you have. For your age, stunning!

As the woman said to me: 'With perhaps a plain pant?' And it wasn't dear.

She shows SUSAN *the price tag.* SUSAN *grimaces in unfeigned shock.*

Not for what it is.

SUSAN. If you say so!

It's lovely all the same! Special occasion coming up?

NATALIE. No, not really. It's not that! Just fancied it.

SUSAN. Indulge yourself!

NATALIE. Why not?

SUSAN. Nobody else is going to!

NATALIE. Well… Ajay indulges me all the time actually, but I've got to not leave it up to him to do the choosing. Men, eh? They'd have you running around in raunchy, red-lace, see-through bra-and-thong sets – oh, which you've to wear below butter-wouldn't-melt, duck-egg-blue, retro, angora twinsets that make you look like a cross between Nigella Lawson and the first teacher they ever adored in the mixed infants!

I go, 'Ajay, thank you, but exactly *who* is this a present *for*?'

NATALIE *catches sight of the heart-patterned tie sticking out of the top of* DAVID*'s bag, and pulls it out like a lovely silken snake.*

Oh, hearts, look! I'm sure it's silk! My, that'd be a lovely little Valentine's Day extra.

SUSAN. Does he wear ties?

Because men don't much these days, do they? Mine never –

NATALIE. No?

SUSAN. Not really.

NATALIE. Oh, Ajay really likes to get dressed up.

SUSAN. Lucky you. Mine was a slob.

NATALIE. When we go out. Like tonight he's insisting we go out for dinner. Well, it's not that it's Valentine's Day as such; it's more that it's our anniversary, two years to the day since we actually… you know! For the first time.

Course I'd fancied him for absolutely ages!

(*Of tie.*) I have to get this. I really do!

Tell you, tonight quite frankly I'd as soon stay home. Honestly. Heartburn. It's really shocking. I'm nearly two months pregnant and nobody told me that morning sickness was more like morning, noon and night!

I'm getting married in a month's time too. I hope to God it's stopped by then or I'll not be the bonny blushing bride, I'll be the pale green and permanently puking bride!

Course he's over the moon; well, men always are, aren't they? They just love pregnant women.

SUSAN. Mine didn't.

NATALIE. No?

SUSAN. Not really.

NATALIE. Ajay's signing up for the breathing classes, the lot.

SUSAN. I suppose it's not actually his fault. I went into labour a month early and he was in Barcelona at the big match while I was getting an emergency Caesarean – but oh well… He's always been a great dad, I'll give him that. Once our daughter was born, he enjoyed that. We both did. When she was little…

NATALIE. How old is she now?

SUSAN. Fifteen.

NATALIE. Oh, don't! My step-daughter's fifteen! Great lump, so she is, that Stephanie. Ajay says, 'Natalie, there's no need to put up with cheek from her, she knows I won't tolerate it.'

SUSAN (*reeling*). Excuse me, it's just occurred to me I think I might know where that shoe is.

SUSAN *exits backshop.* NATALIE *looks around puzzled. Then she holds out, and rolls up the tie, savouring it.*

NATALIE. Gorgeous…

SUSAN *steams back on with the shoebox containing the left shoe wrapped in tissue.* FRAZER *comes running on after her.*

SUSAN. Here it is!

NATALIE. Gosh! I'm in luck then.

SUSAN. Looks like it!

FRAZER. What are you doing? I think you'll find, I think you'll find the heel's broken! You can't sell that shoe, it's dangerous!

NATALIE. Nonsense, it looks absolutely fine! Give me a little shot of the other one again.

FRAZER. They're very expensive.

NATALIE. Not at all! Because they're normally extortionate!

SUSAN. Frazer! You must have them! Of course you must.

NATALIE *puts them on, and kicks her heels in pleasure.*

NATALIE. Oh yes! Yes! YES! They are divine!

SUSAN. Take them!

NATALIE *stands and sashays across the room in them.*

FRAZER. For God's sake!

She twirls, then stops, takes a dithering beat or two.

NATALIE. ...But you know, the left one does pinch a little bit...

SUSAN. It'll stretch!

NATALIE. Maybe... (*Beat. Walks again. Considers.*) I'm not sure it will.

FRAZER. It's a mistake to buy a shoe that doesn't fit you perfectly!

NATALIE. I know. I know, but I just –

FRAZER. Big mistake. Bunions before you –

NATALIE. God forbid. But they are *so* lovely...

FRAZER. But they don't fit you!

NATALIE (*long beat*). You're right. You're right. It is so, so weird too because normally my left foot is slightly smaller than the right, I can't understand it.

She takes them off, shaking her head in disappointment. FRAZER *grabs them.*

FRAZER. There you go! You made the right decision.

NATALIE. I'll take that tie though.

FRAZER. This? It's not priced.

NATALIE. How much do they normally go for?

SUSAN. £1.99. Invariably.

FRAZER. Or more!

NATALIE. It's immaculate! I'd have paid a tenner.

SUSAN. Done!

FRAZER. But it's not priced!

SUSAN. Well, I've sold it! Ten quid to you!

NATALIE. Gosh, I don't actually have any cash! Do you take credit cards, I don't suppose so…

SUSAN. Or cheque!

NATALIE. Well, great! (*Begins writing a cheque.*) Ooh! He'll love it! He'll just so so love it!

SUSAN. Good!

NATALIE. Do you want my card? Will I put the number?

SUSAN. No, it's fine, I'm sure we can trust you.

NATALIE. You sure?

NATALIE *exits with the tie, but without the shoes. As she goes:*

Oh, do you know, I could just spit about those shoes!

FRAZER. That was a close thing!

Ruby slippers! Talk about lucky! I'm buying you them, I am, as a belated birthday present next week once they've survived Marjorie's six-weeks-on-sale-before-staff-eligible-to-purchase rule.

SUSAN. I don't want them.

FRAZER. What's the matter?

SUSAN. That was Natalie.

FRAZER. You mean…

SUSAN. Natalie. Antony James's, sorry, Ajay's, new little…

She waves the signed cheque in front of his face, then puts it in the till.

FRAZER. Her? No! She's practically young enough to be his –

SUSAN. – girlfriend. Yes. Exactly.

FRAZER. Well, at least she never got your shoes!

SUSAN. She might as well have, she's got everything else. Go on! Take my husband, buy my daughter's affection by giving her everything money can buy, letting her do everything that Bad Old Mum won't let her do because she's too young, give her the thrill of being a Big Sister…

FRAZER. You mean she's –

SUSAN. Yup!

FRAZER. Well, I suppose it was on the cards.

SUSAN. Yup!

FRAZER. You had already come up with that particular 'someday' scenario yourself.

SUSAN. Yup. Stephi will be thrilled!

FRAZER. Susan, you said your Stephi couldn't stand the Dreaded Natalie –

An enormous and horrible realisation hits SUSAN*: 'What a bastard!'*

SUSAN. Oh my God!

FRAZER. What?

SUSAN. Huh! Now I know where Tony was and exactly what he was up to on my forty-seventh birthday!

FRAZER. You said to me things between you and Tony were dead long before –

SUSAN. Okay! Okay!

FRAZER. You'd nothing in common really except Stephi, you never had sex except once in a blue moon –

SUSAN. I know, I know.

FRAZER. – 'A very very blue moon, with the lights out and over in no time and personally you'd have preferred a cup of tea.' These are your own exact words. I'm quoting.

SUSAN. I don't think that's uncommon, Frazer, not after twenty odd years!

FRAZER. Well, perhaps not, what would I know, nothing, I've never been married and the way you describe you and Tony, well, if that's typical, I can't say I've missed much. I know one thing, my mother never felt like that about my dad. Adored him. When he died she couldn't begin to cope without him –

SUSAN. Frazer, it's one thing going along as usual, living quite the thing in a flatline marriage with a fairly friendly semi-stranger, and another being all of a sudden dumped and having to witness your husband be far from flatline with a girl half his age.

FRAZER. Plus seven!

SUSAN. Oh shut up, you!

DORIS*'s hand comes through curtain, holding out some garments.*

DORIS (*off*). No, these are definite no-nos, you can hing them back up. I've a couple of mibbes, but.

SUSAN *goes and takes them.*

SUSAN. Lovatt not do it for you? Just you take your time, Doris…

A thought planted by NATALIE *crosses* SUSAN*'s mind.*

Frazer. Frazer, listen, darling, you did send me these roses for my birthday, didn't you, not for Valentine's?

FRAZER. Me? I never sent you the roses at all, Susan.

SUSAN. Then who did?

FRAZER *shrugs and holds up the 'ruby slippers', plays with them, puts them on his hands to wear and points them at* SUSAN *throughout the following.*

FRAZER. Ooh! Absolutely no bloody thanks to you they're still here, madam! My heart was in my mouth there. I could've brained you! 'Positive Steps'? 'Positive Steps'? You've got a real streak of negativity, you have.

SUSAN. Me?

FRAZER. Because you do deserve these (*Of the shoes.*) and there are attractive, available men out there. Without you resorting to desperate measures.

SUSAN. There is nothing desperate about me, Frazer, if I manage to meet someone on the internet or via the lonely hearts' column or however so be it. If not, I'll live. I would like to, I'd like for that whole side of my life not to be totally over, but I'm really not banking on it.

MARJORIE *comes swanning out from backshop, carrying* SUSAN*'s flowers in a vase –*

MARJORIE. Say what you like about similar demographics, but the stuff they sent over from the other branch isn't a patch on what we sent them.

– which she puts on the counter with a flourish.

My, Susan, you're a dark horse!

Flustered, FRAZER *catches himself with the shoes in his hands, so pushes them deep into* DAVID*'s bag with the ties on top to hide them.*

FRAZER. Oh, err, I was just saying to Susan that there are attractive, unattached, available men you can meet, eh, Marjorie? Even in middle age. I mean, take me, take David.

SUSAN. Who's David?

FRAZER. David! You saw him, he's a widower, he's –

MARJORIE. – In a relationship, Frazer, sorry to disappoint you!

FRAZER. Eh? David? I don't think so, Marjorie, he certainly never gave me that impression.

MARJORIE. Well, I'm sorry, but he's got a girlfriend.

FRAZER. Has he?

SUSAN. Of course he has! (Whoever he is…)

MARJORIE. Oh yes. He made that very clear to me in our little chat. The first thing he made sure he told me! He's a normal heterosexual male, Frazer…

SUSAN.… And your normal heterosexual male doesn't lack female company for very long! Widower? Do you know how long the average widower goes before he has another relationship?

FRAZER. No, but –

SUSAN. How long?

FRAZER. Oh… A couple of years? I dunno, but –

SUSAN. Six months! And how long for the average widow?

FRAZER. I don't know. Longer. Presumably. Three years?

SUSAN. Thirteen. Widowers, six months. Widows, thirteen years. On average.

FRAZER. You're hell of a keen on numbers and statistics these days, Susan. (This that bloody magazine at the dentist again?) I mean, people are people, they don't necessarily fit into statistics.

MARJORIE. Nor do leopards change their spots, Frazer. Just think about it, pet, please, for your own sake.

FRAZER. Eh?

MARJORIE. Because I wouldn't like to see you getting hurt, that's all.

SUSAN (*looking out of the window*). Oh my God, there's that guy, that I… He's coming in! I'm away –

DAVID *enters, just in time to see the very back of* SUSAN *as she flees.*

FRAZER. David! Back again!

DAVID. I am. Thing is… This is embarrassing, but I brought over something I shouldn't have. Can I take a look?

MARJORIE. Of course! If you just brought it over, David, it'll be still there. Nothing's even priced yet. Can I help you? What exactly is it?

DAVID. Oh, it's okay, Marjorie. It's just a… it was a present in fact, a tie, and I should never –

FRAZER. Were there hearts on it?

DAVID. Yes.

FRAZER. (I knew it…)

MARJORIE. Well, it'll still be there. Definitely. Hearts?

She begins to look with him.

On a tie? In a pattern kind of thing? (*Shouting.*) Susan! Did you see David's tie? Susan! Come here!

MARJORIE, *in her rummaging, finds the ruby slippers deep in the bag. She stands them up, in all their glory, on the counter.*

Well, would you credit it! The pair! Because, David, I know these were a kind donation from you and I tell you we could have sold them ten times over in the past few weeks only there was only ever the one of them could be found, it was a total mystery! (*Shouting.*) Susan! Susan, you definitely never sold a heart-patterned tie of David's, did you?

FRAZER. But they weren't even priced yet, Marjorie!

MARJORIE. I know! You sure you brought it over, David?

DAVID. Yes, I'm afraid that I did.

MARJORIE. I'll away through and see if by any chance it fell in the box with those books of yours, David!

MARJORIE *exits backshop.* DAVID *keeps looking, delving to the bottom of the bag, ever more worried. The phone rings.* FRAZER *answers.*

FRAZER. Hello. (*Beat.*) Yes, it is, yes! (*Beat.*) Yes, she is. (*Calls.*) Susan, it's for you. SUSAN! PHONE!

Reluctantly, SUSAN *enters and takes the phone.* FRAZER *takes* DAVID *aside.*

SUSAN (*phone*). Hello, hello, who is this? (*Listens.*) Excuse me? (*Listens.*) No, no, I did not send a Valentine message to you, you're dreaming.

DAVID. It really doesn't seem to be here anywhere…

FRAZER. No.

SUSAN (*phone*). No, I told you at the time, there really isn't any point. How did you? How did you know where to…?

FRAZER. Thing is, David… Susan sold it.

SUSAN (*phone*). No, I did not see you on the bus. I did not signal for you to get off and follow me, you're deluded. That's not… that's not so, I'm sorry.

Don't call me here again, I mean it.

SUSAN *puts the phone down firmly and stuffs the roses into bin. Both* DAVID *and* FRAZER *watch amazed.*

FRAZER. Hey, steady on, Susan.

SUSAN. Frazer, they were from You Know Who, I really don't want to discuss it, thank you!

FRAZER. Eh? – Oh right, from Mr Speed –

SUSAN. Frazer!

DAVID (*puzzled*). But could you not have…? I mean, if you didn't want them?

SUSAN. What? Given them to charity?

SUSAN *fishes the roses back out of the bin.*

Yes, yes, of course, they're perfectly good roses, oh, only a little bit bashed and past it and worse for wear – do you want to buy them?

DAVID. No… just, sorry –

SUSAN. Sure? Because I could get Marjorie to give us a price. No? Oh well, they'll just have to go back in the bin – goodbye! – because if there's one thing worse than not getting flowers on Valentine's Day, it's getting flowers on Valentine's Day from someone who is the last person you'd ever want flowers off of on Valentine's Day, or any other.

FRAZER. We might have known, eh? How did he get the address?

SUSAN. I said I don't want to talk about it!

DAVID. Frazer says you sold it?

SUSAN. Does he?

SUSAN *glares at* FRAZER.

DORIS *comes out of the changing room with a garment*

DORIS. I'll take this, I suppose. There was nothing else. I've just left the rest all in there.

SUSAN. Fine, Doris.

DORIS *claps eyes on the ruby slippers on the counter. She flings the garment aside.*

DORIS. Oh here, look at these! These're lovely, leave that, I'll take them!

FRAZER. But, Doris, they'll no fit you!

DORIS. They will. Likely. What size are they, a four?

FRAZER. But they're awfully dear!

DORIS. A tenner! No for what they are.

SUSAN. Certainly, Doris, they're yours!

SUSAN *stuffs them into a bag takes the money from* DORIS *and rings it up. She thrusts the bag at* DORIS*, who exits, taking them, thoroughly delighted.*

DORIS (*to* DAVID *as she goes*). Cheeritata! Never let it be said your dancing days are over, eh?

DAVID. I mean, it's my own fault, totally. It is! Let me be the first to admit it. I'm an idiot, I really am. Careless! I brought them all over, these ties. Big clean sweep, you know? It was just that no sooner was I back in the door than I thought to myself, aaah!

I mean, I cannot believe I was so bloody stupid. Thoughtless.

My fault entirely!

Then I thought, well, I could go over, buy it back, but…

Listen, you wouldn't have any idea at all where the tie went?

MARJORIE *shouts out from backshop*

MARJORIE (*off*). No sign of it, David, I'm sorry!

DAVID (*calling*). Yes, yes, it's okay, Marjorie, thank you. (*To* SUSAN.) I mean, who bought it? Because if we could track them down, I could offer them double – more – to get it back?

I mean, I don't know if it's feasible at all, but…?

(*Beat.*) Frazer, you don't happen to know, I don't suppose?

Who the tie was actually sold to?

FRAZER. Well… (*Beat.*) Susan, you don't think you –

SUSAN. No!

DAVID. You see, it's not the value of the thing, not at all, not the monetary value, what is it worth to anyone else but me and the person that made it, nothing, it's a handmade thing, you see, and it's not a question of would I ever wear it again or not – I probably wouldn't, that's absolutely not the point – the point is I really shouldn't have thrown it away, oh, I don't know if you've ever had a case before where somebody like me was silly enough to donate something they –

FRAZER. It happens all the time! Course it does.

Well, not all the time, no, but it happens, it does.

But we're usually lucky enough that they realise before we've actually sold it.

MARJORIE *enters*.

MARJORIE. No! No sign anywhere! So I'm pretty confident that in point of fact you never brought it, David, so check for us at home, eh?

DAVID. But this lady here sold it –

MARJORIE. No! That's quite impossible, because –

SUSAN. I did! I bloody sold the bloody thing! So don't you start either, Marjorie, I'm warning you. I used my gumption and I sold it for ten whole quid. I sold it! I looked at the stupid article and I thought: Valentine's Day, this is the day if ever there is a day you can sell this bloody hideous handmade-looking monstrosity; tomorrow and it'll be on the shelf for another year, she wants it, so sell it, so I sold it!

And, sorry, I'm not bloody sorry.

I work in here for sweet fanny nothing, for this charity, three days a week in good faith, out of nothing but the goodness of my heart, and I am sick, tired and fed up to the back teeth being treated like an idiot by idiots that run around after idiots that don't even know what they want to hand in and what crap they actually want to keep.

DAVID. It's just that it has sentimental value.

SUSAN. Does it? Present was it?

DAVID. Yes, as a matter of fact. You see, it's hand-painted on silk –

SUSAN. A present, very nice. From a young girl, I suppose?

DAVID (*puzzled and taken aback*). Well... She is just young, Helena, as a matter of fact...

SUSAN. How old?

DAVID. How – ?

SUSAN. Yes, Helena, how old?

DAVID. Twenty-one, no, twenty-two, but I really don't see –

SUSAN. Twenty-two? So you're what... Times two is forty-four plus seven – you're fifty one!

DAVID. I am! (How did you know?) I am. But –

SUSAN. And, David, you're a widower! David. Bet your wife wasn't six months in her grave before you were off cavorting with all the young Helenas of the day, typical! And now you want me to get my daughter – my innocent little fifteen-year-old daughter! – to steal some heart-spattered tie out of her estranged father's wardrobe just to get you out of a hole! Sure! Why not? I'll do it and we'll get it back for you, no bother, and I hope it chokes you!

SUSAN *marches off backshop in a rage. The other three stand amazed.*

MARJORIE. Well, poor Susan, she must be menopausal!

Blackout.

Music: 'My Funny Valentine'.

End of Act Two.

Interval.

ACT THREE

HAVE YOURSELF A MERRY LITTLE CHRISTMAS

Music: first verse of 'What is This Thing Called Love?' (Frank Sinatra version).

24 December, later that same year. The shop is now spectacularly spangled and decorated again, but very differently from the previous year. Though there is different tinsel and baubles, there is the same slightly sad, skew-whiff fairy on top of the (taller? more silvery?) Christmas tree.

A POLICEMAN *talks on a crackling radio.*

SUSAN *sits shaking, wrapped in a blanket, head in hands.*

The circling blue emergeny lights recede. Maybe a siren going away.

POLICEMAN. Fatality's name, a Robert Gilmartin, according to witness. Says you've got him on file. According to witness, he was under an injunction not to come near her because of reported harassment –

SUSAN (*blurts*). He was a stalker –

A young POLICEWOMAN *comes from backshop with a steaming cup of tea for* SUSAN.

POLICEWOMAN. Drink this.

SUSAN *takes a drink and grimaces.*

I know. It's very sweet. You've had a shock. Drink.

The POLICEWOMAN *moves away from* SUSAN, *and the* POLICEMAN *continues on his radio, which crackles responses.*

POLICEMAN. Yes. Taking full statement.

A Mrs Susan Love.

That's right. That's it. Yup.

No. No. Witness doesn't know next of kin or address herself, but says you'll definitely have it all.

Now, Mrs Love, can you tell me exactly what happened?

He gets his notebook out and SUSAN, *who takes a deep breath, begins.*

SUSAN. He came into the shop. Thing is, it's been kind of quiet recently on the Robert Gilmartin front. Comparatively. I was getting kind of lulled into a sense of false security. I thought perhaps he's getting the message, perhaps it's sinking in at last. Since I got the injunction I…

POLICEMAN. Is he your ex-husband? Or a former partner?

SUSAN. No. No. I don't even know him. I met him. Once. Once only, it was a… speed dating they called it, it was a… (*Peters out.*)

POLICEWOMAN. Oh I know! You get an equal number of men and women…

SUSAN. Yes, there's an organiser and she books the room and everything. After seven minutes the gong goes and the guys move round one place. It's like a Paul Jones. Well, I did this. Once. Almost a year ago. I'm divorced. Anyway, the one time I tried it…

POLICEMAN. Yes, could you – ?

SUSAN. Sorry! Robert Gilmartin was the last guy I met that night. I look back and I think it was only the luck of the draw but was it because I was the last woman he met and perhaps he was getting desperate? Anyway, I don't remember anything much about him. Was he weird? No weirder than some of the rest of them quite frankly.

Not interesting.

I knew I wasn't interested, but by then I was getting quite used to being pleasant enough, blah-blah, and the seven minutes'll be up soon, we can all go home.

That was that.

See, how it works is if there was anyone you wouldn't mind your details being passed on to, you tell the organiser –

Anyway, I got two or three e-mails from the organiser over the next month, a Robert Gilmartin wanted her to pass on his details to me although I hadn't singled him out, because he was sure I'd like to be in contact with him. I asked her to tell him very firmly, thanks but no thanks, and on no account to pass on mine.

POLICEWOMAN. And she did?

SUSAN. No, she didn't, it was just bad luck he saw me on the bus – I didn't see him, this was a good few weeks later, I wouldn't have recognised him if I did see him – and he followed me here. Then he followed me home. Once he had my address I was bombarded by flowers, presents I didn't want…

POLICEMAN. Did he threaten you?

SUSAN. No. No he didn't. But it was very threatening.

POLICEWOMAN. Of course.

POLICEMAN. They're not generally dangerous.

A look from the POLICEWOMAN.

SUSAN. And I was worried for my daughter too. He used to just stand there for hours. Across the street. Outside here as a matter of fact. All evening. Creepy. Outside this window. Looking up, looking over. Phoning. My dad has lived there for over forty years and had the same phone number, I had to change it, get a new unlisted number. It's been a nightmare. All year long. There was nothing I could say to get through to him. I had to let all the neighbours know on no account were they to… Humiliating. The police couldn't help much at first, but once I spoke to a female detective, she advised me, and I persevered and eventually I got the injunction. I could phone the police and they'd remove him. They did a couple of times. But sometimes I'd feel he'd never, ever, give up –

POLICEMAN. They do eventually.

SUSAN. Really?

The POLICEWOMAN *gives him a withering look. He witters, less confidently, a little deflated.*

POLICEMAN. Well, they are supposed to. Eventually. The ones who aren't violent. Or paranoid with jealousy and kill someone. (*Beat.*) That's the exes mainly.

SUSAN. Today he came into the shop – he must've been watching, he waited till I was alone – and said – (*Breaking*.) he had a beautiful necklace he'd bought me for Christmas and we must spend the day together tomorrow, he knew I'd been sending him messages over his TV. I said I wasn't taking his present and if he left it, it was going in the bin and I dropped it straight in there in front of him and reminded him of the injunction and told him I was calling the police.

POLICEMAN. Is that it?

The POLICEMAN *retrieves a small parcel, nicely gift-wrapped, from a jewellers'*. SUSAN *flinches and shudders*.

SUSAN. Yes. Take it away. Take it away! Please!

POLICEWOMAN. Yes. It's all right. Ssh.

SUSAN. He said if I didn't agree to come with him for Christmas dinner… He said he was going to commit suicide.

(*Trembling*.)… And I said, 'Go right ahead, do what you want, it's nothing to do with me.'

The POLICEWOMAN *gets down to* SUSAN*'s level and gets direct eye contact*.

POLICEWOMAN (*gently*). And it isn't.

SUSAN. He's dead.

POLICEMAN. I don't think he really meant to do it, though. First bus driver said he ran right across his path looking right at him, dodging him and screaming. And straight into the other one coming the other way.

Poor guy never had a chance. That'll be his Christmas ruined!

The POLICEWOMAN *glares at him*.

SUSAN. A man's dead.

POLICEWOMAN. Can you go home? Is there anyone you can call to be with you?

SUSAN. No. No, I'll wait till the other two get back.

POLICEWOMAN. I really think you should call someone. Obviously you've had a hell of a shock –

SUSAN. But I didn't even know him…

POLICEMAN. She's right enough, you should go home.

SUSAN. I'm all right.

POLICEMAN. Well, we're off. And don't let it get to you, okay?

The POLICEMAN *goes out of the front door. The* POLICEWOMAN *goes to exit with him then at the last minute comes back and pauses by* SUSAN, *crouches by her and says her piece.*

POLICEWOMAN. Don't let this ruin your Christmas. He was a nutter, and yes, okay, it's a shame. Pity for him, but he's dead now and it's nothing – nothing – whatsoever to do with you. He didn't care about you. He didn't care about anyone but himself. Remember that.

The POLICEWOMAN *goes.* SUSAN *sits, stricken, for a moment or two.*

DAVID *enters, smiling. She doesn't look up or register who he is.*

DAVID. Hello, hello, err, is Frazer…?

SUSAN. No.

DAVID. It's, eh, Susan, isn't it?

SUSAN (*flinching*). Oh you – !

As DAVID *speaks,* SUSAN *gives tiny, almost imperceptible answers to his questions.*

DAVID. Frazer phoned and left a message on the machine, said to pop in for a second, he had something to tell me that he thought would please me…?

I'll come back later. Will he be in, could you tell him – listen, are you okay?

No, you're not, are you?

You weren't a witness to that accident, were you?

Oh God. That's terrible, you don't think you should – are you in here on your own?

SUSAN. Frazer will be back soon.

DAVID. Good. You didn't, eh, know the person…?

Thank God for that.

The traffic's moving normally out there again as if nothing had happened.

I was in a bus coming back from down the town and we were just stuck in a big tailback for miles, took ages, finally got here and I bumped into old Miss Llewelyn, my downstairs neighbour, and she said what it was, there had been a terrible accident.

SUSAN. Oh, do you know Margot Llewelyn?

DAVID. Stays downstairs. (*Beat.*) Are you sure you're okay?

SUSAN. Used to teach me piano when I was little. To no great effect, I have to say. We stayed next door. Still do.

DAVID. Do you mean we're neighbours?

SUSAN. Number eighty-two. Just across the road there.

DAVID. Eighty-four. Just through the wall.

SUSAN. So you're the person plays all the loud jazz? Specially on a Sunday morning?

DAVID. Sorry, does it disturb you?

SUSAN. No. I quite like it.

DAVID. So you're a jazz fan?

SUSAN. No.

DAVID. You'll be all right soon. I've just sold up. I'm moving out in a fortnight. After twenty-six years. It was… Time for a change.

SUSAN. Oh I didn't mean… I'll miss it. Sunday morning.

DAVID. It's weird though. I mean, cities are unbelievable, aren't they? So we've been neighbours all these years, presumably? Couldn't have been! Yet we've never met till I'm about to leave…

SUSAN. Oh no, no, I didn't stay there always. It's my dad's house. The family home. We moved in when I was seven, I left home at eighteen when I went to university, so…

My daughter and I moved back in nearly two years ago when Dad was beginning to not cope.

DAVID. Your dad is Archie Dickinson of Dickinson the Plumbers, isn't he?

SUSAN. Do you know him?

DAVID. Put in our new bathroom when we moved in in 1978. I've certainly seen him out and about locally over the years.

SUSAN. My dad went into a home at the beginning of this month. He's so confused and I was scared to death of him just wandering off and going missing…

I just couldn't cope any more and the social worker said… And suddenly a place came up… And I put him in.

DAVID. That's not how to think of it. It must've been time.

Not Rylands, is it?

SUSAN. Yes.

DAVID. My mother's been in there for four-and-a-half years. It's very pleasant as these places go. They're very, very good. They really are.

SUSAN. Oh God, I hope so. (*Beat.*) Mr…

DAVID. David.

SUSAN. Listen, why Frazer phoned you… I think what it must have been… I know it's been ages, but better late than never, eh?… I got back your tie.

She begins with increasing puzzlement then panic to search through a drawer in the counter.

DAVID. My tie, that I…?

SUSAN. I told him to wait till after Christmas, till after I left. Then return it!

This is my last day.

I've got a new job, a proper job that I start on the fifth of January and I… Well, getting that tie back I'd no right selling in the first place… that was sort of a bit of unfinished business, and I… never mind, I retrieved it last week and I asked Frazer to let you… And I put it in the drawer here, I did! And somebody's moved it.

She's nearly crying.

DAVID. Don't get upset, honestly – it'll no doubt turn up.

SUSAN *takes a deep breath.*

SUSAN. David, I've only met you once, all those months and months ago, and I was unforgiveably rude to you. It was unbelievable, it really was, and I don't know how to apologise and I certainly couldn't begin to explain why you, a total stranger, got it in the neck like that.

DAVID. Susan – I can call you Susan? – it's okay. Frazer explained.

You weren't having a good day, were you, to put it mildly, and then this idiot comes in, wanting something back you've already sold in good faith –

SUSAN. But I was totally out of order.

DAVID. You were a bit!

But you were very good value. You really made me laugh. It was very, very funny, Susan.

SUSAN. No.

DAVID. I couldn't take it personally, well, you didn't even know me. I was quite taken aback, I must admit. I just stood there. Then all of a sudden it just cracked me up.

Oh, you should've seen Marjorie's face.

SUSAN. Don't.

DAVID. It was a picture, it really was!

He begins to laugh. Eventually she joins in.

And you got the right answer by the wrong method! The Maths teacher in me would have to give you no marks for that.

SUSAN. Sorry…?

DAVID. You said I was fifty-one. Correct. I am. Fifty-two next month, actually, but who's counting? Frazer explained your theory – well, leaving aside the doubtful premise it's based on – purely as arithmetic, you can't double the woman's age and add seven, you'd have to deduct seven from the woman's age then double that figure, so the age of the man whose ideal woman is twenty-two is twenty-two minus seven equals fifteen, times two is thirty. Not fifty-one.

SUSAN. Oh, right enough.

DAVID. Right enough, I'm right!

SUSAN. Is that what you are?

DAVID. What?

SUSAN. A Maths teacher.

DAVID. Uh-huh! And you?

SUSAN. Office administrator. (*Beat.*) This new job I've got sounds pretty challenging…

DAVID. Well, good! I'm sure you'll rise to it!

SUSAN. I hope so.

DAVID. Course you will!

SUSAN. I'm looking forward to it. Nervous of course. Where do you teach?

DAVID. Just round the corner at the high school.

SUSAN. My daughter goes there.

DAVID. What's her name?

SUSAN. Stephanie Love.

DAVID. I know Stephanie! Super girl, I don't actually teach her but she was one of the group I took on the trip to Paris at Easter.

SUSAN. So you're…? Oh, I heard all about it, what great laughs it all was. There was you and Miss…

DAVID – Collins from the Art Department, and Mrs Copeland from French, it was quite an education!

SUSAN. I thought it was fantastic you all giving up your holidays like that. I don't think I would.

DAVID. Well… the extra-curricular stuff can be really quite rewarding. They were a good gang, that lot. And Paris, anytime…!

I actually enjoy my work. I like teaching. I like teaching Maths. It's great when you can actually see the penny drop.

Oh, it's got its humdrum elements of course, nowadays there is the hooligan factor even in a basically really good school like ours – and the admin is a nightmare… but there've been times in my life when going to my work and taking pride in doing an honest day at the chalkface's been just about the only thing to hold everything together for me.

SUSAN. Are you not going to be the new headmaster?

DAVID. Me? No, God forbid!

SUSAN. Can't imagine there're that many Maths teachers turning up at work in the Jon Snow fancy ties!

DAVID. Oh, you mean the –

SUSAN. I'm sure it'll just be Frazer's put it somewhere safe, David. He knew how important that tie was to you.

DAVID. And to you! After all, you went to the effort of getting it back for me. Susan, I'm very, very –

Enter HELENA, *seen just in silhouette, a good-looking twenty-two-year-old with a Czech accent and an absolutely huge 'just-about-to-drop' pregnant bump.*

HELENA. David!

DAVID. (Hey! Don't mention the tie to her! Okay?)

HELENA. There you are! I need you at home!

Exit HELENA.

DAVID. Sorry, Helena! Oh, I'm sorry, darling! I'll only be a minute, I'm just coming!

It'd have been really nice to wear it at Christmas dinner and please her but, oh well!

Everybody gets into such a lather this time of the year, don't they? Trying to get everything perfect. And she's such a driven kind of a girl at the best of times and what with the pregnancy –

SUSAN. Had you not better go?

DAVID. I suppose so! Susan, take care, eh? And see and have a nice Christmas. Hey! If I don't bump into you again before the Big Move, it was nice knowing you!

DAVID *exits.*

SUSAN *sits down, utterly deflated.*

SUSAN. Oh yes, of course! City flats are murder with a pram, eh? Well, wherever you're going, here's hoping you've got a garden!

Enter TONY.

TONY. Susan.

SUSAN. Tony.

TONY. Listen, Susan, I think our Stephi would be willing to come home to you.

SUSAN. Oh really, well, that's not the response I got from her when I phoned her at your place last week.

TONY. Well, she's stubborn and I know she was still keeping up the huff with you, but I happen to know she was crying her eyes out last night and –

SUSAN. And you and Natalie would like to have your first Christmas at home alone with Baby Whatsit without a stroppy adolescent to entertain, I don't blame you.

TONY. Susan, why do you always have to take a dim view?

Of every single thing I try to do. Of every single gesture I try to make?

I'd like you not to be on your own. And I thought you'd like her to be there. With you. At Christmas. And – oh, she'd never admit it – but I know she'd like to come home. Particularly once she found out that Natalie and I are even stricter with the time she's to be in at than you are.

SUSAN. You'd like me to have company at Christmas? That's rich! Thanks a lot. I'm really grateful for your concern.

He holds out his arms in a gesture of surrender.

TONY. Ah, c'mon, Susan…

They look each other in the eye. A beat.

SUSAN. Do you love her, Tony?

TONY. You know fine well I'm crazy about our Stephi, always have been.

SUSAN. No. No, I meant Natalie?

Do you love her, Tony? Do you love her to bits?

TONY. Yes. Yes I do.

SUSAN. Well, that's good because I'd hate for all that agony and turmoil to have been for nothing.

TONY. It's not easy, not always easy to be a new dad at my age, and – (*Catching on to himself, laughing.*) but I don't suppose you want to be hearing that?

SUSAN (*wry laugh*). Not particularly, my reserves of sympathy remain very finite.

TONY. Fair enough.

Enter DAVID.

DAVID. Susan –

SUSAN. No, Mr… erm, Frazer's not back yet! I *will* get him to call you the minute he does and here's hoping he can shed some light on the mystery, okay? We'll do our very best for you! Bye bye just now!

DAVID *is forced to give in, make a goodbye gesture and exit.*

TONY. Who's that?

SUSAN. Just a guy that comes into the shop.

So, Tony, you're saying I should try again? To phone Stephi?

TONY. Let me talk to her on her mobile. I'll get her to call you.

SUSAN. Okay.

They smile amicably enough at each other, and he goes to exit. But at the last moment he has to blow it with a provocative question.

TONY. Susan, why did you fight with her over that top she wanted to wear to the school dance? It's just what they're all wearing, it really is. Natalie says –

SUSAN. Tony, I didn't fall out with her about the skimpy top, I didn't fall out with her going to the school dance like a cross between a teenage hooker and something out of *Sex and the City*, I didn't fall out with her about the pierced navel or the temporary tattoo or the sequined thong showing right out over the top of the skintight hipsters cut low enough to practically show her entire 'excuse me'. I maybe don't get out much but somehow, by some sort of osmosis, I do seem to know what is de rigeur for fifteen-year-olds these days.

I fell out with her because she wouldn't wear a coat, Tony.

To go to the dance. In December, Tony.

TONY *is laughing at the old* SUSAN. *She's good value. She always was.*

TONY. Well, it's all water under the bridge now. And if you just don't mention it and she thinks you'd like her to come back – I told her I'd ask you if she could come back, Susan.

SUSAN. Well, of course she can.

SUSAN *is nearly managing a smile now too. They look each other in the eye.* TONY *tries an awkward 'bye bye' peck on the cheek, but it doesn't go quite right.*

TONY. Have a good Christmas, eh, the two of you, and all the best.

SUSAN. We'll see.

TONY. I do wish you all the best.

Another flash of bitterness from SUSAN, *surprising herself.*

SUSAN. Of course you do, and you'd like to see me happy because you could stop feeling guilty.

TONY. But I don't, actually. Waste of time. Guilt. Regrets. Load of crap.

Susan… I never really felt you were on my side.

SUSAN. No? No, I suppose I wasn't always. Not latterly.

TONY. All the best. Really.

SUSAN. Yeah. (*Beat.*) You too.

As he goes to exit:

Tony!

Thanks for sending back that tie to the shop when I asked you.

TONY. No problem, Susan. No bother at all.

Exit TONY. SUSAN *alone for a beat, thinking, feeling.*

Enter MARJORIE *through the front door in coat with bags. She's very hyped up and breathless about Christmas.*

MARJORIE. That dear delicatessen is queues around the block! Well, Christmas Eve, what would you expect, I suppose?

MARJORIE *bustles into backshop, then back out again, minus her coat and packages.*

Was that Tony I saw leaving?

What did that so-and-so want coming in here?

SUSAN. Nothing.

To wish me a happy Christmas.

MARJORIE. Damnable cheek!

MARJORIE *begins to ricochet about the shop fussing with things and rattling on so much she leaves no space for a response.*

I popped in to Scandalrags to see if they had anything suitable for the Golf Club Dinner Dance and the woman was telling me there had been a terrible accident!

Course, I had to miss everything because I was round the corner in that queue.

Christmas. It'll be no bloody Christmas for me. Skivvying around after a brood of ungrateful articles and every time I get interested in something on the telly (mind you, there's damn all on) some so-and-so switches the channel!

Last night I'd just finished the tree, and Douglas had managed to fuse the lights as per usual, so I just tried to calm myself by putting a little bit of effort into my festive flowers and I'd done a beautiful arrangement – though I say it myself, you know asymmetric with a twisty twig? – and I had just placed it just so, perfect, on the hall table and stepped back to admire it, when – blam! – a bloody great football comes crashing along the hall and smacks straight into it, broken porcelain, bashed blossoms and water all over the parquet. I sat down and I cried buckets.

That's a brood of boys for you.

Darling, are you just going to sit there in a dream all day?

MARJORIE *stands and stares out the window, lost in her own world, quite unaware of* SUSAN *behind her.*

Oh, look, there's Doris! Looks like she's got on a new brassiere. Och aye the noo!

Wonder if she's coming in? Yes, yes, here she comes, no, no, as you were, she's not, she's gone by. Thank goodness.

It'd take blinking Scotch Doris to come in and annoy us on Christmas Eve, eh? I think I'm going to pop a little note to Head Office next year, there's not much point in us actually opening, the amount of trade we get.

I hate Christmas.

Take last year. Practically had to sleep with the butcher to get on his list for a Kelly Bronze, you know, that's that breed of free-range turkey Delia swears by – an arm and a leg, extortionate – so I thought: 'Live up to the bird, I better pull out the stops stuffing-wise', so down with the Cuisinart and it's the cook-and-peel-your-own chestnuts, the home-made minced pork belly, the Perigord, the Pernod, I don't know what, and it's sitting there ready in the fridge in a bowl with the teacloth over it, I come down Christmas morning and it's empty. Stephen's come back in at midnight with half the rugby first fifteen, turned it into hamburger patties and they've scoffed the lot on buns with tomato ketchup! All I got was, 'Mum, we'd the munchies.' The munchies! He says, 'Mum, these burgers, they were mingers.' Scrimp and scrape to send them to a good school and they still talk like I don't know what!

So that was us reduced to the packet of Paxo sage and onion, and to add insult to injury, Douglas had to say that was his favourite bit of the meal, reminded him of how his old mum used to make it.

Plus Marcus my youngest has decided he's a lacto-veggie and will eat absolutely bugger all but soya sausages –

SUSAN *sinks to the floor, beginning to scream and cry.*

Enter FRAZER.

FRAZER. Guy in the Asian grocer's told me there'd been a terrible acci–

SUSAN *flies into his arms, crying. He comforts her.*

MARJORIE. Tell you, it'll be that blinking nuisance of an ex-husband upsetting her, Frazer, because when I came in –

SUSAN (*sobbing*). It was Robert Gilmartin! And he's dead.

MARJORIE *and* FRAZER *are stunned.*

MARJORIE. Through here! Come on! Through here! A cup of tea and half a Valium, that's what you're needing, dear.

FRAZER *and* MARJORIE *help a practically prostrate* SUSAN *through to backshop.*

DAVID *enters and looks around puzzled.*

DAVID. Hello? Hello?

MARJORIE *enters from backshop, firmly shutting the door with its private sign.*

MARJORIE. Hello! Oh, it's you, David, I'm afraid we're a little bit busy.

DAVID. Marjorie. Erm, I was wondering if I could see Susan, please.

MARJORIE. No, that's just it, she's a little bit indisposed at the moment.

DAVID. But I'd just –

Enter FRAZER *from backshop.*

FRAZER. David! I came by your house and rang the bell half an hour ago but no answer.

MARJORIE. How is she, Frazer?

FRAZER. Well, this is it, Marjorie, I don't like the colour of her at all.

DAVID *goes to the private door,* MARJORIE *bars his way.*

DAVID. If I could just –

MARJORIE (*briskly*). No certainly not, David, we'll pass on any message you've got for her –

DAVID. But I just want to –

FRAZER. Here, David! I've got your tie! (Go away through, Marjorie, and see what you think. I said to her, perhaps we should call a doctor, but she'll not have it.)

MARJORIE *exits backshop.* FRAZER *pulls the tie out of his pocket, hands it over to* DAVID.

Put it in my pocket when I went out there, and I thought I'll just see if I can deliver it in person.

Susan said she'd been feeling guilty all these months about not getting it back for you.

DAVID. No need whatsoever, I was –

FRAZER. I thought you'd be delighted!

DAVID. Well, I am, I am, but –

MARJORIE (*calling from backshop*). Frazer!

FRAZER. Excuse me just a little minute, David –

DAVID. Frazer. Could you ask Susan if she'd like a lift up to Rylands tomorrow? Because I'm going up to see my mother and she was telling me about her dad… I don't know if she drives, but –

FRAZER. No, Susan's not got a car, no.

DAVID. Well, it can be hard to get a taxi on Christmas Day and –

FRAZER. That's awfully kind of you, David, but I've already arranged to pop round in the car at eleven and take her up. It's no bother. I'm not doing hellish much anyway!

DAVID. Oh, well, I just thought –

FRAZER. There's honestly no need.

DAVID. But could you tell her – ?

FRAZER. Have a merry Christmas, David! Excuse me, will you?

FRAZER *exits backshop.*

DAVID *looks at the heart-spattered tie and glumly puts it on in a mirror. It certainly doesn't go with his casual tartan shirt. He pretends to hang himself with it. He sighs, gives up (he's forced to, really), and exits through the front door.*

SUSAN *enters from backshop pursued by* MARJORIE *with a glass of water and a pill, and by* FRAZER.

SUSAN. No, Marjorie, I don't want a pill, honestly! I'm fine now!

MARJORIE. You've had a terrible shock!

SUSAN. Poor guy!

Love. A fatal carry-on. Madness. You wouldn't wish it on your worst enemy.

I remember, oh, two or three years before I met Tony I was in love, mad unrequited love, with a guy called Arthur. Arthur! Ridiculous. Once I stood outside his flat for a whole weekend – it was freezing as well – because I knew he was in there with a girl called Heather Maxwell instead of on a works weekend like he'd said he was. And thing was, I knew he really loved me, he just hadn't realised it yet.

I was, looking back – really – in myself – just every bit as nuts as Robert Gilmartin.

I really never do want to go there again.

Never again will I try any of these… You were right, Frazer, it was desperate, and if you do desperate things, it puts you in touch with desperate people.

Love? Spare me! No, what I want most of all is peace.

MARJORIE. I think you're very wise, Susan. Live for yourself. Have things exactly the way you want them.

I'll tell you, see, if it wasn't for Douglas and the boys, I'd have a pink fitted carpet in the bathroom.

Because the male aim is only ninety per cent accurate, isn't it? If that.

SUSAN. It's a terrible thing to say but I'm glad it's all over.

MARJORIE. If you'll not take a little half a Valium, Susan, I'll tell you, I'm going to pop out to get you some Sleepy-Time Tea out the health-food shop, make sure you sleep tonight. Celia who works in here on a Tuesday swears by it.

MARJORIE *goes backshop from there.*

Frazer, kettle's boiling!

But FRAZER *stands still, staring strangely at* SUSAN.

MARJORIE *bustles out from backshop in her coat –*

That and I'll get you some St John's Wort when I'm at it, it's wonderful for getting you through the winter, so it is, and it's not drugs, dear, it's only herbal.

– and she hurries out the front door. As she goes:

Frazer! Are you not going to make that tea?

FRAZER *rouses himself and goes backshop. The moment he's off,* SUSAN*'s mobile rings with a daft ringtone. She answers quickly, eagerly, the tiny phone clapped against her left ear.*

SUSAN. Oh, Stephi! Stephi, your dad said he'd get you to phone. Come home, love!

Okay.

No, no of course I've not got a tree, why would I bother a tree for just me?

Okay, okay, I'm saying nothing, I'm listening.

FRAZER *enters, launching straight into it as he does.*

FRAZER. I'm not even going to look at you till I get it out but I might as well say it before Marjorie gets back because it's something I've wanted to say for a while, I suppose. Am I wrong to hope that perhaps one day you and me might get married?

I mean, once sex is out of the equation.

Because Marjorie's perhaps decided I'm gay, but I'm not. If I think of what it is to be gay, it makes me shudder, it does, the whole lifestyle. Plus my mother would've had a fit and I suppose her attitude's rubbed off on me and I like women. I really like you, Susan, and I always have and do we not get on like a house on fire?

SUSAN (*on the phone*). Oh, darling, I don't know what I'd do with myself if it came to you and me not getting on!

FRAZER. Face facts, Frazer, you're not a 'costume designer', you're not going back to London – I hated London, I was over the moon to scuttle back home and look after Mother. I'm a part-time dog walker, and a part-time gardener, and a part-time volunteer in a charity shop and, oh yes, I'll run up a lovely frock for a mother of the bride for a very reasonable price in jigtime.

And I get by.

Except it's a little bit lonely at times and if I have a dream – don't laugh, Susan –

SUSAN, *on the phone, lets out a loud snort then a peal of laughter, then –*

SUSAN. Oh, you take the biscuit, Stephi, you really do. Okay, it's a deal, see you later, baby!

She clicks off the phone and goes, smiling happily, to FRAZER.

The prodigal returns! Tonight about teatime.

Only snag is she's booked the very last tree in the Asian grocer's and she and her boyfriend – this is a new development! – are going to bring it up and get down the decorations and do it up in the living room – from which I am banned for the evening, poor old Cinders here's got her full instructions on what kind of pizza to be putting in the oven for them in the kitchen –

Sorry, Frazer, were you saying something?

FRAZER *sits, shattered, but she doesn't notice, so ecstatic is she about Stephi.*

Enter DORIS, *dressed in her usual outfit, carrying a bundle of three peculiarly wrapped presents in a string bag. She picks up a twee little dish from among the merchandise on display.*

DORIS. That's nice! It's a bonny wee dish, that, intit?

SUSAN. Very nice! I think it's Dutch, Doris. Delft.

DORIS. Dutch Delft? Is it? (*Unimpressed.*) You don't say.

Haw, Susan, what kind of a dish would you cry that wee dish?

SUSAN. Dunno. Just a dish…

DORIS. Whit fur?

SUSAN. Well… Frazer…?

FRAZER (*shrugs*). A little bonbon dish, basically.

DORIS. A bonbon dish? It's bonny.

Like for nuts or that?

SUSAN. Exactly.

DORIS. It's nice. Perhaps I should buy myself that bonny wee bonbon dish for my Christmas?

SUSAN. Go on, Doris, make our day! Why don't you be our sole customer and make us feel we've not been totally wasting our time. Tell you, how about a pre-Christmas sale, it's marked at a pound – let's say seventy per cent off – 30p to you.

DORIS. It's no dear.

SUSAN. It is not.

DORIS. And it is bonny.

SUSAN. It is.

DORIS. Mind you, I've already got enough blinking crap and tat at home. A houseful of bloody rubbish! Gloryholes stuffed to the gunnels with gash this that and the next thing. Shite coming out my ears.

So I'll not bother, so I willnae.

Why I came in, a little bird told me you were leaving.

SUSAN. I am, Doris. A paying job presented itself so…

DORIS. Good things come to those that wait!

All the best, hen.

SUSAN. Thank you very much!

DORIS. So I wanted to leave you a little minding.

DORIS *takes three bizarre parcels out of her string bag.*

SUSAN. Oh-ho, don't worry, Doris, I'll not forget you.

DORIS. And seeing it's Christmas… I've brung in something for Frazer and Marjorie as well. I'd that much re-fankled recycled paper, I thought I might as well yase some o it up.

DORIS *leaves these three presents – one clearly a bottle; one obviously a vinyl LP record; one a lumpy, amorphous ball of a parcel with a great big label reading 'Susan'.*

SUSAN. Thank you very much, Doris, honestly, you really shouldn't –

DORIS. No, don't unwrap them, it's no Christmas yit! I'm away. I'm away up the community centre to the carol concert, you get a lovely tea after with hoat mince pies. All the best, eh?

All the best when it comes.

Exit DORIS.

SUSAN. Well, there's a turn-up for the books, eh?

Doris. One thing you'd have to admit, she's totally unpredictable.

Wonder what we got?

Gold, frankincense and myrrh? Possibly not!

No prize for guessing what's in yours, Frazer!

A bottle. (*Feels it.*) Oh well, a bottle of what, that's the sixty-four-thousand-dollar question!

Erm... A bottle of Doris's own home-made elderberry wine decanted into an old turpentine bottle?

Ermm... A bottle of very fusty crème de menthe?

A bottle of bath-oil circa 1965?

An absolutely ancient bottle of Beaujolais Nouveau?

A ship in a bottle!

A message in a bottle –

Sorry. Sorry, Frazer, were you saying something there? Before Doris came in? When I was on the phone to Stephi?

FRAZER. No. No, nothing important, Susan, I can't remember. Doesn't matter.

SUSAN. Will we open them? Early? Put ourselves in the mood. Oh, why not? Why not indeed, give ourselves a laugh, eh? What have we got, for goodness' sake? God knows!

Marjorie's is definitely the size and the feel of an LP.

Remember getting an LP for your Christmas, Frazer? Sorry, *album*! I'm showing my age, eh? Big time.

Will we? Because she said not till –

FRAZER. Oh, open yours! Go on.

SUSAN. Nah. You first...

FRAZER *hums 'The Stripper' tune, and disrobes his bottle of its paper, layer by layer. By now they are laughing. Eventually, out comes a bottle of very nice indeed, thank you, champagne. They are amazed.*

FRAZER. Cold too! Well, well!

Enter DAVID. *The heart tie is still very, very loosely knotted round his neck, incongruous with the tartan shirt.*

DAVID. That looks very nice. Christmas starting early?

SUSAN (*of tie, amazed*). Oh, you got it?

DAVID. I came in. Frazer not tell you?

SUSAN. No!

FRAZER. Oh, I haven't had the time!

SUSAN. Sorry, we've just had surprise Christmas presents from our favourite never-satisfied customer!

Enter MARJORIE *who puts down a little package from the health-food store in front of* SUSAN.

MARJORIE. Just in time, they were closing up. There we are, Susan, those'll sort you. Ooh… I think it's about time we shut up shop ourselves?

SUSAN. Look, Marjorie, Doris left a present for you.

MARJORIE. Scotch Doris? For goodness' sake, I shouldn't have waved to her earlier, I obviously only encouraged her.

SUSAN. Open it up! Go on!

MARJORIE. All right, if you say so. (*Opens it.*) Oh, a record. It's all CDs nowadays, isn't it?

DAVID. Not necessarily!

DAVID *takes it from her, blows on it looks at it in the light.*

It's old, yes. But it looks as if it's in okay nick…

FRAZER. That turntable's in working order you know, we let people try them out on it if they want.

But DAVID *hands it back to* MARJORIE *who looks at it disdainfully.*

MARJORIE (*reading*). *Christmas Classics*? Well, that can join the junk mountain…

DAVID (*quietly, to* SUSAN *and* FRAZER). Listen, why I came over, I wondered if I could invite you pair, well, it's awfully short notice I know, you'll very likely both be busy, but tonight we're having Christmas dinner in our house, and…

My daughter-in-law Helena – you met her earlier, Susan – she's Czech you know, and there they do Christmas dinner on

Christmas Eve apparently, they make baked carp, it's the Christmas fish and… oh, it's traditional, and Colin – that's my son – the pair of them are visiting, anyway, he says it's the being pregnant has made Helena mad to do everything absolutely just so the Czech way for once, and it's very much the more the merrier. Bring Stephanie if she's free. Old Margot Llewelyn has even promised to brave the stairs.

SUSAN. Helena's your daughter-in-law?

DAVID. Of course! Susan, you didn't think…

He begins to laugh. She's embarassed.

You shouldn't believe everything you read in magazines. Really!

Yes, the famous tie was part of the wedding outfits. Helena had a coat lined with this fabric, she made it herself, and she made us all wear matching ties. Colin, the best man, her father, me.

She did Textile Design at art school.

MARJORIE. So you're going to be a granddad, David?

DAVID. I am.

MARJORIE. Not make you feel old?

DAVID. Not really! I'm delighted.

Are you busy tonight, Marjorie, because, of course, you're very welcome to –

MARJORIE. Goodness me, no, David, thank you, but no thanks, my family are all-consuming this time of year.

DAVID. Of course, so…?

FRAZER. I'm actually busy, David, sorry.

DAVID (*genuinely*). Oh, that's a disappointment.

Susan? Helena's a terrific cook, I'll guarantee you that.

SUSAN. Well… (*Laughs.*) I was reconciled to dining on the crumbs from someone's pizza, so –

DAVID. Lovely. About, say, half past seven for drinks…?

FRAZER, *making a big effort to be generous, wields his bottle.*

FRAZER. Why don't we have this now?

MARJORIE. Ooh… Why not? Teensy one for me though, Frazer, I'm driving.

FRAZER. Hurry up and open your Doris doofer, Suze, you'll perhaps have the plum duff. Lay on McDuff!

SUSAN *begins to unwrap her lump of a present.* MARJORIE *picks up a boxed set of champagne flute glasses from among the merchandise.*

MARJORIE. I might as well give these a little rinse and we'll use them, eh?

FRAZER. But Marjorie! They're stock! And they're still in the box!

MARJORIE. Frazer, don't be so bloody stupid. It's Christmas!

And she slips off with them to backshop.

DAVID. And we should surely try the music while we're at it?

DAVID *picks up* MARJORIE*'s LP and sets about putting it on the turntable. He calls through to her.*

May I, Marjorie?

MARJORIE (*off*). Sorry, David?

SUSAN. Frazer, look!

SUSAN, *finishing unwrapping her present, astonished, holds out the 'ruby slippers'.*

Then claps her hand to her mouth, remembering their provenance. But DAVID, *having set the needle in the record's groove and waiting for the music to start, turns and looks on in absolute equanimity.*

DAVID. They're lovely. Are they going to fit?

The record begins, the first line of 'Have Yourself a Merry Little Christmas'. SUSAN *nods solemnly.*

SUSAN (*hushed*). I think so… Yes.

FRAZER. Go on, Susan! Put them on!

She slips them on. DAVID *throws off his jacket, turns and very deliberately straightens his tie, tightening the knot.*

DAVID. Let's dance.

He holds out his arms, and shyly, tentatively, awkwardly at first, SUSAN *and* DAVID *begin to dance.*

FRAZER, *left out, sighs one single small audible breath.*

MARJORIE (*calling from backshop*). Frazer, Frazer! Give me a hand with this tray, can't you?

FRAZER (*a beat*). Coming, Marjorie, coming, I'm all yours.

He exits backshop, flourishing the bottle of champagne.

Alone, still awkwardly, SUSAN *and* DAVID *waltz.*

The record – well, it was a present from half-cracked DORIS *– begins to reveal an increasingly intrusive scratch and a click as it plays.*

They laugh heartily, joyfully, at this audible crack, looking into each other's eyes. At this moment, indoors as it is, magical snow begins to fall.

They close in and dance on together.

The End.